MACMILLAN MODERN NOVELISTS
ERNEST HEMINGWAY

Peter Messent

MACMILLAN

First published 1992 by
THE MACMILLAN PRESS LTD
Houndmills, Basingstoke, Hampshire RG21 2XS
and London
Companies and representatives
throughout the world

ISBN 0–333–51919–1 hardcover
ISBN 0–333–51920–5 paperback

A catalogue record for this book is available
from the British Library.

Typeset by Nick Allen/Longworth Editorial Services
Longworth, Oxon.

Printed in Hong Kong

Series Standing Order
If you would like to receive future titles in this series as they are published,
you can make use of our standing order facility. To place a standing order
please contact your bookseller or, in case of difficulty, write to us at the
address below with your name and address and the name of the series.
Please state with which title you wish to begin your standing order. (If you
live outside the United Kingdom we may not have the rights for your area,
in which case we will forward your order to the publisher concerned.)

Customer Services Department, Macmillan Distribution Ltd
Houndmills, Basingstoke, Hampshire, RG21 2XS, England.

Contents

Acknowledgements

First, I acknowledge my debt to Godfrey Kearns, my tutor when I was an undergraduate at Manchester, who first stimulated my enthusiasm for Hemingway. Both the encouragement he gave me then, and his friendship in the years since, have been of real importance to me.

I gave versions of several chapters in this book to the staff-postgraduate research group in my department, American and Canadian Studies, at Nottingham. The comments I received helped me greatly as I moved toward my final version. My thanks to all the members of that group. Three of them helped even more. Chris Gair, Richard King and David Murray read additional chapters in draft version. The changes that I made as a result of their (always constructive) criticism made this a much better book than it would otherwise have been. David Murray read the complete manuscript prior to submission at a time when he was over-busy anyway. He knows how much it was appreciated.

Finally, I have relied as always on the support and encouragement of my family and friends as I have written this book. To them all, and especially to my children, William and Alice, thank you.

List of Abbreviations

Page references in the text are to the following editions, all published current to the time of writing, in paperback, by Grafton Books (London), unless otherwise indicated. Titles of the books are abbreviated in the text as shown. Initial year of publication in square brackets.

1971) pp. 40–52, 57–66: abbreviated as *AJ1*; 36 (3 January 1972) pp. 26–46: *AJ2*; 37 (10 January 1972) pp. 22–30, 43–50: *AJ3*.

WY   *Hemingway: The Wild Years*, ed. Gene Z. Hanrahan (New York: Dell, 1967 [1962]).

L   *Ernest Hemingway: Selected Letters, 1917–1961*, ed. Carlos Baker (London: Granada, 1981).

To Penny Craig

General Editor's Preface

The death of the novel has often been announced, and part of the secret of its obstinate vitality must be its capacity for growth, adaptation, self-renewal and self-transformation: like some vigorous organism in a speeded-up Darwinian ecosystem, it adapts itself quickly to a changing world. War and revolution, economic crisis and social change, radically new ideologies such as Marxism and Freudianism, have made this century unprecedented in human history in the speed and extent of change, but the novel has shown an extraordinary capacity to find new forms and techniques and to accommodate new ideas and conceptions of human nature and human experience, and even to take up new positions on the nature of fiction itself.

In the generations immediately preceding and following 1914, the novel underwent a radical redefinition of its nature and possibilities. The present series of monographs is devoted to the novelists who created the modern novel and to those who, in their turn, either continued and extended, or reacted against and rejected, the traditions established during that period of intense exploration and experiment. It includes a number of those who lived and wrote in the nineteenth century but whose innovative contribution to the art of fiction makes it impossible to ignore them in any account of the origins of the modern novel; it also includes the so-called 'modernists' and those who in the mid- and late twentieth century have emerged as outstanding practitioners of this genre. The scope is, inevitably, international; not only, in the migratory and exile-haunted world of our century, do writers refuse to heed national frontiers – 'English' literature lays claim to Conrad the Pole, Henry James the American, and Joyce the

Irishman – but geniuses such as Flaubert, Dostoevsky and Kafka have had an influence on the fiction of many nations.

Each volume in the series is intended to provide an introduction to the fiction of the writer concerned, both for those approaching him or her for the first time and for those who are already familiar with some parts of the achievement in question and now wish to place it in the context of the total *oeuvre*. Although essential information relating to the writer's life and times is given, usually in an opening chapter, the approach is primarily critical and the emphasis is not upon 'background' or generalisations but upon close examination of important texts. Where an author is notably prolific, major texts have been made to convey, more summarily, a sense of the nature and quality of the author's work as a whole. Those who want to read further will find suggestions in the select bibliography included in each volume. Many novelists are, of course, not only novelists but also poets, essayists, biographers, dramatists, travel writers and so forth; many have practised shorter forms of fiction; and many have written letters or kept diaries that constitute a significant part of their literary output. A brief study cannot hope to deal with all these in detail, but where the shorter fiction and the non-fictional writings, public and private, have an important relationship to the novels, some space has been devoted to them.

NORMAN PAGE

1
Introduction

Hemingway is a canonic figure in the American literary tradition. Anthony Burgess calls him 'the major prose innovator of the century'.[1] Ihab Hassan judges *In Our Time* 'the best [collection] written by an American in our century'.[2] Robert Scholes places him alongside 'the other major figures of modern fiction since Flaubert'.[3] However, since his death in 1961 his work and reputation have suffered considerable disparagement, and a liking for Hemingway has come to be seen – at least in some quarters – as a sign of both immaturity and ideological wrong-headedness.

This can be seen partly as a reaction to what John Raeburn calls 'the Legendary Hemingway',[4] that public persona which the writer himself was only too keen on occasions to foster. The profile he offered to the world, and to the media in particular, was that of red-blooded, hairy-chested man of action. The advertisement in which he endorsed Ballantine's Ale in *Life* Magazine called attention both to his status as 'internationally famous . . . deep-sea fisherman' and as the 'greatest living American writer', while *Argosy* celebrated him as 'the world's greatest writer and authority on hunting, fishing, drinking and other manly occupations'.[5] Although such manliness was only one facet of an extremely complicated – even divided – sensibility, it was enough to hang Hemingway for many of those of a later generation for whom the cult of masculinity proved less attractive.

Such a response has undoubtedly been heightened by the particular difficulty, in Hemingway's case, of separating biographical detail from the writing performance. The two, for instance, are elided in both the above magazine quotations. This difficulty is indicated too by the presence of a large body of non-fiction work

1

in which a version of the author functions as (active) central protagonist and by the series of fictions that undoubtedly draw, in however modified a degree, on actual biographical circumstance. Life feeds both non-fiction and fiction in a way that has encouraged even contemporary critics to obliterate their crucial difference. Thus Peter Griffin, in *Along With Youth* (1985), takes the passage from *A Farewell to Arms* where Frederic Henry describes his wounding and applies it directly to Hemingway's own experience ('Ernest tried hard "to breathe but my breath would not come . . ."') with no hint that he is taking his description from a fictional source.[6] Private experience connects up with both public persona and creative activity in a way that has proved particularly unfortunate to Hemingway's recent reputation. As Diane Johnson suggests, speaking of the way in which present-day ideology has affected readings of his work

> The modern world of male sensitivity groups and paternity leave has felt uncomfortable with the crudely phallic emblems of masculinity – the gun and the fishing rod – that decorate his plots, with his enjoyment, today so suspect, of killing defenceless wild animals and with his supposed inability to write about women. And so some have derided his books, which is really rather unfair, as if we were to throw out Jane Austen now that women are more independent and need not look to marriage as the sole possible female destiny.[7]

There is more to say here, however, in both literary and biographical terms, as critics have now begun to recognise. The phallic emblems that scatter his plots are matched and countered by the impotence (both physical and psychological) of many of his male protagonists and their insecure sense of their own sexual identity. And in the biographical area, work done over the last two decades has dented beyond repair the myth of Hemingway as male culture hero, as a 'hard-living, hard-drinking, hard-fighting adventurer always in the end the master of his fate'.[8] Kenneth Lynn has effectively examined both life and fiction in his *Hemingway* (1987) to show how anxieties about gender roles and sexuality make any remaining attempt to consign the author automatically and simply to the 'cult of masculinity' bracket misguided in the extreme.[9]

Much of this recent criticism has been productively concerned with relating Hemingway's life and works to the changing patterns and requirements of American cultural life from the late nineteenth century onward. John Raeburn thus traces Hemingway's celebrity to his close relationship with his American audience. He explicates his role as 'culture hero' as a product of his ability seemingly successfully to reconcile the gospels of work and leisure and the realms of art and action.[10] Michael Reynolds links cultural and biographical context to fictional performance when he traces the radical changes taking place in the Oak Park, Illinois, of Hemingway's boyhood. Commenting on the fact that not a single story was written by the author about this world, he sees it as a kind of lost, simpler country standing behind his fiction: 'Oak Park remains beneath the surface, invisible and inviolate. It was his first world . . . lost, not to the war, but to modern times.'[11] Scott Donaldson widens this frame of reference when he links Hemingway's appeal to his contemporaries to shared cultural background and concerns. '[Hemingway's] ideas', he writes, 'came originally from the American middle class in the American Midwest at the turn of the century. . . . He owes much of his staying power, in fact, to the sense of communion which his writing generates. He came from the same culture as most middle-class Americans of his time, and [he] . . . mirrored and helped to shape the thinking of that culture.'[12]

If Hemingway's work comes out of this particular American context, it has a larger reference and resonance too. Reynolds's phrase concerning 'the world [Hemingway] lost . . . to modern times' is particularly revealing here. The forms and themes, contradictions and tensions, of Hemingway's work relate directly to his response to modernity and its conditions. In this study I will selectively examine both the fiction and non-fiction to illustrate how this is so.

In the first chapter of this book, I discuss, perhaps predictably, Hemingway's style. This is after all his most distinctive characteristic. I use Georg Lukacs's essay, 'Narrate or Describe?', as a starting point here. Lukacs's criticism of naturalism and modernism and the language he uses to describe them could, it seems to me, have been written with Hemingway's work specifically in mind. And, though his essay is now somewhat dated, his opposition to the diminished nature of the modernist stance and the partial nature of its representation of reality can be taken as a paradigm for later critical attacks on Hemingway which, whether from a Marxist or even a feminist perspective, would focus on the restricted nature of his fictional world. Responding to such a position, I show what I see as both the intent and the achievement of Hemingway's style.

My middle two chapters examine the twin themes of identity and gender. The status of the subject in Hemingway and her or his sense of sexual identity interconnects with the nature of historical change. In the modern world he depicts, the subject's position is both unstable and uncertain, and the concept of 'identity' is consequently marked off as something very provisional indeed. Similar instabilities come to affect the structure of gender relations as traditional versions of masculinity, in particular, are placed under threat. The sexual concerns of Hemingway's fiction relate directly to such informing conditions.

In my final chapter, I focus on the use of place in Hemingway's writing with specific reference to America, Africa and Spain. The last two function, I would suggest, as imaginatively potential (though actually impossible) havens in a modernised world in which, to use the particularly appropriate title of Jackson Lears's book on late nineteenth-century American culture, 'No Place of Grace' can be found.[13] In Hemingway's most interesting work the private subject struggles to negotiate a changing or changed socio-historical order. It is the way in which this conflict is represented which gives that sense of thematic resonance and of taut narrative power which is so typical of his writing at its best.

2

Style: Personal Impressions

In narration . . . the reader may grasp the real causality of the epic events. And only the experience of this causality can communicate the sense of a real chronological, concrete, historical sequence. . . . With the loss of the art of narration . . . any artistic relationship to the composition as a whole is lost . . . the vitality, vibrance and exuberance of life withdraws into the minute image.

(Georg Lukacs)[1]

The opening lines of A Farewell to Arms cast a spell. They do not altogether make sense except as pure visual impressionism.

(Alfred Kazin)[2]

I

When Hemingway's protagonists act there is a disturbing quality to the nature of such actions. A type of alienation effect is produced whereby, though 'the characters [may] come on with a heavy preponderance of active verbs . . . the effect is passive'. Even when these characters initiate actions 'they influence nothing; events happen to them'.[3] In Hemingway, the desire for authentic individual expression comes up headlong against a set of larger circumstances which deny such a possibility. It is this condition that his fiction represents. His protagonists are powerless in the face of history. The stress on action and sensation in his prose cannot be separated from a type of passive determinism.

I use Georg Lukacs's comments in the essay, 'Narrate or

Describe?', to approach this issue. Lukacs, who writes from a Marxist perspective, believes in the possibility of grasping the 'real causality' (p. 133) of events. This translates in terms of literary politics to a belief in the writer as one who can see and chart the direction of historical sequence and show 'significant human beings' (p. 125) actively participating to affect the life of their society. The forging of Hemingway's style begins with his lack of confidence in such participations. In 'Now I Lay Me', Nick Adams says of his orderly, John's, experience in 1914: 'They had taken him for a soldier' (*MWW*, 129). The undefined nature of that pronoun and its sense of uncontrollable larger force mirrors the deterministic implications of Frederic Henry's belief in *A Farewell to Arms* that 'The world breaks everyone' (*FA*, 178).

In Hemingway the subjective 'I' is out of kilter with an impinging and threatening world. Lukacs sees true realism in terms of the creation of a narrative that in its formal completion makes full historical sense of those episodes it describes. For Hemingway, private sensation and public meaning are in tense relationship. His short stories and early novels foreground the interaction between the subject and his[4] immediate context (presented in terms of a sequence of strong images), but with precise historical detail and fully developed contextual setting absent. This reflects the fact that, for Hemingway, the 'dynamic interaction' between character and 'objects and events' has broken down. Any understanding of 'historical sequence'[5] in which the individual plays a meaningful part has been replaced by the (static) condition of the modern in which the human subject stands in anxious and passive relationship to the surrounding 'gear-and-girder'[6] world, totally unable to influence it significantly.

In the version of modernity Hemingway gives us, history is just there as something that conditions and constrains. His fictional subjects are peculiarly and strongly alienated from the everyday world of historical and social praxis, and seem to exist in a type of ideological vacuum precisely because of their inability to find any meaningful and positive connection with the larger public arena. Thus Jake Barnes in *The Sun Also Rises* is positioned as a spectator and consumer, 'just looking' at a European cultural and social scene to which he does not properly belong. So too in the short stories we are given brief narrative sequences that involve protagonists who are either passing through foreign territory – literally in

'Out of Season', metaphorically in 'The Battler' – or are alien in other ways to the given socio-historical context, like Krebs in 'Soldier's Home'. Alternatively such central characters are spatially at one remove from full social involvement, like Nick in 'Big Two-Hearted River'. These protagonists look, listen, talk, taste, buy and act or fail to act, but this behaviour is peripheral and appears at first glance irrelevant to any larger socio-historical context.

In his early and most influential work, Hemingway practises what Lukacs would call an impressionist mode of writing. 'A series of subjective impressions',[7] a succession of episodic, disconnected and self-oriented details, replace the latter's version of realism as 'chronological, concrete, historical sequence'. Hemingway's impressionism is marked by a focus on 'the beholder's effort to capture one detail after another'[8] rather than to take in the larger picture. While this tactic indicates, as I will show, a resistance to the static and harmful conditions of modernity, paradoxically it reveals at the same time exactly its pressures and conditioning effects.

Hemingway's modernist poetics[9] operate first and foremost through the foregrounding of subjective experience. It is the 'minute image' round which his texts focus as these images substitute for, and battle against, objective 'truth' or historical overview. The individual positions himself through subjective impression as he tries to negotiate a world whose larger meanings all speak of his irrelevance and powerlessness.

Hemingway's protagonists, then, encounter their immediate world impressionistically – through the data of their senses. Hemingway's use of the first-person voice encourages an elision of the gap between the subject who is the reader and the textual subject. His use of a transparent third-person narrator often has a similar effect. The world of external reality does not lose its importance (Fredric Jameson claims this happens in Impressionist painting[10]). What does happen though is that the range of outer experience to which reference is made is limited to the immediate province of direct sensation. So when Hemingway describes Nick's actions in 'Big Two-Hearted River', the essential reality presented is that which the senses can confirm. What Nick sees, what Nick does, what Nick feels – how he acts in and responds to the world which directly surrounds him – is what the reader knows. One detail is captured after another:

Nick went over to the pack and found, with his fingers, a long nail in a paper sack of nails, in the bottom of the pack. He drove it into the pine tree, holding it close and hitting it gently with the flat of the ax. He hung the pack up on the nail. All his supplies were in his pack. They were off the ground and sheltered now.

Nick was hungry. He did not believe he had ever been hungrier. He opened and emptied a can of pork and beans. (*EH*, 345–6)

Nick's actions are described in the exact sequence of their occurrence. He feels with his fingers, carefully drives the nail into the tree. The focus is on vision, touch and (limited) knowledge: how to do things – how to make supplies, for instance, 'safe'. Nick's hunger is 'earned', a natural response to a hot day and a long walk. The reader will soon be told how Nick can smell the simple food cooking, and how good it tastes: '"Geezus Chrise," he said happily.' Here the reader is being carefully led, via the stress on the senses, on basic actions (homemaking and cooking) and on simple emotions (happiness), to a belief that here Nick has touched base, got back to the necessary essentials to enjoy life and to function, apparently, as an autonomous subject.

Thus Hemingway, in focusing on Nick's sensations, what directly 'impresses' him, does not subordinate external reality but rather concentrates only on that which is immediately at hand. Alfred Kazin refers to Hemingway's imitation of Cézanne and sees the greatness of the latter as lying in the 'removal of his subjects from the contingent world'.[11] In Hemingway's case, this is both true and not true. Here, for example, Nick is positioned in relation to that which surrounds him – countryside, river and swamp – but this contingent world is very narrow. The scenes that compose the story initially appear as if within a frame, self-sufficient in themselves. Any larger sense of contingent reality – where and with whom Nick lives, and what he does – drops away, and the relation of these scenes to the extended narrative of his life is repressed. However, and this is central to my argument, the larger defining context for these sharply defined scenes may be repressed, but is never quite forgotten. The conditioning force of wider historical reality may not be directly presented but is indirectly realised as we move through Nick's immediate perceptions and feelings – by means of symbols (the burned townscape and grass-hoppers, and the swamp) and by the veiled references to what lies outside the immediate presented scene – to a clear awareness of its informing presence and powerful and damaging effect.

There is an urge here toward solipsism – the apparent elimination of ideology as the subject negotiates and responds to a very limited presented scene. But it is not, and cannot be, completely successful. For the subject's thoughts and actions are linked irremediably to a larger and oppressive historical frame. Although no full analysis of socio-historical force is given, the crucial nature of its influence cannot be denied. Perception and a stress on the data of the senses may be ends in themselves for his protagonists, a way of asserting their subjectivity and compensating for the impersonal power and damaging effect of external reality.[12] But Hemingway's fictional methods (the repetitions and oppositions that cause interpretation[13]) and the peculiar disconnection and passivities of his fictional subjects suggest that the final power and *impressing* stamp of this reality cannot go unrecognised

Hemingway, then, concentrates on the presentation of brief and powerful scenes. He foregrounds the individual sensibility as it positions itself in relation to those material objects and human subjects, that physical environment and those directly experienced events which compose the immediate and informing context of such scenes. This immediate interaction leads in two directions. First, it suggests the gap that lies between the individual, and necessarily limited, subjective state and what is 'other' to it – both the objective world and those unknown or partially known human actors in it. There is always in Hemingway an awareness of the partial nature of the presented narrative. Such a stress on the protagonist's response to his immediate environment, that which he knows (physically or psychologically) at first hand, means *of necessity* that any larger historical frame is presented only in glimpses and/or as it effects the present flow of consciousness of the protagonist. Immediate sense impression, the capturing of the chain of the detail that hits eye or mind most forcefully, pushes any full sense of the 'contingent world' (the range of socio-historical conditions that contextualise the subject's present acts and thoughts in the presented scene) to the margins of the text.

What results is a representation of epistemological fluidity. William James wrote that the 'world is full of partial stories that run parallel to one another, beginning and ending at odd times. They mutually interlace and interfere at points, but we cannot unify them completely in our minds'.[14] This points to the recognition of the rifts in, and instabilities and limits of, knowledge. Hemingway built such a recognition into both the style and form of his fiction. Grand narratives, fully coherent and explanatory, disappear from view. Different focalisations – points of view and value-systems – vie with one another for authority in a relativistic textual world (I will return to this point in future chapters). His central protagonists engage the facts of their known world within narrow limits.

This epistemological fluidity exists, however, within an over-riding deterministic frame. Again the apparent paradox can be explained. For the second direction in which the self/other interrelation leads us in these fictions is to reveal those conditioning pressures of modernity which Hemingway sees as damaging any sense of subjective autonomy. His focus on individual sensation, brief scene and selective viewpoint is part of the presentation of the world of the isolated self. All the 'bitten-off'[15] narratives we are given, though, and all the bits and pieces of personal and public history they contain, as well as their symbolic frame, combine to persuade of the larger fact of an impersonal power and a conditioning force which would deny the authority and validity of that subject. We remain in his fictional world caught between partial story and general truth.[16] What is lost between the two is any sense of history as ordered and progressive sequence or as something that the individual can influence, or with which he can interact meaningfully, one way or another. This is the excluded middle of Hemingway's fictional world. It is a world with the individual subject on one side and all that conditions him (including that generally monolithic and fixed social order that is the product of modernity) on the other. Only tension and no concord or compromise exists between the two poles. The only way out of this situation is by attempting (against the odds) to redefine the nature of the subject or by (impossibly) returning to what are constructed as pre-modern cultures; those of Spain and Africa in particular. I will examine such attempts further in my second and final chapters.

Hemingway's fiction, then, is peculiarly double-edged as the alienation effects and forms of disassociation we find there suggest.

In his work we find paradox, but a paradox with which most readers will strongly sympathise. For Hemingway both writes and denies the 'myth of the self'.[17] His narratives are filtered through the individual feeling subject but that 'ground' which is history denies the ultimate value of such feelings. This ground figures in his stories as something to be evaded and resisted, but always the difficulty of so doing is built into these narratives, both stylistically and thematically.

The conditions of modernity challenge any notion of the autonomous subject. Broad changes in the patterns of late nineteenth-century life led to the collapse of prior ideas of an independent self. Hemingway's fiction clearly shows how an impersonal and incorporated world impinges on the subject and renders him powerless in the public arena. At the same time, however, his foregrounding of the senses as a 'theme in their own right' indicates a deep resistance to such knowledge. In showing the world through the impressions of a single subject he reconstructs a 'myth of the self' to resist and compensate for that recognised oppressive historical world. The stress on private feeling (direct sensation, individual expectation and desire) is a type of 'containment strategy'[18] in a world that bears down heavily on the subject and is beyond his power of control. Such a strategy is aimed at countering the distinguishing oppressive characteristics of modern life. Hemingway's fiction moves between the necessity for such a strategy if we are to retain any sense of ourselves (the data of our senses compose our sense of the world we inhabit) and the knowledge that such a sense of ourselves is already fatally compromised. For the workings of our senses are in fact a *response to* the conditions that have already invalidated their independence and epistemological efficacy. I will develop this important issue as I proceed.

II

Now, though, I am going to do three things. First, I will briefly sketch the distinctive characteristics of Hemingway's style. This ground has been often covered, so I will not spend very long on it. Rather, I trust that the way it functions will be clearly depicted as I

develop my argument in the chapter as a whole concerning the
negotiations between subjective experience and objective reality
which gives that style its fuller meanings. Next, I will suggest
Hemingway's relation to his modernist contemporaries, paying
particular attention to Ezra Pound. Third, I will examine in detail
one story, 'Now I Lay Me', both to illustrate some of my prior
points in fuller form and to show Hemingway's complex narrative
techniques at work.

Hemingway has a distinctive stylistic signature. His prose is a
'degree zero' type of writing, a bare minimalist style in which
reticence is the order of the day and in which none of the larger
meanings of the narrative are spelled out for the reader's ease of
access. At the same time, metaphoric patterns are revealed, most
particularly by his use of repetition, which lead the reader in the
direction of interpretation. It is a stress on concrete and physical
detail, however, that forms the underpinning of Hemingway's
writing. In *Death in the Afternoon*, he describes his attempt to 'put
down what really happened in action; what the actual things were
which produced the emotion that you experienced' (*DA*, 8). This
would appear to be a claim for transparency – a one-to-one
relationship between text and world ('to put down . . . what the
actual things were') straight out of the realist handbook. Again,
though, his paratactic style, which draws so much attention to the
sequence of events ('Uncle George was smoking a cigar in the
dark. The young Indian pulled the boat way up the beach. Uncle
George gave both the Indians cigars' – *EH*, 271) and to acute and
immediate perception and sensation, in fact conceals a careful
concentration on formal design.

In Hemingway, metonymic surface disguises metaphoric depth.
While he uses realistic techniques to achieve strong intimacy
between text and reader and to present a textual world of certainty
and immediacy (places, objects, conversations, how the weather
was), his simultaneous stress on the text's verbal and figurative
patternings opens up a series of deeper (non-temporal and non-
sequential) meanings that work formally against such transparent
representationalism. Such a tension acts in part merely to position
Hemingway as a modernist writer. It is a particular combination of
qualities, though, that marks his particular distinctiveness. On one
hand there is a stark, paratactic and strongly concrete depiction of
reality and a refusal explicitly to spell out larger meanings (his

famous 'iceberg' theory). This blends, however, with a compositional emphasis on those 'quasi-poetical links'[19] that form the overall abstract literary design and lead us toward that interpretation which his textual surfaces apparently deny.

Further connections can be made between Hemingway and that modernist movement which to some degree contextualises him. The influences on Hemingway's artistic development were many. Michael Reynolds points out his skill and adeptness as a pupil, 'one who always learned quickly, one who could seize anyone's gift and make it his own'.[20] His study of other writers and painters (both modernist and pre-modernist) was crucial to his own artistic self-development. Flaubert, Turgenev, Joyce and Cézanne were of especial importance to him. So too were those earlier American writers – Twain, James, Crane, London – and his older contemporary, Anderson.

Ezra Pound and Gertrude Stein, though, had the most immediate impact on Hemingway as a stylist. I do not want to linger too long on Stein here. I would suggest that it was her use of the 'continuous present' that had most effect on his work. For Stein, influenced by William James, focused in her prose on the flow of consciousness. Time was conceived of as 'a series of disconnected instants, each creating a new situation and requiring a new effort of the attention, each claiming equal importance with all others'.[21] The detailing of the sequence of fact and motion in Hemingway, and the paratactic sentences that are so typical (with their sense of fluid temporal movement and lack of hierarchical distinction) – this happens and then this happens – can be seen as bearing a direct relationship to Stein here, as can his impressionistic method. Epistemological coherence is a myth in Stein's work. A stress on immediate perception and knowledge is foregrounded at the expense of any full sense of a larger unity – of a complete and ordered historical narrative. Although she moves much further than Hemingway in this respect and in her consequent representation of the dislocation of the subject, they both work from similar starting points. Stein's preoccupation with ellipsis and silence – 'Silence is so windowful'[22] – also connects up crucially with Hemingway's writing practice.

In the linguistic patternings of his prose, Hemingway also owed a debt to Stein. Her shift away from rational discourse and toward a focus on the play of language on the textual surface undoubtedly had its effect on his work. He acknowledges, in *A Moveable Feast*, the 'valid and valuable . . . truths about rhythms and the uses of words in repetition' (*MF*, 21) that she taught him. Her concentration on the musicality of language though, on repetition and rhythm, often operate at the expense of direct meaning. Hemingway's own sharp referentiality moved counter to her resistance to the sense-making process associated with conventional rational discourse. Stein's poetry is based on the principle of deferral, with individual words and phrases making sense in themselves but not in combination. Complete and stable meanings are never bestowed on these unanchored words and phrases but always put off, delayed.[23] Stein does not abandon the referential world, though, for the heavy repetition of individual words draws the reader back to their particular (if unanchored) referential base. The odd effect then occurs where we are hammered by, our attention constantly focused on, a particular word and its reference, while our sense of a larger context, a fuller grammatical and epistemological frame, disappears. Hemingway's experimentations never took him this far. Stein's patterns of repetition and the drawing of acute attention to a particular word or words undoubtedly influenced him, but, in his prose, language is clearly referential in a way that Stein often resists. The stress on repetition he learnt from her became in his spatial poetics a way of guiding interpretation. In her case, this is not necessarily so.[24]

Hemingway's referential accessibility and syntactical simplicity help to explain why he appealed to a wider type of readership than Stein. His letters show how clearly he had such a general readership in mind. Discussing the saleability of *In Our Time* with his publisher, Horace Liveright, Hemingway compared his work with E. E. Cummings's *The Enormous Room* (1922). His remarks signal his difference from Stein too. He claimed that those who were not well versed in '"modern" writing' would not be able to read Cummings's book, while his would rather be one that 'will be praised by highbrows and can be read by lowbrows. There is no writing in it that anybody with a high-school education cannot read' (*L*, 155).

It is the influence that Ezra Pound had on Hemingway, however, which is particularly relevant to my larger argument. The stress on immediacy found in Stein is channelled in the direction of physical sensation alone in Pound's Imagist writings and is linked to a severe economy of style. Both fitted Hemingway's emerging artistic needs. Pound said that 'all knowledge is built up from a rain of factual atoms.'[25] Hemingway's praise of Melville in *Green Hills of Africa* for his account of 'how things, actual things, can be' (*GH*, 24) echoes this. Both men believed that the language of a previous generation had lost its signifying effectiveness. Krebs in 'Soldier's Home' looks at 'the bacon fat hardening on his plate' as his mother describes her worry about him: 'I know the temptations you must have been exposed to. I know how weak men are. . . . I pray for you all day long, Harold.' Her repeated 'I know's' reveal a confidence about the way the world works that the returning soldier cannot share. Her religious discourse and abstract categorisations bear no relation to his experience. The hardening bacon fat is something he can see and smell, close at hand. His focus on it proves an effective way for Hemingway to ironise a situation in which the mother's talk of 'aim in life', 'credit to the community', 'no idle hands in His Kingdom' (*EH*, 307) just has, for Krebs, no real meaning. The unpleasant connotations implicit in the image — what was clear, tasty and hot congealing as it cools — also provides a metonymic/metaphoric comment on the lack of appetite he has for her words. The homecomer is in fact a type of alien. He understands the words that are spoken but can relate them to nothing that he knows. Belleau Wood has rendered his mother's pious language and framework of conventional belief a nonsense. The world now contingent to Krebs is one from which he is absolutely disconnected — whose language and values he cannot share.

Jacob Korg foregrounds the change in value systems associated with the modernist movement: 'conventional syntax and vocabulary silently insinuated assumptions about time, space, matter, causality, the mind, the self and other elementary concepts which were becoming obsolete'.[26] Hemingway's reworking of syntax and vocabulary was part and parcel of an altered conception of reality. The fictional subject, as in Krebs's case, is left acting in, or (mainly) reacting to, an immediate contextual frame, with all larger (positive) conceptual frames of reference in doubt. Certain assumptions about the deterministic nature of reality are inherent in Hemingway's early writing but they only leave his characters decentred — able to function only by concentrating on immediate sensation and event, on private details eccentric from that world of public history which should, in Lukacs's terms, properly give their lives its meaning. The stress both on visual process and the particularity of the immediate response – Pound's intention to 'paint the thing as I see it'[27] – become in Hemingway's case, too, a way of questioning and rejecting the traditional meanings of the past.

Undoubtedly, Pound's stylistic pronouncements and practice considerably affected both Hemingway's thinking and his writing. Pound's stress on factual atoms and his rejection of 'ornamental metaphor' (where the encroaching hand of the artist is obtrusively felt) might be used as a direct explanation of the differences in stylistic presentation of *In Our Time* from the more ornate descriptions of the early journalism. There, writing of the Parisian 'apaches' who occasionally held people up, he tells how 'they sometimes hit too hard, or shoot too quick, and then life becomes a very grim matter with an upright machine that casts a thin shadow and is called a guillotine at the end of it' (*WY*, 81). The figurative play and shift away from the thing itself to its trace or shadow in this sequence is a long way removed from the technique used in 'Soldier's Home', where figurative effect arises directly from the sharp and immediate presence of the object itself, the bacon fat hardening on the plate. The statements on Imagism associated with Pound (his directives to cut unnecessary words and to 'go in fear of abstractions'[28]) point directly to Hemingway's prose. His poetry too shows Pound's influence, sometimes to imitative excess. Although it cannot necessarily be taken as his final or fully considered word on the matter, Hemingway wrote in 1933 that he 'had learned more from Pound than from any other person'.[29]

Pound's watchwords were concreteness, precision and accuracy. His idea of 'luminous detail' is, however, I would argue, one that especially influenced Hemingway but which the latter modified to suit his particular needs and beliefs. Pound proposed that the writer should concentrate on those details that 'give one a sudden insight into circumjacent conditions, into their causes, their effects, into sequence and law. . . . The artist seeks out the luminous detail and presents it. He does not comment.'[30] This reads in its latter part like an alternative version of Hemingway's own 'iceberg' theory.

The vignettes that appear in *In Our Time* (1925) provide a working illustration of such luminous effect. I would ask my reader to remind her/himself of vignette five – that commencing 'They shot the six cabinet ministers' (*EH*, 292). It is the very form of the vignette – a fragment, a brief narrative, something removed from a full context – that gives the occurrences depicted in it their luminosity. I will argue, though, that this works against an understanding of immediate historical context. This mini-narrative is broken-off both in terms of time and space from anything that might surround it.

The narrator or author is invisible within the vignette. Events stand by themselves, and it is the details of those events to which our attention is drawn. We see what the narrator sees. His focalisation (or point of view) is the one we share. The whole story (what happened) is given in the first sentence of the sketch: who was shot and where and when. We cannot, however, fail to be aware of what is *not* given. What country did these cabinet ministers serve? What are their names? Why are they being shot? Which morning is this and what hospital? What are they doing there? Pound's 'sudden insight' into cause and effect, sequence and law, initially appears to be denied as we are just given the details, the minutiae, of the immediate scene – 'pools of water', 'shutter . . . nailed shut'. The background knowledge we are given is minimal and comes from the informed narrator. He chooses to tell us of the men's status as cabinet ministers and the fact that one of them has typhoid. Presumably he could fill in all the other absent information too if he wished. The fact that he does not do so suggests that that is not the point of the exercise.

Here a brief but powerful series of images 'shine forth in their unique reality',[31] to quote Laszlo Gefin on Pound, but also work to further effect. The insights we gain from them, however, bear no relation at all to 'circumjacent conditions' and it is this that marks one difference between the two writers. What insights are realised from the vignette? Robert Scholes suggests that, as a general rule, we can move as readers from what is given on the page to our interpretation of it (what is unsaid and implied) by looking for the oppositions and repetitions that are evident in the text. In other words, we have ways of moving beyond the immediate clear scene. This connects up with the modernist conception of spatial form. In this vignette the main repetition concerns water ('pools . . . water . . . wet . . . rained . . . rain . . . puddle . . . water . . . water'), though variants of standing and sitting are also repeated. So too is the notion of death – the described 'dead leaves' connecting by association with the firing of the volley, the shooting with which the passage starts and (almost) ends. The oppositions of the passage can be organised round concepts of indoors and outdoors with the hospital, a place for the care of the sick or wounded but also a place of hospitality, sealed off behind those nailed shutters and contrasted with the courtyard outside, the sodden place of death. This yard is, however, enclosed by the hospital itself as if to emphasise the claustrophobic and constricted nature of the presented scene. Death is of course contrasted with life, with the sick minister initially a type of transgressive figure positioned between these two states: suffering from typhoid but still alive. He ends up dead but, ironically, from a different cause.

There are two final noteworthy oppositions in the vignette. The civilian world is set against the military one, and the fact here that civilian leaders are victims of a military firing squad tells us clearly that this is a time of political change and disturbance. Only in such circumstances could this particular interrelationship between the two (normally separate) kinds of authorities come about. Secondly, the passage also hinges on vertical/horizontal oppositions: the standing men, the wall and the shutters counterposed by the nails, the paving, the pools and the volley. The man seated with his head on his knees disrupts this patterning. That sick minister is thus twice presented as a transgressive figure and readerly attention is consequently centred on him.

We can get this far in terms of the symbolic resonances of the vignette. Its sharp details lead in the direction of insight (though not, in this particular case, in the 'sudden' way triggered by Pound's use in his poems of the immediate contrast and con-junction of images). But we are unable to position the scene in an extended narrative sequence which might give it fuller meaning. We are, though, given knowledge of a general condition – and its consequences – which, as it were, cancels the very concept of cause, effect and sequence as it relates to immediate historical context. For there is a jump here from sharp detail to general truth that bypasses any sense of developing history. The larger condition revealed here is one of individual powerlessness and passivity (effect) in the face of greater force (cause). To return to Lukacs, 'the opposition between the individual and the objective world is so stark and crude that no dynamic interaction is possible' (p. 144).

On the one hand we have the brief and static scene – for though action does take place it is strictly enclosed within a fixed and very limited spatial-temporal frame. On the other, we have the static condition of the modern – a world where larger, dislocating and uncontrollable force operates over and over again. Lost between the two is 'sequence', the notion of historical process and the development, change and improvement that it makes possible.

It is in examining the repetitions and oppositions of the vignette that what Hemingway posits as the larger (static) condition of the modern is evident. All the fragments of history on which he so intently focuses – he refers to the interchapters of *In Our Time* in terms of 'looking at [something] with 15× binoculars' (*L*, 128) – fit the same general sense of haphazardness and meaningless repetition. To give a fuller sense of 'adjacent circumstance' would gain nothing since the individual incident cannot be fitted into any progressive historical narrative.

It is, however, possible to fill out the historical detail from which Hemingway has constructed this sketch. Kenneth Lynn and Michael Reynolds quote respectively a news story and a news headline (of 29 November 1922) reporting on the 11.30 a.m. execution of six men, including ex-Premier Gounaris of Greece, in Goudi Square outside Athens, for their part in bearing responsibility for Greece's defeat by Turkey in the recent war.[32] Both critics give these news stories to show how Hemingway only used these reported facts in order to rework them imaginatively. In reworking them, though, the immediate historical context drops away. Hemingway is not interested in the 'circumjacent conditions'. He is concerned with what he sees as a general truth, and it is this to which he keeps returning us in *In Our Time*. The vignette does radiate outward from 'the stark statement'[33] of the scene itself. Its details, and the foregrounded sick figure who dies sitting in the puddle with his head on his knees, do suggest a larger picture of a world of death, pain, violence and political confusion and one without pity or charity (so those nailed shutters connote). This is a world (and *In Our Time* is a text) of brief broken episodes where the only larger whole in sight is that of random victimisation and institutional oppression. The inevitability of biological collapse and a return to physical basics, both also illustrated here, complete his grim picture. Any kind of heroic meaning is shorn away in a sketch which focuses on the slumped body, not the dignified end. A random and uncontrollable external reality does not allow for any 'dynamic interaction' with it on the individual's part. Passivity of response is the only option. The syntax of the vignette emphasises this: 'One of the ministers *was sick with* typhoid.' All he actually *does* is to sit down (twice).

In Our Time operates generally in the manner described above. Hemingway's stress on concrete detail – or as Lukacs might call them, 'delicately delineated minutiae' (p. 131) – relates directly to a view of the world where individual sequence cannot be fitted to progressive historical narrative and where subjective impression and objective 'truth' are in conflict. In the vignettes that have war or political turmoil as their context, a rigorous dehistoricisation of the immediate event occurs.[34]

Carlos Baker's comment about the bullfighting vignettes suggests a similar type of writing practice on Hemingway's part as he turns to a different subject. Again it is exactly the larger sense of situation that is omitted. Baker stresses this in his judgement of the 'They whack-whacked the white horse' (*EH*, 314) sequence as:

> a writer's apprentice exercise. . . . He puts down what he sees, exactly as he sees it. He eliminates from his view the panorama, the weather, the crowd, the waiting matadors, the price of the seats, the hardness of the bench on which he sits, the odour of his neighbour, the colour of the sky, the degree of the temperature. Instead he watches the horse, and what takes place immediately around the horse, with a tremendous intensity of concentration.[35]

To describe the vignette as apprentice work is again somewhat to miss the point, in that the very essence of Hemingway's early technique lies in such an intensity of concentration on the individual concrete details of a scene. To stress such details *at the cost of* any larger narrative whole explains in part the very effectiveness of *In Our Time* and the vignettes in particular. For in the vignettes we move from one concentrated visual image to another. These are broken fragments, shifting us as readers from scene to scene, some of which connect and some of which differ entirely in terms of geography and immediate subject. Their overall (as well as their individual) effect depends on the repetition of certain key words and images. Words like 'wall', 'road', 'up', 'down' and 'drunk' recur insistently: so too do certain types of image. The bull's 'legs [are] caving' (*EH*, 323) presumably like those of the cabinet minister as he sits down in a puddle of water. The young girl is 'scared sick' (*EH*, 275) while watching a childbirth, sharing similar emotions both to the man in the bombardment who 'lay very flat and sweated and prayed' (*EH*, 302) and to the horse which is 'nervously unsteady' (*EH*, 314) in the bullfight (notions of both fear and collapse come together in this last).

Through repetition, cross-reference and analogy – both within and between individual vignettes and between vignettes and stories – the general state of what it means to live 'in our time' begins to emerge. A sense of pain, fear, danger, violence and dislocation connect scenes that together fail to compose a unified sequence. Questions about control and the lack of it, and the related issue of where the margins between human and animal behaviour lie, are constantly raised by such means. Hemingway moves thematically in the vignettes between the worlds of warfare, politics, urban crime and bullfighting – between Europe and America too. Any meaningful sense of social and historical difference is obliterated as such a move is made, since all subject matter shares the same general condition.

Hemingway then departed from Pound's theory in a highly significant way. It can be argued that Pound's own movement away from Imagism was a recognition that the move from acute detail to larger sequences of cause and effect could not be successfully accomplished within its limits. His urge, which the Cantos evidence most clearly, to move from the part to the coherent whole (however personal a form that might take) and to reconnect historical fragments in a larger chain of positive meaning, together with his related concern for *politics*, runs quite counter to what Hemingway was attempting. What Hemingway learnt from him cannot, however, be underestimated.

Pound's pronouncements on, and practice of, literature correlate with Hemingway's writing practice in a number of important ways. Precise observations juxtaposed with one another lead to moments of striking insight, often as a result of implicit metaphoric connection. 'Luminous detail' presented without authorial comment operates as a dominant stylistic mode. This stress on particulars, on concrete objects, leads to sequences of clear and hard images put before the reader with all excess description pared

drastically away. Emotional and intellectual complexity come
directly from the presentation of the physical image. There is a lot
more to Pound than this but his importance as a tutor to Hemingway is evident in the above. His letters reinforce this notion of the
master–pupil relation, with Pound always offering sharp advice:
'keep your eye on the objek MORE, and be less licherary. . . .
ANYTHING put on on top of the subject is BAD. . . . The subject is
always interesting enough without the blankets.'[36]

III

I will now use one Hemingway story, 'Now I Lay Me', to illustrate
how the deceptive simplicity of his writing masks his careful
control of narrative technique. This is to examine in a single
instance how he creates his narrative effects. I will also continue to
pursue my earlier general arguments. For this story, like the other
Nick Adams stories, is a partial narrative that roots the reader in
the subjective impressions of the protagonist as he meets, and
retreats from, the realm of contemporary public history. Subjective
states (thought, feeling and memory) and objective world (the
realm of material things and events) are bound together in-
extricably in the story. Reality in Hemingway is known through
the power of the senses. Full and coherent overview and controlled
analysis of either a private or a public narrative are impossible to
the subject whose damaged being results from his very positioning
within a story whose beginnings (or at least their effects) are cloudy
and whose endings are unknown. This subject's senses are foregrounded as a 'theme in their own right', but the validity of such a
theme is contradicted by the prior damage dealt that subject.
Where such damage is clear, it can only be countered by a reliance
on those same senses whose message signals the collapse of
autonomy and control. This same double bind runs throughout
Hemingway's early texts.
    As I focus my attention on how the fictional effects of the story
are created, I will show how the powerful visual and aural images
that are so central to it relate directly to Nick's emotional and
psychological state. The larger historical context, the area of public
meaning, is pushed to the margins of the text as we focus in on

Nick's damaged and solipsistic consciousness (solipsistic due to his need to resist that very context). The workings of this consciousness as it reflects and struggles with the nature of private and public experience as it knows them and as it renegotiates them in memory (the damage has *already* been done in both realms) constitute the story. Nick's senses and impressions, described in a kind of vacuum, take on heightened significance as the possibility of constructing a linear narrative, where his life can gain coherence and meaning from the things, experiences and events encountered, just drops away to nothing – or rather, to repeated and repressed realisations that any meanings which can be found take overwhelmingly negative form.

One aspect of modernism is its habit of engaging the literary and cultural past in dialogue, and of highlighting the disjunction between traditional meaning and modern displacements of such meaning. Hemingway's version of this appears in his (typical) ploy of taking a traditional quotation, and either emptying it of meaning, or ironising its original meaning, in the use he makes of it. So just as *In Our Time* offers ironic play on the phrase from the Book of Common Prayer ('Give us peace in our time, O Lord'), so the title of this story refers ironically to the simple belief and passive trust in divine protection, both here and in the hereafter, contained in the child's prayer, 'Now I lay me down to sleep'.

The narrative line of 'Now I Lay Me' is straightforward, though, typically for Hemingway's short stories, very little actually happens in terms of action. States of mind (subjective impressions) as they situate themselves in relation to object and event are what concern him most. There are a series of strong material images in this story – the silkworms chewing the mulberry leaves, the jars of snakes preserved in alcohol, ten worms in a tobacco tin – which make for that 'language . . . made out of concrete things . . . clamped to reality'[37] for which Pound called. At first reading this seems a straightforward transparent and mimetic narrative. One third of it, approximately, is made up of one big chunk of straight dialogue with no external interruption at all except the very infrequent 'I said', 'he asked' and 'he said'. But cutting against such initial representational clarity is something quite different. For attention is also drawn to the prose medium itself, to what is happening in terms of the spatial arrangement of language on the printed page, in a way which is unmistakeable. If this is accessible writing, it is also writing of the most 'modern' type. With some elision, parts of it indeed stand as a kind of Steinian experiment in repetition and linguistic rhythm: 'since I had been blown up at night . . . finally it would be light . . . I do not remember a night' (*MWW*, 125, 7, 8).

The whole story operates indeed around principles of repetition. The sound of the silkworms chewing the mulberry leaves, a detail repeated in various forms some ten times in this short narrative, is perhaps the most obvious example of this. Nick's sensitivity to this sound both suggests his emotional state and triggers the textual release of further information concerning his disturbed condition. This type of tactic and method, where one or more strong physical images both dominate and condition our reception of a narrative, is constantly employed in the early work. Such a strong and repeated focus on this one eccentric detail (to our readerly knowledge Nick is the only person aware of such a noise) suggests the way in which we as readers are drawn into a world of private sensation, here through the use of the first-person narrator. The stress on immediate sensation and private image, the concrete detail of childhood memory, relates directly to a need on Nick's part to repress any extended thought of – or detailed reference to – public history (the war). Nick's experience of being 'blown up' and its effect on him are described and act as initial explanation for his mentally unstable condition. But all information about the war is skimpy. Nick is in Italy. He has been wounded, it seems, several times, but has apparently physically recovered. It is implicit that he takes part in 'the October offensive' (*MWW*, 132) – no further detail given – and is then hospitalised in Milan. This is as much of the public story as we know. Public historical context fades to almost nothing as we focus in on one subject and his current and acute sensations.

In terms of the charting of these sensations, it is worth noting that a more complex movement occurs here between present and past time than is usual in Hemingway's short fiction. The time of what Genette would call the 'first narrative'[38] is 'that night' (*MWW*, 125) when Nick lies on the floor listening to the silkworms. This night is one of a whole series of similar nights which Nick remembers and which extend on either side of this date. The story is being narrated by Nick from a point in the future when his state of mind is altered. He is 'now . . . *fairly* sure' [my emphasis] that his soul would not have escaped his body had he allowed himself to go to sleep that summer. This, and the fact that he no longer fishes made-up streams, an activity now referred to in the past tense, might suggest that the period of trauma described in the narrative is over. Other textual signals, however, strongly counter such a reading as I shall show later. If it is initially implied that Nick has managed, at least partially, to work or find his way out of those patterns of repetition that control the time of the first narrative, such an implication is then questioned by the way in which the story develops.

This story is, of course, one of a whole series about Nick Adams, composed at different times and moving back and forth over parts of his life. They illustrate both as a group and at an individual level the same thing. Partial fragments, brief glimpses, of Nick's life are all that we are given, with the lack of a larger sequential coherence suggested by these compositional disruptions of chronological linearity. This in turn brings questions into play about what, if anything, has been learnt by the central protagonist and whether he has developed and changed in significant ways. I return briefly to this issue in Chapter 3. I would argue, however, that we can lay the Nick Adams stories against each other for purposes of comparison and contrast. Thus 'Big Two-Hearted River', a story set later in Nick's life, might suggest that relief from mental distress can be brought about by repetition of past actions – actions there repeated physically rather than mentally. No renewal or new start, though, seems likely. The best Nick can hope for, if we agree to read these two stories in terms of chronological linearity, is someday to be able to fish that swamp he has already fished in the past; someday to repeat again what he did successfully before.

To look at the temporal shifts of 'Now I Lay Me' is to see a to-and-fro movement from the time of the first narrative (the night described at the story's start) to all those other nights when Nick needs, and has needed, to keep himself awake. These latter date from his initially being blown up to some indefinite point prior to his narrating of the story. To look at these shifts is also to see a movement between the time of this general period and those times in the past which locate the series of past remembrances that Nick recounts. These remembrances include the fishing trips he took as a boy, the 'earliest thing' (*MWW*, 126) he recalls (the attic of his grandfather's house), and the people who inhabit his past. The

moment of being blown up which precedes the time of the first
narrative provides both a bridge between that present (and the
time surrounding it) and the recovered past, and a catalyst for
those recaptured memories.

The story's straightforward language and sharp images are
contained within complex chronological patternings. These patternings are further complicated by that other story – that of John,
the Italian orderly – which is bracketed, as it were, within Nick's.[39]
By my count, twelve different chronological periods are introduced
within Nick's story alone. We are, however, continually pulled
back to the time occurring round that of the first narrative – his
sleeplessness 'that summer' (*MWW*, 125) during that war. Any
escape from the constraint and fear associated with this time is
very provisional. If we look, though, not only at the pattern of
temporal to and fros but bring another factor into play – the length
of the relative scenes – we note that past memory clearly, initially,
overwhelms this wartime experience. Such memories comprise, in
terms of text time (the amount of textual space given them)
roughly two-thirds of the first part of the text. With the
introduction of John, Nick's orderly, in the second half of the
narrative (both its sections are approximately the same length) a
shift to dialogue takes place and references to other time periods
become much briefer. Only once that dialogue has ended do we
again get an extended move away from the time of the first
narrative – first into the past, then into the future.

In the first half of the text, where the focus is on Nick alone,
there is one sequence of pronounced mental and emotional activity.
This sequence runs from 'But some nights I could not fish' to 'I
would pray for them both' (*MWW*, 126–8). The depth of Nick's
disturbance here is signalled by the intensity of the activity that
occurs in terms of temporal shifts and the contrast, in terms of
such activity, to the long fishing sequence that textually precedes it.
In the later passages, Nick's memory swoops backward through
time to focus strongly on a series of different – and chronologically
separate – prior scenes. The importance of those particular scenes
involving the 'new house designed and built by my mother'
(*MWW*, 127) within this latter sequence is then further signalled by
the shift of tense that accompanies them and the use of direct
discourse which marks the final recall. Such signals mark this
whole sequence out as of particular narrative interest.

I will examine this sequence, and the calmer (fishing) one that precedes it, in more detail. In the case of the one I have highlighted, the range and selective force of the memories recovered mark their greater significance (in terms of their meaning for, and effect on, Nick) than his earlier remembrances. For the movement and varied intensity of this sequence – as measured in narrative duration – stand in strong contrast to the long and static fishing memory previously recovered.

The fishing passage is generic. One day stands for a whole series of days with any individual variant then foregrounded. It starts with Nick as narrator referring back to the (general) time of the first narrative and to his ways of occupying himself while laying awake at night. One of these is the careful recapturing of a typical morning's fishing as a boy and the activity associated with it. The word 'carefully' (*MWW*, 125) is itself repeated textually here, carrying the reader from the process of Nick's mental activity to the original act of the fishing itself. This memory might be seen, speculatively, as initially calming and comforting to the troubled Nick; the care he takes to recover it matched by the memory of that early well-ordered ritual. Nick then moves on to the subject of bait. This is the point at which it here becomes clear that Nick is not talking of one fishing trip, but a whole series of them. A discussion of the difficulties of finding bait leads, though, into a remembrance which carries for the reader (and certainly, in the second case, for the protagonist too) unpleasant connotations: the cutting up of Nick's own catch to provide more bait and the one-time use of the delicate salamander for similar purpose.

This last act bears symbolic weight. This returns me to Lukacs and his comment that in terms of 'epic interrelationships' – for him, the decisive individual actions which inform and effect historical change – 'not much is gained . . . when a novel is based on the lyrical, self-oriented subjectivity of an isolated individual; a succession of subjective impressions no more suffices to establish an epic interrelationship than a succession of fetishised objects, even when these are inflated into symbols' (p. 134). Hemingway writes his fiction from the belief that epic interrelationships are no longer possible in the modern era. The weight his symbol carries here refers back precisely to a self-oriented subjectivity in that its reverberations attach only to Nick himself. At the same time its very point is to show just how provisional the notion of subject-

ivity has become, given the larger conditions which affect, indeed
help to compose it.

The symbolic effects here cluster round the word 'salamander'.
This word refers to a lizard-like animal supposed to be able to live
in fire and never to be consumed, but has also come to denote 'a
soldier who exposes himself to fire in battle' (*OED*). Nick's own
lack of fireproofness in battle draws together his past concern for
that salamander's fate (he repeats the word 'salamander' three
times in close succession), his own later personal condition, as well
as the concern for fire, burning and destruction that is to be
recurrent in the narrative. More immediately, though, it is evident
that even the best of the past is no secure haven for Nick. Fishing
memories are not all pleasurable. The fact that it is in the swamp
that he cuts up his own catch of trout – destroys that which is
described with so much aesthetic appreciation elsewhere in
Hemingway[40] – points forward to 'Big Two-Hearted River' and to
the possibility of fishing as a 'tragic adventure' (*EH*, 357). After the
discussion of bait, the anxiety implicit there recedes; is controlled.
'Open meadow' (*MWW*, 126) replaces swamp. Routine and con-
sistency are highlighted: regular up and down fishings of streams
from source to exit and vice versa. Creative activity, the powerful
imagining of new streams to the point that they are confused at the
time of narration with streams really known, brings once more a
sense of recovered balance and even of pleasurable excitement as
favoured past activity spurs constructive fantasy ('like being awake
and dreaming') at a time when fear and threat appear the norm.

This solid focus on fishing, then, generally signifies a past time
of safety and pleasure, though even here glitches occur. These
scenes are followed by a much more unstable series of remembrances as Nick's mind – as if time itself were that river to be
traced from source to outlet and then back again – sweeps over his
whole known past. Nick's personal vulnerability in the realm of
public history spurs a return to 'self-oriented subjectivity' as he
plumbs private memory and impression to try to find the coherence and meaning that the public world denies. Nick engages here
on a broadscale fishing of time's river with all its holes and
shallows, a search that takes him back to origins as he returns as
far into his past as he can recall. This long sweep of memory has,
though, very definite boundaries. He recovers significant personal
memories but can only remember back to the attic of his grand-

father's house, a memory consisting of things only, before people enter his mental landscape. He will only remember forward as far as the war. Presumably he avoids that which has happened since as too painful or unpleasant to face. Nick can be seen as a substitute salamander, out of control of his fate just like that 'hooked' creature. He also has been (psychologically and physically) burnt by a series of fires – those which literally occurred in his childhood and the metaphoric ones of war. Nick, though, unlike the the salamander of myth, is not impervious to this element.

Nick's memories are distinctive and not very comforting. Peculiarly, as he conducts his sweeps of memory, the things he first remembers and lingers on are from marginalised areas – the attic and the basement – of the houses he lived in. These areas appear in fact to be spaces shared by both father and son in this narrative. For if the theme of 'Fathers and Sons', to use the title of one of the Nick Adams stories, is a major one for Hemingway, here the father and his belongings seem pushed to the edges of the households described. The houses are not his. His possessions are kept in attic and basement, from there to be taken out and burnt. Two fires are described in this narrative sequence: the first describing the nature of the things burnt; the second, both the things burnt and the people involved. In both cases the things burnt are Nick's father's. It is specified that it is Nick's mother who feeds the second fire and it seems likely (especially in a narrative so locked into repetition) that she also fed the first. Nick appears as an unspeaking bit player in the second of these scenes, at the beck of his father's imperatives: 'Get a rake. . . . Take the gun.' The mother, however, has no communication with him at all. After the commands, which convert Nick into the role of orderly (thus foreshadowing the Nick–John relationship in the second half of the narrative), the father does end with that statement, 'The best arrow-heads went all to pieces' (*MWW*, 128), which suggests an attempt to communicate loss and perhaps elicit sympathy. Such a reading, though, is tentative: he could just be talking aloud to himself. The thrust of all this is, however, to see Nick as sharing his father's marginalisation in the home environment. Nick is only seen in the attic and he has no direct communication with the powerfully active figure of the mother. His marginalisation may in fact be more acute than the father's. In the second incident, after

all, he is initially left alone outside the house when both parents
have entered.

Nick's memories centre on strong physical images. These – his
parents' wedding cake, which hangs from the rafters in a tin box in
the attic, the 'jars of snakes and other specimens' (*MWW*, 126)
popping in a fire, and the chipped and blackened Indian
artefacts – all speak of loss. The cake, symbol of union and
celebration, stands against the given illustration of marital discord
and lack of shared values. The loss of the snakes is an obliteration
of the father's personal history, of those things from his boyhood
that had remained meaningful to him. The same is true of the
Indian artefacts, though this collection may be that of an adult
rather than a boy. The loss of such artefacts might possibly also
signify the loss of an alternative cultural tradition.

The narrative of 'Now I Lay Me' is based around repetition – of
words, images and events. A series of phrases recur in the story.
Nick himself has been wounded (more than once) already and
presumably is wounded once more in the October offensive, given
his hospitalisation in Milan several months after it. He returns in
memory to repeated fishing trips and returns also to the two fires
which stand out in his memory. Repetition can be constructive or
negative. It can lead to development and transformation (to repeat
in order to understand and progress: Ike repeating his past in
Faulkner's *Go Down, Moses* in order to transcend it) or to stasis, to
sheer repetition without difference.[41] Here, the repetitions of
language and image parallel and reinforce the repeated actions of
the protagonist Nick. Caught between the fact of being blown up
at night and the fear of dying in the dark which that experience
has given him, he can only endlessly repeat those actions (praying,
remembering, listening) which form his only defence in the face of
those unsurmountable fears concerning the nature of his own
mortality. This is a story in which there is only repetition and no
renewal, and that fact is formally recognised (if not at a conscious
level by the protagonist) because, as far as Nick's thoughts at night
go, the narrative moves from thinking about fishing to thinking
about fishing. One might claim a minimal form of renewal in the
fact that Nick finds that there is 'always something new' (*MWW*,
132) to remember about those streams he once fished, but the
mental return is only to a past which is already closed and over.

This story's close account of how Nick's consciousness works centres on the psychology of sensation. Certain overdetermined moments are presented as resonant of meaning in a world where coherent larger narrative interconnections have been lost. Sheer repetition here undercuts notions of development and growth. Both the fires described appear to signify not Thoreau's *bon*fires (my emphasis) – 'purifying destruction[s]' of 'trumpery'[42] – but only a bleak sense of an ending of that potential for family harmony and unity that the wedding cake had initially signalled (though faintly so: it is only seen in a box in the attic hanging from a rafter, like a suicide). Fire here is harmful in the way it consumes and destroys. Repetition replaces change; change which is for the worse anyway.

Trawling his past, Nick may find partial comfort and relief in the fishing trips, but as his own mental state deteriorates – 'cold-awake' on the 'nights I could not fish' (*MWW*, 126) – he ranges his memories in search of 'everything that had ever happened to me' (*MWW*, 127). The use of this particular wording together with the consequent focus, not on the developed biographical description one might expect but on the presentation (rather than the analysis) of a brief number of intense scenes suggests that in the personal past as well as the immediate past of public history, Nick is one to whom things have been done. In both areas he remains a puzzled and passive recipient of experience rather than one who is either in control or in full understanding of it. Nick's personal history seems to focus round repeated images of fire, pain, damage and discord. What he finds in the past only confirms what he knows in the present. Praying – or trying to pray – is his final calming ritual as he remembers, and prays for, both father and mother (he makes no judgements on them here). But prayer has already been signalled as ineffective in the ironic gap between the title and what follows.

The power of past events to disturb Nick is indicated by the shift of tense that occurs in the course of this sequence. Immediately the subject of the mother's house is raised, a subject that leads into the detailing of his parents' interactions, this tense change occurs. From the past tense of 'I could only remember', an unusual move takes place in the shift to the present with the words 'I remember' being repeated four times in two paragraphs.[43] Here, as Nick retells his story (this is a retrospective narrative) he apparently repeats the process of remembering activated earlier. He relives these memories so powerfully as he writes that a transgressive effect occurs as the distance between the narrating present and the past (the time of the first narrative) is elided. The alert reader notices this sign of narrative stress. Nick is caught within patterns of repetition from which he cannot fully escape. At the time of narrating, he may be psychologically more stable in that he implies that he can now allow himself to sleep. But his inability to fully free himself from those series of fires which have scarred him is marked by the present strength of those memories of that summer in Italy when he was lying there listening to the silkworms munch, and by their physical immediacy. Indeed the use of direct discourse in the second of the two memories of the childhood burnings takes Nick and the reader one stage further back, transporting them both from the time of the first narrative and the recovery of that powerful memory as though it were just happening, to that of the occurrence of the original event itself as the parents voices are heard to speak.

The narrating present fades from view, in fact, for the majority of the second half of the narrative, with the replaying of the (past) dialogue between John and Nick. Once again we are repositioned with Nick in that past time, recounted as if it were happening in the (narrating) now. This only emphasises the point I have just made. Nick's replaying of the past, of losing himself in it, is a sign of his failure to transcend it. Domestic history and public history (the war) together have made him what he is. If his memories take him – to borrow David Wyatt's terms – from origins (as far back as he can remember) to ends (he cuts his remembrances off at the war), both are 'witness[ed] . . . as violent'.[44] The war remembrances also point in the direction of his final end: his soul leaving his body. There is no 'going forward' for Nick. His physical wound only returns him to the memory of prior emotional wounds.

What is evident from the above is that when we look at the temporal patternings in 'Now I Lay Me' there are a series of particularly noticeable shifts at one particular narrative point. These shifts range through as much of Nick's personal history as he remembers, to focus on key memories. We are given glimpses of the broken narrative of his life in which both beginnings and ends are provisional. The large-scale sweeps through time that Nick makes are a measure of his personal distress at the time of their occurrence. Battling to keep sleep away, and that death with which it has come to seem synonymous, he takes himself back through these large-scale tours of his past. These sweeps through time are revealing in that the strong impressions to which he returns reinforce a message received in the different context of battle. Pain, loss, fire and loneliness are repeated thematic refrains in the narrative. Fishing the stream of Nick's personal history alongside him, we linger at those 'deep holes' (*MWW*, 125) which contain the biggest fish: those objects and memories that signify most in his memory and link repeated trauma, present to past.

IV

My analysis of the temporal patternings in 'Now I Lay Me' has been, of necessity, piecemeal and I have focused most of my attention on the early parts of the text. I wish now to comment on the development of the narrative and its patternings before returning to the matter of repetition in terms both of its spatial and symbolic effects. The story takes a change of direction halfway through. This transition point occurs when the move is made outward from a focus on Nick's solipsistic mental activity to his awareness of, and communication with, John, the other person awake in that room. Once this shift occurs the narrative's temporal patterns get much more regular and, until John falls asleep, almost all of the text time is located in the time of the first narrative.

This outward move comes about in a quite specific way. After the fishing memories, Nick says that there are some nights that this resource was unavailable to him. No information is given as to why not. This is part and parcel of Hemingway's elliptical style. It seems, however, to connect up with the depth of Nick's fear or terror. 'Cold-awake', he cannot make the transition to the comforting and dreamlike activity (invented streams merging with real ones; dream merging with wakefulness) that fishing comes by and large to mean to him. He then moves to prayer, put into effect by his memories of those people he has known in the past.

This too breaks down, since on some nights he cannot even remember his prayers – a memory interference that again suggests both the extent of his trauma and of the waves of deep anxiety consequent to it. This particular memory loss might also signal Nick's unconscious awareness of the failure of religious discourse to fit the needs of his present situation. For prayer is generally ineffectual in Hemingway's fiction. In *A Farewell to Arms*, for example, Frederic's recourse to it is seen as singularly inappropriate. The disaster which he and Catherine undergo at the novel's end is seen as 'just a dirty trick' (*FA*, 235) rather than as something that prayer can affect one way or another.

My reference to *A Farewell to Arms* also connects up with Nick's next response in this story. For when prayer fails, he attempts to remember the names of animals, birds, fishes, countries, cities, types of food and streets. This calls to mind that famous passage from the novel when Frederic Henry says that only such things as 'the concrete names of villages, the numbers of roads, the names of rivers' (*FA*, 133) have meaning in a context where the abstract language of patriotism has been shown to be hollow. Nick's focus on concrete things here – things with none of those emotional connotations of the things in his grandfather's attic – can be read as minimalist activity. His mind holds on to the very basic defining qualities of the things it used to know rather than putting itself under any of the kinds of emotional or psychological pressure which comes when other modes of remembering are engaged. Again, though, the presented world is a disconnected one where Nick is stuck in individual class categories (animals, cities, types of food) that cannot be combined to positive effect. Foucault's words are suggestive here: 'the real world, as it presents itself to the gaze, is not merely the unwinding of the fundamental chain of being, but offers jumbled fragments of it, repeated and discontinuous'.[45] Even Nick's attempts to remember the fragments, the basic facts of the world he once knew, fail him at times. He reports that 'when I could not remember anything at all any more I would just listen' (*MWW*, 128). Nick fishes his memories, with the reader in tow, until these break down absolutely. He is then left stranded in the time of the first narrative with all larger sense of continuity and sequence – any sight of a 'fundamental chain of being' – lost. He is entirely caught in the realm of immediate sense impression, lying there listening to the sounds of the silkworms eating and to John 'being awake' (*MWW*, 129). The acute hypersensitivity Nick evidences here is reminiscent of a protagonist in a Poe story, his nerves shot to pieces. The first half of the story provides a perfect lead-in to the second. Nick's failure to find any sustaining grip in memories of the past evidences a loss of coherence to the narrative of his life which strands him in a present where all he can do is lie anxiously listening to the sounds inside and outside of that room.

My final comments on the temporal patternings of the narrative concern the relationship between Nick's story and John's. In the latter's case there is a regular pattern between information about the past and plans concerning the future. We are told of John's past – of his living in Chicago for ten years, his marriage and the having of a family, and of his entry into the army. There is then, though, a regular progression charted forward beyond the point of the first narrative. John's removal from active service prior to the October offensive and his hospital visit to Nick mark stages in a confident process leading back to America, to the 'nice [and profitable] place' (*MWW*, 129) he will be running there and to the boy he then hopes to father. Nick's narrative is much more past oriented. John's talk of marriage leads Nick straight back into the past, to think of 'all the girls I had ever known'. His consequent speculation on the 'kind of wives they would make' (*MWW*, 132) is temporally vague. It may be past-centred in kind, with an implied 'would have made' hanging there. It may be a return to the time of the first narrative or beyond – what kind of wives would those girls make now or eventually? This speculation is only a prelude, though, to a return to the trout streams of the past (or of his imagination) which do not blur in his mind like the girls do. In the time which follows that described in the first narrative lies – as we are to find out in the last paragraph of the story – further wounding. Nick has previously referred to the future and his intention to get a job on a paper but he does not know where ('Chicago?' 'Maybe'), and when John suggests marriage to him as a cure for his 'worry' he can only say 'I'll think about it' (*MWW*, 131) – twice. The regular chronological pattern of John's story suggests that his 'nervous' (*MWW*, 130) state just does not bear real comparison with Nick's. The latter is alone in the seriousness of his condition. It also suggests a confidence about the future and about the institution of marriage that Nick cannot share.

The reasons why this is so lie, implicitly, in Nick's memories of his own family life. The temporal patterns of this narrative suggest a protagonist psychologically 'blackened and chipped' (*MWW*, 128) both by the 'fires' of war and of his childhood experiences.

Fire and the ways of surviving it come to resonate symbolically within the text. The different aspects of such repetitions fail to mask their deep similarity for both have contributed to the making/unmaking of Nick as we see him. His response to repetitions that damage from without is to engage in patterns of recovering the past, to repeat (mentally and within) that which he already knows well: memories of fishing, of family, of events, of things. These latter repetitions do not cure anything. Although some of them may bring relief from pain, others merely remind of that which damaged him in the first place. This is a narrative where repetition encloses repetition; a narrative of damage limitation where to stay caught between wound and wound is at least to avoid more of the same. Nick keeps coming back to those incidents and events that have caused him social and psychological harm. Notions of narrative and biographical development and progress are questioned by the strength of those few distinct and powerful memories of a passive protagonist 'burning' in fires that he did not light. The generalisations we can make from this are similar to those made about the 'They shot the six cabinet ministers' vignette earlier. Brief and vivid images are not revelatory of 'circumjacent conditions', for the full details of Nick's biography and particularly of his war experience are irrelevant here. The presence of repetition points to a condition of damage and victimisation that is both social and psychological in kind. This is revealed *through* the startling clarity of the presented scene.

The idea of the symbolic resonance of fire referred to above returns me to Hemingway's classic modernist move between narrative transparency and symbolic depth. His particular version of it owes, as I suggest earlier, much to Pound and his insistence on concrete particularity. Pound believed that symbols should not intrusively signal their presence in a text but should be rooted in and emerge naturally from the very being of the material object itself: 'the natural object is always the adequate symbol . . : if a man uses "symbols" he must use them that their symbolic function does not obtrude'.[46] So here the salamander is placed in its solid reality before the eye of the reader, with the tiny feet trying to hold on to the hook by which it is pierced. The symbolic function of the salamander, the way its supposed ability to withstand fire connects up with all the symbolic activity in the text about fire damage and fireproofness, is never overt. The clear material image remains in the foreground. The salamander remains first and concretely a salamander (to echo Pound on the hawk) before it begins to work as a symbol. Kenneth Johnston's discussion of the symbolic reverberations of the silkworm motif – the way, for example, that Nick tries to 'weave' his 'threads of memories' into 'a kind of protective shield, not unlike the cocoon which the silkworm constructs in response to its instinct for survival'[47] – provides another illustration of this same technique.

This movement found in Hemingway's prose between the presentation of a clear and concrete image and that implicit symbolic function which emerges from it suggests his ability successfully to negotiate an artistic pathway between the syntagmatic (the textual chain of immediate connecting sequences that makes up its narrative movement and its direct representational life) and the paradigmatic (the static network of linguistic recurrences and symbolic patternings that give the text its deeper meanings). What is very noticeable in this narrative is both the overall spread of its verbal patternings and, at the same time, the degree of movement as one cluster of such patternings modulates into the next.

In terms of the complete story, then, there are certain words that insistently recur in much greater proportion to the textual whole than would normally be found in prose writing. Variants of the word 'sleep' appear twenty-six times; 'remember', nineteen times; 'night', fifteen times; 'stream', fourteen times; 'fish', twelve times; 'listen', eleven times; 'marry', ten times; 'pray' and 'father', nine times; and 'silkworms' and 'awake', eight times. We might rearrange these words into a set of three groupings, the last of which would consist of just a single word, to suggest the major shifts and concerns of the narrative. Such groupings would correspond to three different time schemes:

First narrative		The past		The future
sleep		remember		
awake		stream		
night	*	fish	*	marry
listen		pray		
silkworms		father		

The first cluster of words are grouped around the time of the first narrative and refer to the condition (static, passive and silent) of the narrator, the main immediate external influence working on him (the silkworms) and the immediate time of action. An obsessive concern for sleep and the lack of it at night, and what most concretely comes between Nick and sleep, is evidenced here. The second cluster is grouped around time past, the time of memory. The words repeated here refer to the context (the stream) which metaphorically sites both the act of memory and the activity with which it is most pleasantly associated. They refer too to the central figure in Nick's life (his father) and the activity (prayer) to which he keeps (pointlessly?) returning. This might suggest his inability to free himself from ineffectual but traditional ideological frames of reference. Time future has no signification in this scheme of verbal repetition except marriage, the odd term out in the entire verbal pattern (alone by itself in this third 'time' category). This may prove a possible escape for Nick from his present torture. As we have already seen, though, this seems an unlikely option in terms of the first narrative present. And such a notion returns us, too, to time past and the figure of the father, whose damage within this institution has been clearly suggested. Again repetition is foregrounded in terms of the dangers implicit in Nick following in his father's footsteps. The verbal repetitions of the text here give triggers to textual interpretation and to the thematics of repetition that such interpretation highlights.

Hemingway uses here, then, networks of repetition to help create the textual unity of his work. The impact of the Hemingway text generally depends on its semantic as well as its narrative continuity. David Lodge suggests that by 'drawing our attention . . . to similarities rather than contiguities' in the prose, repetition can focus the mind of the reader on given particulars, converting the temporal into the spatial and making 'an apparently metonymic style . . . serve the purposes of metaphor'.[48] Thus metaphoric connotations also attach to the stress on darkness within the text. Nick is in the dark for the entire time of the first narrative. This state is metaphoric in the sense that his perception of reality has been adversely affected by the psychological damage that has been done to him. He lacks the knowledge that in Hemingway is a corollary of vision (the ability to see clearly is generally signified by light). He repeats the words 'I don't know' both when he is asked about his past (why he entered the war) and when he is advised about his present/future: 'You ought to get married' (*MWW*, 130–1). The wife in 'The Doctor and the Doctor's Wife' lies 'with the blinds drawn . . . in [a] darkened room' (*EH*, 277), her Christian Science a blind to a correct reading of reality. The darkness in which Nick lies is that of one whose reading of reality has been shattered by what has happened to him, by being 'blown up at night'. His incipient panic (his fear of his soul leaving his body), his uncertainty and his lack of confidence are all signs of one who is in 'pretty bad shape' (*MWW*, 130), who has been so traumatised that unlike those trout in 'Big Two-Hearted River' he cannot hold himself stable in his surrounding environment. The self-control and ability to act deliberately and positively that he evidences in that story are not available to him here. He cannot see and is caught hypersensitively in a world of small sounds. Nick here has metaphorically lost his bearings, unlike that later version of himself who 'did not need to get his map out' and who 'knew where he was from the position of the river' (*EH*, 342). His lying awake here in the dark is a measure of his disassociation from the world of everyday reality and his failure to cope with it.

V

Hemingway's particular brand of impressionism starts off, as I have described throughout, with the capturing of immediate detail through direct sensation. His stated intent as an artist was to represent 'what really happened in action; what the actual things were which produced the emotion that you experienced . . . the real thing' (*DA*, 8). This he attempted to achieve through his use of the perspective of protagonists whose vision is brilliantly sharp but partial, fragmented and solipsistic. In my first section, I used Jameson to suggest that the way in which reality is channelled through the exercise of his protagonists' sense data is a way of holding on to 'the myth of the self'; to the importance and validity of the independent seeing and feeling subject in a modern world which would deny it. Hemingway's fiction, I suggested, operates through (controlled) contradiction, where a desire to hold on to, and assert, the myth of the self underlies his use of point of view and narrative technique while other aspects of his style, narrative technique and thematic content continually evidences the fragility of this myth. His need to endorse 'the fiction of the individual subject'[49] is met and matched by the realisation that such an endorsement cannot hold water in the face of what is to be learnt from history and psychology.

I suggested earlier that this contradiction has further implications. For if the notion of the valid subject is linked to the way in which the external world is filtered through the immediate sensations and perceptions of that subject then *the form that those senses take* offers evidence of the way in which the larger historical world has already affected that subject and has already shaped his response to external reality. This notion needs gradual development.

Hemingway's stress on 'the real thing' raises problems here. The dubious nature of any appeal to unmediated 'reality' becomes instantly apparent in the fact that the above phrase has become, at the time of my writing, Coca-Cola's main advertising slogan. Who is the 'you' who experiences the emotion to which he refers above? Authorial consciousness, that of the fictional protagonist, and that of the reader seem curiously blurred here. I would suggest that there is in fact a type of double play in Hemingway's fiction whereby the reader is shuttled between the particular *limited* version of reality with which his protagonists are identified and a fuller version of reality that (the author knows) those protagonists cannot, but would wish to, evade. Immediate sequences of motion and fact constantly indicate the repressed knowledge of a general lack of meaning to events, and it is this knowledge which helps, in turn, to explain such immediate action. It is this double 'reality' effect that operates in Hemingway's best fiction.

The 'authenticity' that Hemingway presents as synonymous with the direct charting of immediate sensation and sequences of motion and fact thus needs careful positioning. I quoted Lukacs at the start of this chapter. For him, the best form of fiction was that which depicted '*real* chronological, concrete, historical sequence' (my emphasis). Concrete historical sequence gives way in Hemingway to an episodic and impressionistic observation and description. This alone – and misleadingly, given the double effect I have noted above – he calls 'the real thing'. When his prose charts 'what really happened in action' he is giving a version of reality that concentrates on immediate event and generally reflects the way his protagonist(s) see and react to things. Both this, and the 'deeper' version of reality which becomes apparent when we 'read through' such surface effects, differ, however, from the way in which Lukacs would define 'the real'.

To decide what is real and what is not is, of course, always problematic. It is a product of 'thought about the real':[50] that which results from the interaction between the ideology of the subject and the historical conditions which site her or him and to which he or she is responding. In Hemingway, the concentration on immediate 'real' fact and sensation is a way of illustrating the avoidance or resistance techniques his protagonists have developed. For such a concentration has become, on their part, a way either of repressing thought about the threats to the self that arise once a wider 'reality' is acknowledged, or of countering the implications of such a reality.[51]

Nick Adams's concentration on the details of the activity of fishing in 'Big Two-Hearted River' can accordingly be seen as a tactic aimed at avoiding thought about his own damaged status as a subject. The things on which he focuses and the way in which he focuses on them are *predetermined* by the psychological and social pressures of which he has been a victim. To choose a realm to signify as 'real' and meaningful is to eliminate that part of the real – history, the war, the family – which has previously threatened his sense of autonomous identity. His reading of the real is a product of his experience of other and more deadly aspects of reality. The 'real' is a construct forced on him (if he is to recapture mental stability) by the text of history, a text which it is impossible for him to escape.

What has 'real' value and worth to Nick (the real and the valuable become here conterminous) is what is 'natural and untinkered with'.[52] In 'Big Two-Hearted River', the trout, the countryside and the weather fulfil this criteria. Adorno suggests the impossibility of equating the natural with the real or true and of separating it off from the cultural (in the way Nick does). He comments on the ears of corn which blow in the wind at the end of Chaplin's *The Great Dictator*: 'Nature is viewed . . . as a healthy contrast to society, and is therefore denatured. Pictures showing green trees, a blue sky, and moving clouds make these aspects of nature into so many cryptograms for factory chimneys and service stations.'[53] Caught within a historical and social order which would deny individual autonomy and worth, Nick's concentration on sensation and immediate surface is built precisely on his desire to avoid such an historical and social analysis. However, that which is repressed cannot be kept completely repressed. The limited version of the real which the story foregrounds, covers over, with only partial success, a different version of the world which Nick would prefer to deny. To interpret the story in terms of its symbolic and paradigmatic structure, in the light of Nick's own brief acknowledgements of a prior context to his present actions, and in the larger framework of the other Nick Adams stories, is to draw attention to just how limited are the aspects of that 'reality' to which Nick now pays such attention; just how impotent he is once wider historical contexts are taken into account.

So, similarly, in *A Farewell to Arms* Frederic Henry is directly involved in the war, and in his description of the Caparetto retreat Hemingway produces some of the most effective writing in the book. The war, however, is presented in terms of its effect on the individual consciousness of Frederic Henry. His perception of it conditions the reader's. All we see is a very partial version of a larger whole. The use of first-person narration and the stress on immediate physical sensation again operates at the initial cost of any larger understanding of a historical situation. What Frederic *sees* provides the narrative focus. So, in the first chapter, the reader is geographically and politically absolutely dislocated. We see what Frederic sees – the road, the troops, the flashes from the artillery in the mountains – but we do not know who is fighting, or on what side, or even in which country, until we are given the reference to Udine at the chapter's end. We are completely caught within Frederic's consciousness, within his subjective frame of knowledge. To focus so narrowly on the facts at immediate hand is a survival tactic where a more general sense of his validity as a subject and the meaning of the events around him has been lost (I will examine this issue in more detail in my next chapter). Here though, positioned within what Sam Girgus calls 'the universal "we" of the community of soldiers and state',[54] Frederic's response to such 'things' only puts off what he already knows, and what the reader comes to know – that this larger political and institutional frame has invalidated the meaning of that individual response. In his best fiction Hemingway constantly works between these two poles. The more his characters try to escape from history into a pure reliance on immediate reaction and direct sensation, the more they have to accept its conditioning presence. This is the paradox at the core of his work and one that results from his own version of the 'real'. That engagement with politics which Lukacs would see as an alternative to getting caught between determinism (objective force) and interiority (subjective impression) is not (normally) a viable option in his fictional world.

3

The Status of the Subject

[Hemingway] is an elegiac poet, who mourns the self, who celebrates the self (rather less effectively), and who suffers divisions in the self.

(Harold Bloom)[1]

The idea of a unifying unity of the human condition has always had on me the effect of a scandalous lie.

(Jacques Lacan)[2]

I

The problematics of identity is a major concern in Hemingway's fiction. A recognition that the notion of coherent subjectivity is a myth vies with the urge to represent the self as autonomous and independent. A presentation of the self as unstable, caught between subject positions, confined and partly defined by the social formation in which it is positioned, conflicts with the urge to celebrate the self, to endorse individual freedom and authority. Michel Leiris in *Manhood* refers to 'events of my life that relate to the theme of the "injured man"'.[3] The injuries suffered by Hemingway's protagonists do not just relate to physical wounds suffered in war but to a whole series of social and psychological factors that place the notion of the sovereign subject under acute threat. The attraction of the latter notion, though, remains strong. Traditional beliefs in the 'transcendental sanctity and stability of the subject'[4] die hard. In Hemingway's case, in fact, such beliefs strengthen rather than diminish.

In this chapter I will argue that it is Hemingway's foregrounding of the difficulty of 'fashion[ing] a self'[5] that accounts for the generally recognised superiority of the short stories and early fiction to the later novels. The stylistic and thematic changes that occur in the later fiction are related to the change in presentation of subjectivity. Hemingway's best effects occur when he is charting the uncertainties and instabilities of the subject's position in the modern world. His later protagonists act with an authority and power that the earlier ones entirely lack. For while the constraints of historical and social forces beyond the individual's control remain apparent in this later work, the internal self-divisions of his fictional subjects have been contained, controlled and mastered in a manner impossible to their predecessors. This leads to a loss of fictional power on the author's part, since his very distinctiveness and originality as a writer had been in the ways he had found of representing damaged and limited selfhood. I would suggest that the growing interest in the 'posthumous' fictions, *Islands in the Stream* and *The Garden of Eden*, is because there he once more returns to the theme of the incomplete and self-divided subject.

The question of selfhood and autonomy is a deeply troubled one in Hemingway's work. In this he gives fictional form to the uncertainties and worries of that American culture whose product he was and whose problems he shared. Jackson Lears, the intellectual historian, analyses cultural change and disturbance in America at the end of the nineteenth century.[6] He suggests that the bourgeois belief in autonomous individualism, which was so central a part of late nineteenth-century American ideology, could not in fact be squared with the actual conditions of a modernised world marked by increasingly strong patternings of rationalisation and bureaucratisation. Such a gap between active individual energy and effectiveness and larger and unnegotiable repressive force provides the very conditions of Hemingway's fictional world. In it he plays variations on the tensions Lears describes. My comments here relate closely to my discussion of style in the previous chapter. By focusing now directly on the status of Hemingway's protagonists I wish both to reinforce my earlier arguments and to account for the changes that occur in his fictional vision. I see the two chapters, though, as interlinked and interdependent.

II

Hemingway focuses many of his short stories around one central protagonist, Nick Adams. *In Our Time* – where the majority of stories centre on Nick – can be seen as 'a repressed or broken *bildungsroman*'. For the introduction of stories and vignettes that do not centre on Nick leads to a questioning, in the volume taken as a whole, of 'the ideology of the *bildungsroman*' since their presence 'decentre[s] Nick and his subjectivity upon the stage of his time'. Such an ideology is more fundamentally questioned by a set of stories that fail to illustrate Nick's development or his real connection with 'the stage of his time' and thus fail to 'obey the law of the novel of growth'.[7] Rather the stories obey the law of repetition and stasis as we see brief glimpses of a subject damaged over and over again.

Here, and in the larger collection of Nick Adams stories, it is Hemingway's method of writing that foregrounds the fragmentation of his subject. 'A Way You'll Never Be' can serve as exemplar. We are thrown into the narrative in the middle of things. The details given in the first paragraph seem initially to float unanchored in time and space. We are told of an 'attack' (*WTN*, 84), but no information is given of which attack is being referred to, or where exactly it is occurring. The geography of the description is purely local, with the relationship given of field to sunken road, to group of farm houses to river, but with no larger contextualisation or sense of relatedness.

All the verbs of action in the first sentence have 'the attack' as their subject. Any human involvement in this activity is thus subordinated to the abstract military force that contains and controls it. Although it is what Nick Adams sees – the bodies which mark the route of that attack – which makes up the initial content of the story, his name does not appear until the paragraph's end and his position as a subject is far from structurally central to it. Nick is distanced from what he sees, as confirmed by the defamiliarising tactic of having him come along the road on a bicycle, as if an amateur naturalist on a country jaunt who finds 'clumps' of dead bodies (*WTN*, 84) where he might have expected clusters of flowers. The intertextual references to 'A Natural History of the Dead' encourage such a reading.

The story is about Nick's damaged sense of his own identity.

The concentrated focus on what he sees suggests the same 'displacement of self into seeing' that Thomas Strychacz notes of him in *In Our Time* (and of Jake in *The Sun Also Rises*).[8] This displacement points to self-protectiveness and a loss of confidence in subjectivity itself. For a gap exists between the objective and the subjective, between what is seen and what is emotionally felt, and between life and consciousness,[9] which is, on the part of the fictional protagonist, disabling in the extreme.

If we are thrown into the narrative *in media res*, so its ending similarly lacks the (traditionally) expected formal closure. Nick is returning to his bicycle, to shuttle about pointlessly between one section of the army and another. An image from the past strikes him ('The horses' breath made plumes in the cold air') but in the process of recollection he realises he has misremembered its locating context. This failure of memory, of positioning himself clearly in relation to the past, is then followed by his talking to himself, with the stress again on the possibility of dislocation: 'I'd better get to that damned bicycle . . . I don't want to lose the way' (*WTN*, 96). Things are left unfinished, the story incomplete, the reader still looking for a subject (in both senses of the word).

The story itself thus functions as a fragment, with no real beginning and no real ending. The narrative of Nick's life as represented in all the stories about him is itself unfinished – one that wanders back and forth in time, is full of gaps and absences and where we are given glimpses of him as child, as adolescent and as adult, without such pieces adding up to a complete and satisfactory whole.

Nick's schizophrenic discourse in 'A Way You'll Never Be' points to his status as a wounded subject. It represents one whose previous sense of self just does not connect up with recent experience and present condition. The incoherence of Nick's sense of his own status as subject is evident in the way his mind shifts uncontrollably from present to past reality – from recent wound and present mental distress (shell-shock) to past incidents now 'so damned mixed up' (*WTN*, 90) in his mind. This incoherence is evident in the linguistic shifts that occur. For what are rational and appropriate responses to his immediate circumstances slide suddenly into a formal disquisition on natural history (on the characteristics of 'the American locust' – *WTN*, 93) entirely at odds with the prior mode of speech.[10] That self known in the past and its knowledge and concerns is radically out of synch with that of the present. Nick's schizophrenic discourse indicates his lack of mental balance, that badly damaged sense of his own self of which his wound was physical mark and final confirmation.

Sandra Gilbert celebrates the costume changes that occur in female modernist texts by saying that 'no one, male or female, can or should be confined to uni-form, a single form or self'.[11] The playful acceptance of the multiple possibilities of self is not available to Nick Adams. His education is an ironic one, teaching only one repeated message: how vulnerable selfhood is and how subject to (acutely painful) divisions. Metaphorically, Nick's uniform is all that holds him together: having suffered 'severe dissociation . . . his "self" . . . is solely the uniform; the clothes are . . . [a] barely adequate package for his violently disturbed inner terrain'.[12] Kenneth Johnston discusses the way in which the whole question of identity is self-consciously raised in the early stages of the story: 'For Nick, who has only a tenuous grip on his sanity, the question of "Who am I?" is of paramount importance.'[13] If Nick's uniform gives him at least a provisional sense of identity, the nature and worth of this identity is questioned both by Nick's own inability to play out his military role successfully and by Captain Paravicini's initial response to seeing Nick again. For the Nick he knows is not the one he sees: 'Hello . . . I didn't know you. What are you doing in that uniform?'(*WTN*, 87).

Nick's broken sense of his own identity is in 'A Way You'll Never Be' linked to the wound he has received in war. This wound, though, is, if we take the Nick Adams stories together, a repetition and culmination of what has come before. The notion of growth implicit in the *bildungsroman* is contradicted by that sense of an 'abject terror in the face of potential selflessness' which commonly marks Nick's 'education'. Steven Hoffman uses the phrase to describe 'Now I Lay Me'. As I suggested earlier though, the terror in that story arises not only from the damage done to Nick in battle, but from the psychological damage that pre-dated his physical wound; a physical wound that in its turn caused more psychological damage. Both private and public history combine to render Nick uncertain what rules to follow and how to act in life – to leave him in the case of 'Now I Lay Me' suffering from a type of paralysis.[14] Such uncertainties provide the recurring conditions of the Nick Adams stories.

Nick Adams is both a wounded subject and a self-divided one. In 'Now I Lay Me' his desire for rest, recuperation and security is resisted by his knowledge that home, the place that should signify all these things, is rather, in his experience, identified with loss and emotional pain. His earliest memories deny his route to recovery. Desire and knowledge are incompatible with one another. The idea of the 'centred subject' is a myth.[15] If Nick's family history has contributed to his self-diminishments and self-divisions (the psychological damage caused in the above case by parental inter-action), such a history also connects up with more general forms of social repression associated with the culture to which he belongs. Lacan's words that 'Law and repressed desire are one and the same thing'[16] pertain directly to Nick, whose father (the Law's representative) opposes his desires with the voice of cultural restraint. Nick himself then appears to re-create his father's role, to a degree at least, in his subsequent relations with his own child.

I wish briefly to focus on 'Fathers and Sons' to show how such self-division is suggested in Nick's difficulties in finding a com-fortable position in regard to his own sexuality. The story depicts Nick both in the role of son and of father and gains its effects in the play between the two. Sexual desire and spontaneity mark Nick's boyhood/adolescent behaviour in the text. His love-making with Trudy, even in her brother's presence, is contrasted with his father's extreme sexual puritanism. This latter is indicated by the force of his hyperbolic and morally prescriptive pronouncements: masturbation, he tells Nick, 'produced blindness, insanity and death' (*WTN*, 168). Nick's father's voice is that of repressive authority, responding negatively to Nick's curiosity about sex and outlawing the expression of his sexual desire.

Nick does not follow his father's advice. He recognises (retro-spectively) that his father was 'unsound on sex' (*WTN*, 166) and much of the story is about Nick's rebellion against his influence. However, his father's codes are – in exaggerated form – those of his culture. The expression of Nick's desire for Trudy runs counter to the requirements of official morality. Although Nick appears to have evaded cultural restraint in the rejection of his father's values implied by the relationship with Trudy, I would suggest that this free expression of the sexual self is not thoroughgoing. It is only a temporary evasion of social norms and conventional restraints. The force of patriarchal law cannot be thrown off by Nick, and a tension between its requirements and that of instinctive desire will continue to exist in him.

For though Nick reports that he 'had shared nothing with [his father]' (*WTN*, 172) from the age of fifteen, in his relationship with his own son he does share exactly his reticence. His father, he remembers, had only ever given him 'two pieces of information' (*WTN*, 167) regarding sexuality and that information was neither expansive nor helpful to Nick's developing needs. Nick has not the puritanical attitudes of his father, but he is equally tight-lipped on the subject of sex. When his son asks him about the Ojibways and what it was like, being with them, Nick replies 'It's hard to say.' The information, the detailing of sexual initiation and pleasure, the reader then receives as he or she shares Nick's thoughts ('Could you say she did first what no one has ever done better' – *WTN*, 174) is withheld from the son.

Both Nick and his father 'lived with' the Indians as boys. In a draft version of 'Fathers and Sons', Nick evidently does mention Trudy (Prudy) to his son:

'There was an Indian named Prudy Gilbey that I was very fond of. We were very good friends.'
'What happened to her?'
'She [had a baby] went away to become a hooker.'

Paul Smith points out that Nick's words parallel his father's in the same draft copy. Nick speculates on his father's life and wonders 'what my father knew beside the nonsense that he told me and how things were with him because when I asked him what the Indians were like when he was a boy he said that he had very good friends among them, that he was very fond of them'.[17]

A gap appears on Nick's part between the sexual spontaneity evidenced in the relationship he had with Trudy as a boy and a later suppression of it in conversation with his own son. Such a suppression (on the evidence of the draft version) may well echo that of his father before him. His father's sexual puritanism now takes on a rather different look. Extreme though it undoubtedly is, it may signal a larger cultural failure to reconcile sexual self-expression and desire with the conventional codes of middle-class American morality. Such a failure to reconcile sexual need and cultural prohibition becomes even more acute where desire occurs in a transgressive context – that of miscegenation. That theme is foregrounded in Nick's response to Eddie Gilby's designs on his sister. This analysis is speculative as far as Nick's father is concerned. The fact that Nick's own early sexual experiences occur with an Indian girl and that as an adult he can not freely admit this to his son, suggests though that, for both men, the sexual 'self' as spoken by cultural law cannot be squared with that driven by the force of desire. The fact that it is an Indian girl involved here only heightens the moral/cultural stakes.

'Fathers and Sons' has much more to it than the particular strand here discussed, but the gap that appears between conventional morality and forbidden desire is significant. Despite the presence of a son, Nick is never shown as an adult in a full sexual–emotional partnership. This might point to a failure ever to reconcile deepest need and social pressure. I would note that 'The Last Good Country' has as its central theme the incompatibility between these two areas with, in effect, two Nicks presented there: he who lives within society and he whose deepest wishes cannot be fulfilled by it. The fact that no satisfactory bridge exists in that story to connect these two selves (which may explain its unfinished form) makes it a perfectly logical end to one branch of his fictional output. I shall discuss this story further, though from a slightly different perspective, in my final chapter.

In 'Fathers and Sons' and 'The Last Good Country' the most extreme form of self division to be found in the Hemingway protagonist – that between social existence and individual need – is represented. Elsewhere the one stands in complex and entangled coexistence with the other. To look at the Nick Adams stories generally, though, is to look at a subject lacking both autonomy and self-certainty. His relationship to his parents is an insecure one. 'The Doctor and the Doctor's Wife' begins what David Seed calls that 'erosion of domestic stability'[18] which will be such a feature of the stories concerning him. The mother with her pious gentility and sentimental naïvety is associated with a form of emotional claustrophobia on which Nick turns his back. Nick's ambivalent attitude to his father is again most forcefully expressed in 'Fathers and Sons' where love and pathological rage are uneasily combined. David Wyatt makes an illuminating remark when he picks up on Nick's first question in 'Indian Camp' – 'Where are we going, Dad?' (*EH*, 271) – to comment that 'Nick begins as a lost son.'[19]

Nick Adams fails to progress as a subject. The different glimpses presented of his life are indicative of his self-divisions. Caught between male and female worlds, disturbed by and uncertain in his relation to his parental figures, his desire for 'at-homeness' compromised by his failure fully to find or feel it, Nick cannot move positively forward in his life. In Wyatt's words, he 'lives but he does not develop. . . . None of [his] experiences lead to emotional development. Nick's life has no middle. It emerges as pure reaction.' Wyatt dismisses claims that would see 'Big Two-Hearted River' as a ritual of return (to well-known ground) in order that Nick may face the future afresh with a certain confidence and a knowledge of his own limitations. Rather, he sees the narrative as one of repetition, of doing what has been done before (see coffee *à la* Hopkins) in an obsessively controlled way: 'nothing can be left loose, surprising, open-ended'.[20] A similar sense of repetition might also be seen in the way that, when Hemingway came to write other Nick Adams stories, he did not proceed by way of a straightforward linear movement into Nick's future, but rather circled back over past events. And when Nick was taken into the future in 'Fathers and Sons', it would be partly to show how he reproduces the patterns of his father's life. The fact too that the story concludes with a reference first to where Nick will be buried and then to a proposed visit to his own father's tomb, only confirms a sense of (deathly) repetition without change. Nick's failure to construct any sense of full and positive selfhood reveals the insecure grounds of his subjectivity. His status is that of one who is faced with events that cannot be controlled and whose response is in terms of passive reaction rather than any kind of positive and forward looking action. Nick's sense of his own identity is very shaky indeed.

III

The theme of damaged subjectivity also stands as a major concern in Hemingway's first important novels, *The Sun Also Rises* and *A Farewell to Arms*. In these novels, the questioning of the notion of the autonomous self that accompanied the coming of the conditions of modernity is put by Hemingway into sharp relief by his use of war and personal injury as a way of metaphorically representing individual vulnerability and lack of controlling influence in a secularised and reified world. In both texts, Hemingway criticises the notion of the sovereign self.

My analysis begins with a brief reprise and development of the arguments I make about *The Sun Also Rises* in *New Readings of the American Novel*. Catherine Belsey's statement that 'at times of crisis in the social formation . . . confidence in the ideology of subjectivity is eroded'[21] is a helpful basis for discussion of the earlier works. Hemingway's values had been formed in the pre-modern environment of Oak Park. His fiction, though, is informed by the conditions of modernity – conditions that are certainly not accepted with enthusiasm. Large urban centres are strikingly absent in his work generally and Paris in *The Sun Also Rises* largely figures as the place which lacks those values associated with a more traditional Spain where earlier social forms are still, apparently, in place. The problems with such a contrast will become clear in my final chapter. All Hemingway's early work is, however, imbued with the sense of crisis to which Belsey refers, and the fragmentations and self-divisions of his fictional subjects are a product of the tensions and complications of modernity, and the 'dizzying social changes' with which it is associated. In both *The Sun Also Rises* and *A Farewell to Arms* the damage suffered by the subject in war points in the direction of a more general condition – the subject diminished in what Marshall Berman calls the 'inexorable order, capitalistic, legalistic and bureaucratic' of the modern.[22] This relationship is more clearly evident in the second of the two novels here examined, but neither novel can be seen in isolation from the self's loss of coherence in this larger conditioning set of circumstances.

The dislocated subjects of *The Sun Also Rises* have no centre. Their defining context is hotel rooms and bars. The room Jake rents in Paris contains, as far as we see, only a bed and an 'armoire' with its mirror. In James's *The Portrait of a Lady*, Ned Rosier marks his presence on his Paris flat by the lace bibelots he puts on his mantelpiece. Place thus becomes expressive of personality. Here, the space these subjects travel through is curiously impersonal. Their lack of stability is represented physically as well as socially and psychologically. Cut off from both family and native land, the characters here avoid solipsism by bonding together – however temporarily – in a form of group identity that gives their lives an element of stability. Here though lies the rub. For in asserting their membership of this group and living (or failing to live) by its agreed codes, their sense of individual differentiation tends to be lost. It is noticeable how the fact that they share conventions, codes, catch-phrases, forms of wit and tonal nuances means that their separate voices tend to blur and become indistinct.

> As to [these characters'] differentiating characteristics, there seem to be almost none. . . . The minor differences existing between [them] are secondary to their repetitiveness. . . . Names and faces are blurred . . . drunkenness contributes to this blurring of selves. Indeed, one cannot speak of clear-cut identities in this novel . . . alcohol and absence go hand in hand.

If names and faces, voices and tones, blur in the text, so too are character traits duplicated among the group. It is, for example, the analogy between Jake and Cohn as romantics/sentimentalists that ironically collapses a first-person narration premised on the notion of their difference.

The lack of individual definition in the group of characters presented, their disconnection from any larger social network and the accompanying loss of firm grounding for behaviour leads in the direction of a questioning both of the notion of discrete identity and of autonomy. Robert Elbaz claims that 'there is absolutely no purposefulness to what is being done'[23] in the novel. One of the main traits associated with Jake is passivity, and the 'displacement of [his] self into seeing' is evident at the start of chapter 3 when he sits and watches the Parisian life around him. Variations of the verb 'watch' are repeated four times in seven lines and all verbs of action (save Jake's catching of Georgette's eye – an act that needs a minimum of movement on his part) are associated with other people or, perhaps more significantly, things. The 'poules' go by. The electric signs 'come on'. The horse-cabs go 'clippety-clopping along at the edge of the solid taxi traffic' (*SAR*, 15). Throughout the text a similar dissociation between seeing and doing is evident, with Jake presented as one whose capacity for forceful action has been badly compromised.

Not only is Jake a passive character, he is also a self-divided one. His distinctive narrative technique is to report what he sees and

knows of the outside world – 'in his obsession with objectivity . . . restrict[ing] his narrative largely to a neutral, almost
monotonous registration of external facts, actions, and dialogues'[24]
– but consistently to minimise comment on his internal one. If we
explore the silences of his text we find that the solid and
apparently reliable objective description that forms the textual
surface is a way of taking attention away from a narrator riddled
within by inconsistencies and uncertainties. It is due to his own
awareness of this internal confusion that such silencing occurs.

Jake's self-divisions emerge most clearly in regard to Brett. The
laconic and hard-boiled realist who can tell Cohn that Brett is a
drunk and responds to his 'I don't believe she would marry
anybody she didn't love' with a 'Well . . . She's done it twice'
(*SAR*, 35), is also the one caught up emotionally with her. He is so
unsure as to how to respond to these mixed feelings that he can
move from saying 'We'd better keep away from each other' (*SAR*,
25) to pleading 'Couldn't we live together, Brett? Couldn't we just
live together?' (*SAR*, 48) in successive days. Shifts in tone from the
ironic to the sentimental and from the coolly distanced to the
hopelessly engaged mark a narrative in which Jake is never quite
in control of himself despite a style which suggests otherwise.
When, after Cohn has hit him, he says 'It all seemed like some bad
play' (*SAR*, 159) that might be because of the sense of *déjà vu* about
his whole situation. Caught in patterns of repetition that he cannot
step outside, Jake may be aware of the gap between his part in the
action and how his more rational and 'ironic' side would judge
what is a pretty poor performance.

Jake's self-divisions are also clear in the way in which his
romantic and emotionally unstable side clashes with his status as
aficionado. His subjectivity is not coherent or continuous but caught
between a series of (incompatible) positions. Jake's knowledge of
bullfighting and very un-American 'passion' (*SAR*, 110) for the
aesthetic satisfactions gained from it may relate to the cultural
drabness of American daily life left behind him. It certainly relates
to his need to find measured rituals and meaningful forms to
compensate for a personal experience that has offered only the
opposite. The injury which occurred on that 'joke front' (*SAR*, 28)
invalidated both his own sense of positive control over his fate and
that masculinity with which it is associated. Jake's *aficion* and
celebration of bullfighting's 'very special secret' (*SAR*, 109) are his

substitute for the rituals of that religion which he can no longer practice successfully (another subject position – the protagonist as believer – now difficult to sustain with conviction).

When Jake, tied to Brett in an emotionally binding but hopeless relationship, introduces her to Romero, he loses the prop to his life which his status as *aficionado* has given him. His self-division is clear. He advises Montoya against setting up a meeting between Romero and the American ambassador. In reply to Montoya's fear that Romero will get caught up with 'this Grand Hotel business' to the detriment of his career, he refers to 'one American woman down here now that collects bull-fighters' (*SAR*, 143). However, when his 'own true love' wants to start off her collection he helps her to do so even though this means his future exclusion from that brotherhood whose membership has meant so much to him. His disgust with his own actions here is thinly veiled in the text.

Notions of character as unified or autonomous tend to explode in one's face in reading *The Sun Also Rises*. If every subject is 'a particular arrangement of the various social or ideological voices available in our culture',[25] then Jake moves between a series of overlapping and often contradictory subject positions as he plays out the various voices that constitute him. His decentring stems from a tension between romantic and religious conceptualisations inherited from a nineteenth-century world and the secular irony produced by the sudden collapse and discreditation of such norms. His 'masculine' position clashes with his invalid status. His profession as newspaperman fits uneasily with his attempted retreat from confining socio-historical networks. So in Brett's case a 'Victorian faith in sexual polarity' conflicts with an ideology of liberation associated with the 1920's New Woman.[26] In *The Sun Also Rises* Hemingway inscribes the demolition of the myth of the authentic and centred self.

IV

The issue of identity is foregrounded from the start in *A Farewell to Arms* in the questions raised about the name and status of its central protagonist. The first chapter has 'we' as its subject. The narrator is part of a larger and undefined group, presumably (and in retrospect) those members of the division who 'lived in a house in a village' (*FA*, 7). In the second chapter a shift takes place as a reference to 'our house' is replaced by a narrower focus on the individual subject: 'I was very glad' (*FA*, 8). In the next two chapters the definition of the subject continues to waver between 'I' and 'we', but it is noticeable that an intensified use of the former pronoun (nine times in the first paragraph) at the start of chapter 3 marks the protagonist's return from a winter's absence. This can be linked to his realisation, soon to be formulated, that professionally speaking he has not been missed: 'It evidently made no difference whether I was there . . . or not' (*FA*, 16). The stress on his presence as a subject can be seen as a defensive ploy in a situation where his suspicions of his own irrelevance to a larger process and activity are about to be confirmed. It is only at this point that we learn the protagonist's army function. It is also here, in chapter 4, that we learn that he is not an Italian (though his American nationality is not given until the next chapter). There is, then, a very gradual early release of information about this subject and the sense of his dislocation and potential futility is strong, both in the detail given about his professional role and in that general sense of the random and coincidental exemplified when he gives his reason for joining the Italian army.

The text initially withholds the name of this central protagonist. Both the mechanics and Catherine call him by his professional rank ('Signor Tenente', 'Tenente'). Even this can confuse the English-speaking reader who may not know the Italian for lieutenant and may be thrown onto the wrong track by the 'Signor' which initially precedes it. He is eventually defined as Mr Henry by Miss Ferguson at the start of chapter 5, and Catherine repeats this in a peculiarly formal manner (given that he now calls her 'darling') in the next chapter. His first name, or rather the Italian variant of it, Frederico, is not given until the end of chapter 7. It is here, though, that the potential confusion between first and last names that already exists is compounded as Bassi, who first identifies the protagonist by his full name during a drunken conversation in the mess, plays with its two elements: 'He said was my name Frederico Enrico or Enrico Federico?' (*FA*, 33). Only at the start of Book Two, when he has already experienced that sense of non-being that occurs with his wounding – 'I felt myself rush bodily out of myself' (*FA*, 44) – does the protagonist name himself unequivocally as Frederic Henry (*FA*, 64); the reader having been further confused meanwhile by the major's repetition of Bassi's 'Federico' (*FA*, 60). As Scott Donaldson notes, 'People are always misspelling Frederic Henry's name, and no wonder: only once in the book does Hemingway supply it, in full, and those who know him best usually do not call him by any name at all.'

This sense of uncertainty concerning the identity of the major protagonist is continued in different forms as the book proceeds. His youth, inexperience and lack of awareness are implicit in the 'suggestive' term of affection, 'baby', which Rinaldi constantly employs in conversation with him, and in the way that Catherine, the priest and others refer to him as a silly (or poor or good) 'boy'.[27] This is linked to a stress on an unformed and provisional quality to his selfhood which constantly recurs. For the notion of role-playing and false identity is one consistently associated with Frederic. Even before we have been given that first clear naming of him in the hospital, reference has been made to him, to achieve speedy medical treatment, as 'the only son of the American Ambassador' (*FA*, 47) and then, jokingly, as 'the American Garibaldi' (*FA*, 60). This type of deliberate misidentification goes together with less jocular forms of the same activity. Catherine gets him to play the role of her dead fiancé when, 'nearly crazy', she first meets him and has him ventriloquising the words she would have that fiancé speak (*FA*, 26). The barber in the hospital mistakes him for an Austrian. During the retreat the battle police mistake him for a German agitator in an Italian uniform. Frederic, in fact, 'is continually being mistaken for someone he is not'.[28]

The notion of uniform as expressive of a dissociated self that I raised in regard to 'A Way You'll Never Be' is again crucial here. For Catherine, initially, one 'nice boy' (*FA*, 27) in uniform can, in her disturbed condition, be replaced by another. When Frederic is talking about the marble busts that line the office of the hospital where Catherine works, he says 'they were all uniformly classical. You could not tell anything about them' (*FA*, 25). A description of his own military equipment follows: cap or steel helmet, English gas-mask and automatic pistol. All of these, when worn, disguise distinctiveness and difference. In the hospital, Frederic's uniform is off; in the retreat, he is suspected of wearing it fraudulently.

I would suggest that, until the end of chapter 30, Frederic is dependent on his uniform for his identity. It confines him – to recall Sandra Gilbert – to 'a single form or self'. The fragile nature of such a 'self' is, though, evidenced by Catherine's initial response to him and by his anomalous position in the army in which he serves. It is evidenced too by his own lack of real commitment to the cause with which it is identified (he allows his subordinates to voice their disaffected opinions) and by his use of metaphors of illusion to describe the war in which he fights. He compares, for instance, the matting screening the road to the front to 'the entrance at a circus' (*FA*, 37).

The way the 'painted horse' metaphor functions in the novel[29] connects up here in its relevance to a central protagonist who performs under a false identity. For Frederic's uniform offers him a very provisional sense of self-definition indeed. The military framework in which he serves only diminishes the subjects at its command. The serious criticisms aimed at it are evident in the references to strong anti-war feeling, both inside and outside the military, and to officers shooting their own troops; to the grotesque sense of 'patriotic' discipline shown during the retreat, and to the pointlessness of military manoeuvres and the falseness of the language associated with their achievement. Frederic's rejection of all this and his making of a 'separate peace' (*FA*, 173) is a response to the uneasy fit of the uniform that contains him.

In the army and wearing that uniform Frederic is closer to an object than a subject – shaped and manipulated rather than actively independent. The theme of identity loss and of the collapse of a sense of control over one's circumstances and fate figures centrally in the novel. It is introduced in the reference at the end of the first chapter to 'only seven thousand' (*FA*, 8) of the army dying of the cholera in the rainy winter of that year. Robert Gajdusek suggests that Hemingway starts Book Two of the novel with 'a dominant "they" who manipulate the questionable "I"'.[30] I would suggest, rather, that this 'I' is questionable from the first. The chain of 'there was's' and 'there were's' in the first chapter ('there was much traffic . . . there was fighting . . . there were mists') imply exactly the same sense of personal passivity and lack of autonomy.

Such a collapse of autonomy in the presented world of the novel is also implicit in the text's focus on the way in which individuals are reduced to their constituent parts. Right at the start of the book we are told of Catherine's fiancé that 'They blew him all to bits'

(*FA*, 19). The 'dominant "They"' are already active at this point. The theme of the maimed subject takes on more immediate physical dimension as Passini has one of his legs blown off and as the unseen man in the stretcher above Frederic is reduced to a stream of dripping blood as he haemorrhages to death. The differences between the human and the object world are elided to confirm this sense of the reduced self. Another man on a stretcher in the ambulance has only a nose emerging from his bandages visible to Frederic, and that is 'waxy-looking' (*FA*, 48). Frederic's legs, when first treated in Milan, have the 'look of not too freshly ground hamburger steak' (*FA*, 72). And even when he introduces a comic touch, when he describes them after the injury as 'full of old iron . . . trench mortar fragments, old screws and bed-springs' (*FA*, 65), it provides a reinforcement of the same theme.

If, in uniform, Frederic's status as a subject is extremely vulnerable, we might suppose that once it is discarded the 'true' colours of his identity might show through. In fact, though, his sense of self becomes even more attenuated. After he has escaped the battle police and crossed the Tagliamento he first cuts the stars off his sleeves and then discards his uniform for civilian clothes. His thoughts at this point are significant: 'In civilian clothes I felt a masquerader. I had been in uniform a long time and I missed the feeling of being held by your clothes' (*FA*, 173). If his uniform gives him a provisional but thoroughly unconvincing identity, once it is removed his self apparently loses rather than gains shape (no longer held by its clothes). Instead of the revelation of this self's 'essence', just another false front appears. The stripping-off of uniform reveals a masquerade self not a 'real' one.

Once the uniform is gone Frederic's sense of his own identity is further and more radically compromised. He remains 'absor[bed] in the war' even after his desertion. His sense of playing truant signals his feeling of a loss of role and purpose.[31] The masquerade motif stays strong in the 'happy' (*FA*, 216) time he and Catherine have together as they establish their domestic routines in their Swiss chalet. The knowledge of the provisional and artificial nature of this arrangement is indicated in the constant references both to the war and to the delayed break in the weather. Their partnership is falsely represented – they are described first as cousins and later as a married couple. The uniforms that have given them both a function and some sense of identity have been stripped to leave the couple locked in a (fraudulently presented) relationship where the diminished one (Frederic) is reflected in Catherine, his mirror other. I will extend this analysis in my next chapter.

The attenuated state of Frederic's selfhood at this point is indicated by his passivity, apathy and lack of direction once the military has been left behind and life in Switzerland established. This passivity is suggested by his growing of a beard to 'give me something to do' (*FA*, 211). Such minimal activity – growing a beard after all requires less positive effort than shaving – only further compromises his sense of himself. For when he takes up an active sport, boxing, he feels alienated from that physically altered man he now sees in the mirror before him: 'it looked so strange to see a man with a beard boxing' (*FA*, 220). A loss of contact with his own sense of himself has taken place. It is as though the apathetic self he has become is projected into a more active double to schizophrenic effect. Similarly, when he projects a version of himself as having a useful and active professional function – as a doctor – the same alienation effect is produced, as he judges himself a fake: 'I looked in the glass and saw myself looking like a fake doctor with a beard' (*FA*, 226).

Michael Reynolds uses such examples as illustrative of 'the piling up of negative identification' in the text (Frederic is 'not a boxer . . . not a doctor') to 'finally produce a non-heroic figure'.[32] While this makes sense, I would rather stress the type of the disorientation of selfhood and loss of active being which those two reflected images suggest. When Frederic was in uniform he had a social function even if his own sense of personal identity was very shaky. Once that social function is cast off, the only option he finds open to him is to lose himself as insufficient subject in a merger with the desired other. Although his unease with such a type of behaviour is also evident, no alternative options are available.

This novel then focuses throughout on the vulnerability of the self. Such a vulnerability is also indicated in the failure of conventional social and religious frameworks to sustain the two main protagonists. Frederic's and Catherine's position in the institutional matrix is an insecure one with the loss of religious belief associated with an earlier and more stable world and with the types of atomisation consequent on a loosening of the familial and other social structures in a modernised world. There is a sense of almost complete disconnection on Frederic's part from his prior social frame, and both his and Catherine's references to family are generally dismissive and brief in the extreme. Frederic's question to her, 'Have you a father?' (*FA*, 113), comes with a note of surprise that reinforces this sense of separateness.

Religion, too, does not sustain in this novel. The early conversation about Catherine's dead fiancé (*FA*, 18) suggests both her rejection of religious belief and Frederic's more equivocal stance toward it. Such equivocation is a sign of Frederic's self-doubts and divisions, his lack of certainty concerning his relation to the social values and institutional frames that surround him. Such uncertainty is evidenced in the military realm when he acts numbly as 'a kind of moral policeman'[33] in the retreat, senselessly shooting one of the sergeants who disobeys his order, yet will make his separate peace once similar acts of arbitrary and life-threatening authority threaten him.

In terms of Frederic's response to the area of religious belief (and the institution of the church which represents it) his friendship with both Rinaldi and the priest suggests the splits in his self-image, torn between a cynical realism and an idealistic generosity of spirit associated with a (Christian) selfless love. In Frederic's case the latter urges will redirect themselves toward Catherine rather than God. The non-transcendent nature of such a form of secular devotion will mean, however, that the loss of self he suffers in such a relationship cannot – like its religious counterpart – be directed to any kind of future pay-off.

Frederic's continuing self-divisions, his inability quite to reject the realm of religion is seen in his concern with its formal rituals at the book's end. He can say 'I had no religion' but still knows that 'he [the dead baby] ought to have been baptized' (*FA*, 232). It is he too who asks Catherine if she wants a priest when she is dying. This self-division is also represented stylistically. For Frederic's language at the end of the novel moves between two poles. On the one hand there is his use of flat description, which formally reflects a desperate attempt at self-control as his world falls apart: 'I ate the ham and eggs and drank the beer' (*FA*, 233). Such a style endorses the notion of a world in which we are all 'cooked': 'There isn't anything, dog' (*FA*, 223). On the other, there are his desperate, even hysterical, prayers, as he realises Catherine might die. These are the product of a different kind of sensibility, which cannot completely let go of the notion of a transcendent and sympathetic divine presence: 'Please, please, please, dear God, don't let her die' (FA, 234). These self-divisions are not explicitly recognised by the narrator himself. As in The Sun Also Rises, it is the reader that does the work as he or she explores the gaps, silences and self-contradictions in the discourse of this fractured and unstable protagonist.

At the end of the novel Frederic extends the image of the ants burning in the fire. He thus implicitly draws an analogy between himself and those of the ants who escape, 'their bodies burnt and flattened' and who 'went off not knowing where they were going' (FA, 232–3). Such an analogy suggests his own sense of reduced and damaged subjectivity, lack of autonomy and utter loss of direction at the text's end. As such it is an entirely appropriate conclusion to the book. But a man is different from an ant. Autonomous individuality may be a myth and the individual subject may contain contradictory aspects, but that is not to say that one cannot negotiate some sense of one's own place and definition in the interstices of that social formation which confines and partly defines the self. This is exactly what Jake Barnes struggles – and implicitly continues to struggle – to do: to find out how to live in the world (to paraphrase his words) as you go along.[34] Frederic, the retrospective narrator, is not able, at this psychological point, to see how to repair the damage done to him. Devastated at the story's end, the notion of the functioning self is in abeyance.

V

Hemingway's short stories and his first two major novels present protagonists whose instability, uncertainty and fragile sense of their own identity is foregrounded. This sense of damaged subjectivity is linked in the short stories to a particular narrative style, marked by brevity and inconclusiveness, and by that stress on dialogue and spare description which typifies the use of a detached and invisible narrator. In the early novels, it is linked to the use of the first-person voice. Personal disorientation is reflected here in a deadpan narrative that concentrates on the depiction of immediate detail to disguise that sense of larger disconnectedness which the situation and actions of the protagonist clearly reveal. Such disorientation is suggested too in the way that the authority and self-control that the first-person voice apparently suggests is contradicted by physical gestures or (often brief) verbal outbursts which reveal psychological and emotional dislocation, and by the way in which the protagonist's description of his relationship to others gradually – and without explicit recognition – reveals a sense of his own self-divisions. The fact that this first-person narrator often fails to describe his own motivating impulses combined with his narrow focus on 'the solipsistic truths of perception and sensation'[35] alerts the reader to a sense of something unsaid and provisional in his sense both of his world and of himself.

All Hemingway's major novels take a new direction in terms of both style and genre.[36] After *A Farewell to Arms* the presentation of the self as damaged and uncertain gives way to the depiction of more assertive and self-confident central protagonists. Major changes also occur stylistically as Hemingway looks to find effective means to present such characters. I would suggest that this combination of factors explains that falling-off in the quality of his work that most critics recognise. Hemingway was not necessarily writing badly but he was certainly writing differently in the novels that followed *A Farewell to Arms*. The short stories and early novels formally and thematically reflect Hemingway's concern with fragmented subjectivity. It is this fiction, charting the anxieties of the subject and the personal and public history to which they relate, that speaks most strongly, I would contend, to a contemporary audience. With *To Have and Have Not* a significant shift occurs away from such concerns.

To Have and Have Not departs considerably from the earlier novels in terms of narrative technique. The text has a patchwork quality to it which perhaps betrays its origin as a series of short stories. Both narrative voice and character focalisation shift to disorienting effect in the novel. Its explorations of the theme of class operate through a rather clumsy juxtaposition (see especially pp. 130–1 and 186) of the lives of Harry and the other working-class protagonists with those of the 'tourists' first introduced in chapter 7.

It is the language of the latter that initially signals their vacuousness, egocentricity and totally irresponsible economic power.[37] This language, meant to illustrate a selfish and inconsiderate childishness, tends to fall somewhat flat: '"Nerts, nerts, double nerts to you" . . . Just then Harry came in and the tall tourist's wife said, "Isn't he wonderful? That's what I want. Buy me that, Papa"' (*THHN*, 98). Chapter 16 is largely devoted to the representatives of this exploitative class and the description of the Henry Carpenter–Wallace Johnston relationship and the focalisations of the grain broker and the Hollywood director's wife (Dorothy) are used to make crude points about the relationship between wealth, sexual dis-ease, and the abuse of economic position. These read particularly baldly after Hemingway's subtle explorations of the problematics of sexual identity in his earlier novels.

If such narrative tactics suggest the novel's final failure to cohere, they also suggest that Harry Morgan cannot bear the same kind of weight, as psychological and emotional centre of the text, as either Jake Barnes or Frederic Henry. This in part results from Hemingway's use here of the simplest formulas of 1930s hard-boiled fiction. We get none of that sense of real uncertainty and anxiety about the status of the subject evidenced in the two former protagonists. Here we are given the proletarian man as hard-boiled egg. He reacts simply and unselfconsciously to his condition in a way that Frederic and Jake never do. The heavily deterministic nature of his world is never in doubt. It is indicated straight away by the way in which Harry is cheated by Mr Johnson. It is indicated more fundamentally by the 'no choice' nature of his Depression context. Lawbreaking (and the consequent punishments and injuries involved) are inevitable for one who has 'got a family and he's got to eat and feed them' (*THHN*, 64).

All Hemingway protagonists are placed in a context of larger conditioning factors that drastically reduce their ability to control their final fate. In the novels that follow *A Farewell to Arms*, though, the protagonist's sense of his own uncertain subjectivity by and large disappears (exceptions to this rule will be noted later in the chapter). Here the world might 'break' Harry but he is and remains entirely sure of his own identity. 'You know how it is' (*THHN*, 9) is how he starts the narrative. As his thoughts are described, we see a man confident in the rightness of his own feelings and the knowledge that they are shared by the like and right-minded audience to which he speaks: 'I felt bad about hitting him. You know how you feel when you hit a drunk' (*THHN*, 34).

Harry's thoughts and feelings are expressed directly and fully –
see, for example, chapter 2 of Part Three and the end of chapter
10.[38] There is none of that uncertainty about motive and
psychological condition that is in the short stories or earlier novels.

Harry Morgan knows who he is, knows that 'a man's still a
man' (*THHN*, 75) despite the loss of an arm. That loss is the result
of uncontrollable larger circumstance, the unpredictability of
Cuban behaviour as Harry pursues his bootlegging activities –
'Somebody didn't pay somebody' (*THHN*, 68). It is significant that
Harry's identity, though, is undiminished by such external
influence. His injury is not the same as Jake Barnes's and the sense
of his own manhood remains fully intact. He is the one with
'cojones' (*THHN*, 62). Marie knows 'there ain't no other men like
that' (*THHN*, 88) and his masculinity and pragmatic negotiation of
even the most desperate situations are structurally opposed in the
novel to the effeteness and destructive egocentricity of the
representative of the middle-class world, the writer Richard
Gordon.

Harry may recognise that 'a man alone ain't got no bloody
fucking chance' (*THHN*, 165)[39] but Scott Donaldson illustrates the
spuriousness of these sentiments. For this book, unlike the prior
novels, celebrates individualism. Harry's self-sufficient masculinity
operates – and can only operate – against the grain of modern
social and political conditions. And though these conditions finally
render Harry's manhood void, Hemingway is *not* arguing for
socialist collectivity, or even for community. Far from it. To quote
Donaldson:

> One thing Hemingway clearly *did* admire about his protagonist
> was his strong self-reliance . . . he saw [the book's] theme as 'the
> decline of the individual'. . . . When Charles Poore was putting
> together his Hemingway Reader, Ernest specifically asked him to
> include . . . the first five chapters of [the novel] . . . which
> showed 'Harry Morgan pretty much in the round when he could
> still get by on *cojones* and improvising and his luck'. . . .
> Throughout the novel . . . Hemingway deplores the alternatives
> to individualism. Big government oppresses, revolution brutal-
> izes, communism attracts the fashionable and insincere, politics
> ruins art and there is precious little that any man can do for his

fellows. . . . In a better world, one man alone *would* have a chance.[40]

Hemingway changes tack in his presentation of the subject in this novel. Firm individual identity, and the possibility of heroic behaviour associated with it, are placed in opposition to constraining historical circumstance. In the earlier texts such a tension between the two is attenuated and any sense of heroic individualism is provisional, to say the least (as far as his central characters are concerned). There the relationship between social reality and the status of the subject could not be divorced in the way that *To Have and Have Not* suggests. The theme of the damaged subject, which the injuries and uncertainties of Nick Adams, Jake Barnes and Frederic Henry all indicate, is directly bound in with the shifts in social and ideological formations that have occurred. Harry Morgan appears to have an existence as an autonomous and self-sufficient self *prior to* his engagement with that social world which will inevitably diminish him.

This kind of thematic turnaround on Hemingway's part is not so unexpected as it might appear. Although the depiction of Nick, Jake and Frederic would deny the notion of the sovereign subject, the appearance of a character like Pedro Romero in *The Sun Also Rises* and Jake's early comment that 'Nobody ever lives their life all the way up except bull-fighters' (*SAR*, 12) suggests the attraction the idea of the heroic individual subject had for Hemingway. Romero's feats – and the feats of the bullfighters in the non-fictional *Death in the Afternoon* – take place in the sporting arena and would seem accordingly to occur at one ritualised remove from the 'everyday' world (I will modify this statement in my last chapter). However, the qualities Hemingway associates with such figures – knowledge, style, passion, courage and control – speak of an alternative to the constraints and emasculations charted elsewhere.

Throughout Hemingway's work (and life) there is strong evidence of his attraction to the idea of autonomous individualism. As I suggest earlier, he was at least partly in the business of constructing 'desperate myths of the self' to oppose to the reification, social atomisation and decline of potent subjectivity which marked the conditions of modern culture and which his fiction also recognised. His novels taken as a whole might be termed schizophrenic in their treatment of subjectivity. In this respect they are illustrative of a more general tension between actual conditions and ideological frame in American (and Western) society – what Richard Godden calls 'an absolute contradiction between what capitalist production does to the individual and what bourgeois ideology claims for the maimed and individual- ized self'.[41] *To Have and Have Not* marks the fictional beginnings of Hemingway's interest in pursuing the possibilities of actively heroic behaviour *despite* the constraining circumstances of an oppressive and complicated modern world that his next major novel would pursue in a more developed form.

VI

For Whom the Bell Tolls is one of Hemingway's most popular novels. Robert Jordan shares many of those heroic qualities Hemingway associated with the bullfighter. He too has – or comes to have – knowledge, passion, courage and control. Harry, in *To Have and Have Not*, is strongly aware of the determining conditions that limit every aspect of his life and operate to render his strong sense of himself ineffectual. Like so many protagonists in the hard-boiled novel of the 1930s, he is associated with action rather than consistent thought as he looks to survive, physically and economically, in an oppressive world. The reader is also held at one remove from Harry. Questions about ends and means link his illegal activities to those of the Cuban revolutionaries and raise unresolved doubts as to his ultimate status (heroic or otherwise). The narrative techniques used, moreover, remove him more and more from the novel's centre as it proceeds.

Jordan is much more obviously a heroic figure. The novel closely focuses around him from start to end. Although again there is a strongly deterministic element to the novel in the sense that Robert's fate (and that of the Republican cause) is preordained, he has freely chosen to place himself in this situation and is acting not for himself but with larger ends in mind – for 'the future of the human race' (*FWBT*, 45) may be at stake here. This ability to see any distance beyond the immediate facts of the situation marks him off from previous protagonists. Robert is a university professor who is associated with a wider outlook and a more consistently reflective intelligence than Harry. The narrative techniques used endorse such differences in that his thoughts and feelings are given in more extended form than those of any prior Hemingway protagonist.

In this novel, Hemingway continues to move away from the limited narrative perspectives of *The Sun Also Rises* and *A Farewell to Arms*. Such a move suits the broadscale intentions of a novel which works outward from Robert's own specific experience to that of the Spaniards with whom he is most directly involved (the members of Pablo's and El Sordo's band and, to lesser extent, Berrendo) to those Republicans and their supporters (both Spanish and foreign) in Madrid and in the military lines. Robert's experience is thus placed in a wider context than that given for Frederic Henry or Nick Adams, Hemingway's previous men at war. When Hemingway had just begun *For Whom the Bell Tolls* he wrote to Ivan Kashkin, the Soviet literary critic whose name he borrows in the novel. Referring to 'stories about the war', he says, 'I try to show *all* the different sides of it . . . examining it from many ways. So never think one story represents my viewpoint because it is much too complicated for that' (*L*, 480). In the shift from the short story to the novel form such complications could be tackled. In *A Farewell to Arms* the view of war is a largely one-sided one, necessarily so since Frederic Henry's first-person narration acts as a filter on its presentation.

The larger concern with the meaning of the Spanish civil war, and the political, military and social issues involved, lead now to a complete change of narrative tactics. Thus not only is the narration from an omniscient third-person position but the range of focalisation in the novel is extensive. This produces the odd aberrant effect as, for instance, when Pablo's horse's thoughts (*FWBT*, 63) are represented, but for the most part is a highly effective way of extending the text's range of voices and positions. So, for example, in the last few pages of chapter 28 and the start of the next chapter, we are given at least eight different perspectives on the action: those of the Fascist sniper, Berrendo, El Sordo, Joaquin, Ignatio, Jordan, Maria and Anselmo. The use of omniscient narration contributes to this sense of breadth. In chapters 34–42 the narrative swings back and forth from Andrés's journey across the lines to division headquarters to the actions of the guerilla band just prior to their attack on the bridge. As the reader follows Andrés toward the front line, switches of focalisation again occur which add to our general understanding of the politics and psychologies of command. André Marty's mentally disturbed condition is revealed as the workings of his own mind are set against his actions and the way others talk about and behave toward him. We follow Duval and Golz's thoughts when they finally receive the dispatch, which reaches them too late for it to influence events. All these devices add to the broad-scale and multi-faceted picture of the war presented.

In this novel, then, the reader is presented with a whole series of larger locating points and frames to the central protagonist's actions. Hemingway's earlier war fiction lacks such contexts. Pilar's long story of what happened in Avila at the start of the revolutionary movement is the type of extended exercise in personal and public history marked by its absence in the earlier texts. It is intended 'to complicate Jordan's and the reader's understanding of the ethical responsibility inhering within any particular action'.[42] We are also given a much fuller picture of the central protagonist than appears in the earlier texts. David Wyatt speaks of this novel as being a 'long book about a short time' and contrasts it to *In Our Time* in the fact that 'it leaves nothing out'. It is he says, with reference to Frederic Henry's earlier activities, 'a book that fills rather than kills time'.[43] In previous novels the use of unreliable first-person narrators, the number of gaps and inconsistencies in their stories, and the concentration on immediate event and sensation rather than considered reflection were all means of indicating the protagonists' instability and incompleteness. Here Robert is – or at least becomes – a centred, unified and complete self.

Hemingway makes much greater use of interior discourse than he does in *The Sun Also Rises* and *A Farewell to Arms*. We get to know Jordan fully from within as he reflects on immediate events but also spirals away mentally from the present to take in a variety of subjects which include his past, his political position, the Spanish people and his relationship to them, and his projected future. Two of the most conspicuous examples of this use of interior discourse occur in chapters 13 and 18. In the former, we are given his thoughts and feelings as he makes love to Maria. The time of the present narrative then comes to a full stop ('because now he was not there' – *FWBT*, 147) as he thinks about the immediate military situation that confronts him. Jordan goes on to reflect on his effect on the lives of those now being 'used' by him for the necessary military ends and to think about the military command in Spain, his own politics and the language in which they were expressed. He then returns to think about Maria, her past and their future. This takes his thoughts back to his present 'strange life' (*FWBT*, 150), forward to the book he wishes to write about it, and back once more to the importance of the present moments; the fullness of his life as he is now leading it. This provides a selection of his thoughts during the brief period in story time before the narrative picks up where it had left off ('and he came back to the girl' – *FWBT*, 154). Seven pages of text are given to this representation of his interior discourse. Similarly in chapter 18, Jordan moves mentally away from the immediate problem with Pablo to think about Madrid and Gaylord's. There is an eighteen-page digression from the time of the first narrative as he reflects on what he has learnt about military and political realities in this war and about what Karkov has taught him concerning their complexity. Chapter 19 brings him and the reader sharply back to the narrative present with Maria's 'What do you do sitting there?' (*FWBT*, 222).

The text's extended explorations of the central protagonist's thoughts and feelings is accompanied by a stylistic expansiveness far removed from the taut understatement that is the norm in earlier texts. Such a shift is to be seen in the use of long sentences, of chains of adjectives – 'the dry-mouthed, fear-purged, purging ecstasy of battle' (*FWBT*, 211) and of extended figurative device (see, for example, the 'He did not want to make a Thermopylae' passage – *FWBT*, 150). Jordan is fully known to the reader. There are none of the kind of difficulties of interpretation concerning his motivation and psychological position that problematise earlier texts. This is not to say that Robert Jordan is not a complex protagonist, or that he is initially presented as a fully coherent subject. This is far from being the case.

For Robert's awareness of his own self-division is highlighted forcefully on two occasions in the novel. In chapter 26, that part of him which knows that killing is inevitable in the context of war engages in dialogue with the part which is aware of the need to guard against taking such killing as a 'right' and thus allowing its full meaning to be avoided. The distinctions Jordan juggles with here are narrow, but the sense of a man trying to reconcile potentially contradictory aspects of himself is clear in the two separate voices heard: 'Listen, he told himself. . . . Then himself said back to him, You listen, see?' (*FWBT*, 268). What is noticeable here is that Jordan, as he confronts the moral complexities of his position as part of the book's larger argument about ends and means, is able to reconcile these two voices – to move toward a unity of voice and being – as he works out exactly his position on this issue in relation to his larger set of beliefs: 'no man has a right to take another man's life unless it is to prevent something worse happening to other people' (*FWBT*, 269). Although this statement comes from just one of the voices being represented, the tenor of the ending of the sequence suggests that this is the final position taken on the issue; that this is the voice he wishes to speak for him.

A sharper sense of self-division on Jordan's part occurs toward the end of the novel. In chapter 38 he gives way, following Pablo's apparent desertion, to self-contempt and defeatism. In the next chapter, with Pablo returned, he recovers confidence in himself. He is able to balance his possible death against his shared love with Maria without the one cancelling out the worth of the other. He has confidence now in his ability to complete his task. He refers back, though, to his previous state: 'And you, he said to himself . . . you were pretty bad back there. I was ashamed enough of you. . . . Only I was you. . . . We were all in bad shape. You and me and both of us. Come on now. Quit thinking like a schizophrenic. . . . You're all right again now' (*FWBT*, 346). Again we have the sense of different elements of Robert's self struggling against each other, but in this process such self-divisions are overcome. Jordan recovers confidence here in his ability to channel the self to realise its best potential and to continue to move in the direction of significant and necessary action.

The similarities and differences between Frederic Henry and Jordan begin to become evident in such details. Both are caught in a trap. Frederic's is ultimately a biological one (*FA*, 102) while Robert's seems spun by fate and reinforced by political and military circumstance. The stress on the foredoomed nature of Jordan's enterprise is strong from the start with Pablo's question as to whether he would be willing to be left behind if he were wounded in the attack on the bridge (*FWBT*, 26) and Jordan's own recognition, when Pablo asks him if he wants to die, of the 'seriousness' of his position in attempting to carry out his orders: 'You can see it and I see it and the woman read it in my hand' (*FWBT*, 54). There is also here the same kind of attention paid to a larger constraining reality which diminishes individual effort as there was in *A Farewell to Arms*. The strength of the enemy is foregrounded from the first with Pablo's '*They* are very strong' (*FWBT*, 21). The novel was written when Hemingway already knew that 'the Republic was doomed'.[44] The third-person narrator notes that the result of 'Andrés's mission' would probably have been the same even if Jordan's message regarding the Fascist preparation for the coming attack had not been held up by Marty (*FWBT*, 370) – though the later narrative rather cuts against such a judgement. The immediate success of Jordan's mission is compromised by the 'famous balls up' (*FWBT*, 376) of the larger attack.

This does not, however, prevent Jordan from acting forcefully and well to make his part of the mission a success. In this he differs from Frederic who is characterised only by his passivity and whose lack of control over his military environment is apparent in the fact that he is 'blown up while we were eating cheese' (*FA*, 50). Heroic action is an impossibility for this maimed and powerless subject whose one autonomous decision is to run away, to make his separate peace. Robert Jordan, in contrast, is not disassociated. He acts forcefully and confidently in the areas open to him to do so. Larger constraints may be present but they do not diminish the possibility of heroic action; of the self acting autonomously and optimistically, within a limited sphere. 'The greatest gift that he had', he tells himself, was 'that ability not to ignore but to despise whatever bad ending there could be' (*FWBT*, 345–6). He judges his behaviour as he goes along – 'you have behaved OK. So far you have behaved all right' (*FWBT*, 295) – and does what Anselmo calls 'an enormous work' (*FWBT*, 389) in the wiring of the bridge. Like the latter, he is 'one with all of the battle and with the Republic' (*FWBT*, 387) as he does so. He fights for his ideals despite his knowledge of all that work against them and still acts on the belief that the things he does 'may make all the difference' (*FWBT*, 412) as he lies awaiting death. Though he recognises that he has been 'bitched' by the orders that Golz had been given, he still trusts that 'later on we will have these things much better organized' (*FWBT*, 411). He acts on the principle that what he does can make a difference and, in Hemingway's world, that is the very best one can do. He is a heroic figure who blows up the specified military target. This kind of heroism is not an option open to Frederic Henry, Nick Adams or Jake Barnes. Their status as (damaged) subjects is presented as inevitable in a world where the capacity for autonomous will and choice and for the active expression of separate selfhood had already been drastically compromised.

Robert Jordan is a very different case. Described as 'completely integrated' (*FWBT*, 412) at the novel's conclusion, his education (to which frequent reference has been made) is by that stage finalised. This *bildungsroman* is complete – even if Robert's gains in self-knowledge and his maturation cannot prevent his death. Jordan knows when to act and when it is necessary to stifle those thoughts and emotions that hinder such action. He is, despite the claims of a number of critics to the contrary,[45] both politically knowledgeable and astute. Much of the novel, indeed, concerns the political intricacies and ambivalences of a situation in which Jordan, despite an awareness of the similarities of the combatants, can still fight for the Republic because of his belief in it as a system of government and his knowledge that 'if it were destroyed life would be unbearable for all those people who believed in it' (*FWBT*, 149). Jordan has none of the problems about where to position himself in relation to the secular–religious divide of Jake and Henry. He is able to plumb his personal past, unavailable for purposes of therapy or as a marker of growth to those earlier subjects, and to come to terms with his ambivalent feelings concerning it. He can distinguish between love and duty and does not look to the former as a type of retreat from the social self as does Frederic Henry. Rather he celebrates the 'luck' and 'value' found in the intensity of that love which gives him a similar sense of the completion of self in the other, but does not let it blind him to what he sees as his social responsibilities. Both go together in his mind as elements of that complete self which he becomes. The strength of Jordan's commitment to life and his determination to live it fully to its last drop can be evidenced in that change of tense in the passage on one of the last pages: 'I hate to leave it. . . . I have tried to [do some good in it] with what talent I had. *Have, you mean. All right, have*' (*FWBT*, 408). In Robert Jordan's figure and his thoughts, positive and heroic individualism are fully realised. Any sense of uncertainty on the subject's part is worked through and overcome in the course of the novel.

VII

To Have and Have Not and *For Whom the Bell Tolls* signal a change of direction in terms of Hemingway's presentation of his central protagonists. He writes *against* his earlier novels in that a concern with the fractures and divisions of self is replaced and contradicted by a celebration of individualism and inner-directed and coherent selfhood. The subjects presented are still victims of larger constraints in the form of luck, historical circumstance, social condition and institutional and interpersonal action which militate against their larger individual effectiveness and survival. However, there is little doubt (and none at all in the case of *For Whom the Bell Tolls*) concerning the heroic qualities, the worth and attractiveness, of these protagonists, or of their ability to function strongly and successfully within the limited arenas available to them. Hemingway here constructs the type of complete and stable subject that the conditions of modernity would deny. His use of small group situations and spatial settings (the sea and rural Spain), which are associated with expressive movement rather than repressive constraint, allows him to reconstruct the type of myth of the coherent self that the short stories and early novels had so brilliantly deconstructed. If Hemingway continues clearly to depict larger contexts which limit the full and final realisation of that self, such limits (in *For Whom the Bell Tolls* in particular) never diminish the value or 'sanctity'[46] of his later centred and central subjects.

Both Colonel Cantwell in *Across the River and into the Trees* and the old man in *The Old Man and the Sea* fit this developing pattern. In the former novel, however, any reading of the main protagonist as a heroic and unified subject has to remain somewhat provisional. The lack of any gap between the third-person narrative voice and Cantwell's focalisation, his way of looking at things, makes it is very difficult to know if any irony is intended in the presentation of this subject: quite how critically the reader is meant

to respond to the Colonel. When we are told of his elevator ride
that 'it was a good ride with a slight bump, and a rectification at
the end' (*AR*, 82), and of the seating arrangements in the hotel bar
that 'they were at their table in the far corner . . . where the
Colonel had both his flanks covered' (*AR*, 87), we can either
recognise the narrowness of the values and judgements offered or
take it as a serious representation of Cantwell's sharp concern
for detail and a necessary self-protective faculty learnt from
experience. If we do the former, however, we are left in a readerly
limbo not knowing quite where to draw our interpretive lines; not
knowing how far Cantwell's point of view can be trusted and how
far not. There is something very monoglossic (to use Bakhtin's
term) about a text where the protagonist's perspective is so
textually dominant and where the narrator and his protagonist
appear to share the same voice: 'Barone Alvarito came into the
dining-room. He was looking for them and, being a hunter, he saw
them instantly' (*AR*, 96).

This same problem – how far we are meant to distance ourselves
from the central protagonist – is raised in the earlier first-person
narratives. There, though, indications of the problematics of the
protagonist's position are given in the gap between his words and
actions, in the silences of the text and in the relationships between
the main figure and those who surround him. Here the other
figures only reflect the Colonel's own self-image,[47] the type of
direct action that might allow new meanings to emerge is minimal,
and the co-ordination of narration and focalisation operates against
the type of significant reticences found in the earlier work.

If we provisionally accept that we are meant to read Cantwell on
his own terms, then he does show all the signs of inner direction
and self-sufficiency that mark the centred subject. The movement
of the novel, too, does suggest an overcoming of the psychological
conflict that would initially seem to hinder such self-completion. In
some ways Cantwell is a later, but much more authoritative,
composite version of Frederic Henry and Nick Adams. The
intertextual aspects of the novel, as Hemingway feeds back into
this earlier fictional world, are suggested in the references to
Fossalta, to crossing the Tagliamento, to the sense of personal
immortality before the kneecap wound, and to service abroad in a
foreign army. But Cantwell is very different from the earlier
protagonists. Even at eighteen he had the kind of expertise and

personal authority which Frederic never has. Although both are lieutenants, Cantwell is an active and proficient soldier who 'commanded . . . [and] taught his people to shoot' (*AR*, 28), not the passive and non-assertive ambulanceman of the earlier novel. The Colonel is now 'one half a hundred years old' (*AR*, 132) and his age has apparently brought both knowledge and authority over the conditions of his life.

The novel charts Cantwell's preparations for, and movement toward, death. The whole action of the novel is contained by the duck shoot and its immediate aftermath which is that death. Cantwell has his weakness: that 'bitterness' which comes from the remembrance of losses suffered in battle and their cause. Renata's words, 'Don't you see you need to tell me things to purge your bitterness?' (*AR*, 172), triggers Cantwell's retellings of these memories. These take the form of direct discourse, as he tells Renata of parts of this past, and internal discourse, as he uses her – or her portrait – as an imaginary audience for what else there is to tell. The recovery and retelling of these memories forms a main strand of the late part of the novel and would seem to act as a form of therapy. In remembering and relating the past, bitterness can be purged and 'the grace of a happy death' (*AR*, 172–3) thereby made possible. This, at any rate, is what Renata suggests. In fact there are reasons to argue that the success of this therapy remains doubtful. For Cantwell sharply interrupts the flow of his reminiscences by saying to himself:

> I'm through with this whole subject. And what about that company dead up the draw? What about them, professional soldier?
> They're dead, he said. And I can hang and rattle. (*AR*, 185–6).

Physically, Cantwell is a wreck, with his scarred body and dicky heart. Psychologically, he seems to become more whole, his anger cured and 'soul's salvation' realised through the influence of his young and gentle 'confessor-therapist'.[48] Such an interpretation must, however, be tentative given the lack of positive closure to this narrative strand.

Everything about Cantwell speaks self-confident and authoritative selfhood.[49] His ritualised behaviour and formalised knowledge speak of one who has got his responses to life off pat and who is content with those responses. His jokes with bartenders and hotel staff in Venice are repetitions of past jokes. His smiles are repetitions of past smiles: 'It was an old smile that he had been using for fifty years, ever since he first smiled' (*AR*, 70). Cantwell's knowledge of art, of the military 'trade', of hunting, of food and of people, all combine to make his life into a set of fixed responses – ways of controlling and mastering the world in which he moves.

Hemingway's ageing hero here is in control of all elements of his life except his bitterness and his health. The former he (potentially? possibly?) remedies through his 'confession' to Renata. The latter, despite his self-medications, cannot be controlled. Pressing external factors are more or less removed in this novel since Cantwell is moving in his own self-chosen space and seems scarcely subject to the command of larger authority. The biological trap, though, is inevitable. One of the strongest passages in the book concerns exactly death's unpredictability. The spring can snap shut at any time:

> Death . . . comes to you in small fragments that hardly show where it has entered. It comes, sometimes, atrociously. It can come from unboiled water; an un-pulled-up mosquito boot, or it can come with the great, white-hot, clanging roar we have lived with. It comes in small cracking whispers that precede the noise of the automatic weapon. . . . It comes in the metallic rending crash of a vehicle. (*AR*, 159)

Even in this area, though, the Colonel is able to prepare for death in a way denied to others. As Hemingway's protagonists age, so more and more do they become 'completely integrated'; at one with themselves and as much at one with their world as is possible to be.

The Old Man and the Sea is a much more straightforward novel than *Across the River and into the Trees*. In both, however, there is a certain rigidity about Hemingway's prose that reflects the fixed and formalised routines that have now come to mark the lives of his characters. Santiago is an obviously heroic figure and one who is integrated with his world. His eyes are 'the same colour as the sea' (*OMS*, 5). He thinks of this sea as '*la mar* which is what people call her in Spanish when they love her' (*OMS*, 23). The marlin that he kills is a 'brother' (*OMS*, 49) to whom he speaks. His dreams are of the white and golden beaches of Africa and of lions that he 'loved' (*OMS*, 19). His love and respect for nature may be in conflict with his role as fisherman but his awareness of the (necessary) paradoxes of his position and the humility of his final attitude negates any final sense of self-division. The problems of sexuality and the nightmares that stem from past trauma have no place in this protagonist's life. This is a ritualistic fable, a narrative that bears heavy figurative weight, with its references to the crucifixion and its analogies between the arts of fishing and writing. John Aldridge judges it 'a classic parable in stone . . . quite dead'.[50] David Timms suggests a more generous reading in his comment that

> this is a world without a teleology . . . where the only inherent organizing principle or end product is blank sequence. The only way to make such a world meaningful is to force life and death into a context of your own manufacture where they are not arbitrary; for Santiago the assumed moral imperatives of a ritual contest between his own cunning and experience and the fish's strength.[51]

The old man is a figure without the bitterness of Cantwell. He measures his strength, he trusts his skills, he calmly does what the situation calls for. He has exactly that firm sense of his own individuality, identity and place in a social and natural order that Hemingway's early protagonists lack.

VIII

In *Islands in the Stream*, the first of Hemingway's novels published posthumously, dialogue and action once again become much more significant than in the highly monologic published texts of his later years. Such monologism goes hand in hand with his presentation of centred and confident subjects. Despite obvious flaws, perhaps because of them, this novel is Hemingway's most interesting since *For Whom the Bell Tolls*. The narrative technique partly explains this. So too, though, does the fact that both here and in *The Garden of Eden,* which was published later (and which I examine in my next chapter), we are once more given central protagonists who are uncertain in their sense of themselves and their relationship to the world.

The novel is one that depends on a number of narrative shocks. The initial description of the Bimini beach suggests a dualistic world where 'at night the sharks came in close to the beach' but where it is a 'safe and fine place to bathe in the day' due to 'the clear white sand' (*IS,* 9). The clear separation of spheres of safety and danger collapses when David, Hudson's son, is out enjoying spear-fishing on a reef ('I love it underwater . . . more than anything' – *IS,* 83) to find his life threatened – despite the water's clarity – by a shark. The sense of idyll with a nightmare underside suggested in this incident climaxes at the end of the first part of the novel. For the 'very lucky and good' (*IS,* 88) summer that Hudson has spent with his boys is followed by the radio message telling of the death of two of them in a motor accident. Earlier references to Hieronymus Bosch and the art of apocalypse are here reprised as Hudson's life falls apart:

> The end of a man's own world does not come as it does in one of the great paintings Mr Bobby had outlined. It comes with one of the island boys bringing a radio message up the road from the local post office and saying, 'Please sign on the detachable part of the envelope. We're sorry, Mr Tom.' (*IS,* 172)

The narrative shock that occurs with the boys' death is duplicated in the second and weakest section of the novel, 'Cuba'. Here Hemingway returns to the technique used in the Nick Adams stories where a third-person narration gradually allows the unease of the central protagonist to surface. The rather strained opening passages where Hudson talks to his beloved cat, Boise, suggests his psychic dislocation in the fact that dialogue with the outside world has been temporarily closed-off. A sense of despair is explicitly signalled in lines such as 'There's nothing we can do' and 'There isn't any solution' (*IS,* 180). The references to heavy drinking and insomnia reinforce this, together with the use of an interior discourse that spins off in illogical and disconnected directions. The protagonist's move in memory to recover narratives of the past only end in the pointless present: 'And why go on with that? he thought now. The Baron was dead and the Krauts had Paris and the Princess did not have a baby' (*IS*, 203). Descriptions of places and of people continually strengthen these impressions of emotional pain and loss. It is not, however, till he is in the Floridita, drinking one of many double frozen daiquiris with Revello, a 'rummy' and 'damned bore' (*IS*, 227), that we learn, in Hudson's reponse to a casual enquiry about his eldest son, that he too is dead. Details of this death emerge through the rest of this section of the novel, but Hudson's nature as 'grief hoarder' (*IS*, 237) means that even when he tells Tom's mother of his death he does not tell the whole story, and the reader, too, is left in partial ignorance of exactly what he knows.

Such powerfully unexpected turns in the narrative suggest, as so often in Hemingway, the presence of forces in the protagonist's life that cannot be controlled. Here, though, the sense of plot manipulation that results from the violent obliteration of all Hudson's sons has led critics such as Malcolm Cowley to remark 'that the sons have served as a blood sacrifice to the exigencies of fiction'.[52] This may be so. There is, however, in this fiction generally that quality of textual resistance to swift and easy interpretation which marked so many of Hemingway's earlier, and more successful, works.

As I suggest, this may be because of the patchwork quality of a novel released posthumously. There are gaps in the move from Bimini to Cuba and from Hudson's role as practising artist[53] to naval commander in time of war which the reader has to fill as best he or she can. The text is replete with partial narratives about the past and details of the present (Hudson's relationship with his wife and ex-wife and with the military command) which are left unfinished and incomplete. The fact, too, that the balance between action and dialogue and interior discourse (especially in the first and last parts of the novel) tilts in the direction of the former and that the use of obvious patterns of duplication and doubling are not explained by reference to the conscious thoughts of the main protagonist make this a particularly rich text for psychoanalytic criticism.[54] We are caught in our version of Hudson between artist and man of action, failed family man and celebrator of male camaraderie, code hero and melancholic. In this text, I would suggest, Hemingway recaptures something of the sense of doubt and hesitation about the stability and coherence of the subject that made the earlier fiction both so unusual and so artistically successful. *Islands in the Stream* is in many ways a hotch-potch of a novel, but it is certainly not without interest.

4

Gender Role and Sexuality

Hemingway has been attacked by feminist writers for his representation of gender roles and sexuality. The condemnations made by academic critics like Judith Fetterley and Faith Pullin[1] have been casually echoed elsewhere. It would be difficult to provide a strong defence of Hemingway's sexual politics from a contemporary point of view. Biographical detail intrudes power fully in any critical consideration of this area. Edmund Wilson noted Hemingway's 'ominous resemblance to Clark Gable', a resemblance that extended beyond mere physical appearance to a shared form of 'stylized masculinity'.[2] His name became publicly synonymous with bullfighting, big game hunting and fishing. Diane Johnson points to his daring, his 'wartime and sporting exploits', to suggest that by the 1950s his name had taken on 'iconographic magic'; had come to signify 'maleness' itself.[3]

Evidence of a celebration of the cult of virility can be found in his fiction too. Both male and female identity is on occasion presented synecdochally as those bits of the body that comprise the protagonists' sexuality and thus their man or womanhood. 'That boy's got cojones' (*THHN*, 62) is Captain Willie Adams's verdict on Harry Morgan's rough weather crossing from Cuba to Florida in *To Have and Have Not*. While in the notorious passage in 'Fathers and Sons', Nick's sexual initiation is linked to the reductive description of the Indian girl, Trudy, in terms of her 'plump brown legs, flat belly, hard little breasts' (*WTN*, 174). These passages are, though, channelled through particular focalisations, and to focus exclusively on such blatant examples of sexual stereotyping would be to give an extremely unbalanced version of Hemingway's work as a whole.

Another side of the picture is suggested in John Raeburn's perceptive article, 'Skirting the Hemingway Legend'. He claims there that the feminist critics of the early 1970s were paradoxically directly responsible for the revival of interest in both Hemingway's life and his fiction. They found in him an obvious target for their re-evaluations of the American literary and cultural tradition. But their criticism 'led to a fresh examination of his fiction and to the discovery in some of it of a heretofore neglected strain, one which was unusually alert to female sensibilities'. Kenneth Lynn's 1987 biography went on clearly to show the deep ambivalence toward masculinity that underlay, and was perhaps directly responsible for, Hemingway's overt displays of machismo. Raeburn sum- marises an argument that stressed Grace Hemingway's heavy influence:

The maternal figure of Grace Hemingway . . . was 'the dark queen of Hemingway's inner world,' . . . In particular, she was responsible for his undiminishing preoccupation with sexual identity and gender distinction, which made his behaviour at times a caricature of masculine aggressiveness and his art at others almost preternaturally alert to women's sensibilities and to the possibilities of androgyny.[4]

The consensus view of Hemingway until very recently, and one crucial to his literary canonisation, was existentialist in kind. It centred around the 'heroic paradigms' produced as Hemingway's protagonists adhered to a rigid code of behaviour, confronted an indifferent universe in a tight-lipped way, and thereby turned defeat into a kind of victory. Such readings are now accepted as one-sided and Hemingway's work as more varied than this. Susan Beegel in fact suggests that, both in his life and his fiction, Hemingway resists 'closure and consensus'. It is the recurrent themes of homosexuality, unconventional sexual practice and androgyny that have recently caught critical interest, with attention accordingly paid to stories like 'The Sea Change' and 'A Simple Enquiry'. Scribner's publication of *The Garden of Eden* in 1986 was at least partially prompted by their awareness of the present public acceptability of this different side of Hemingway's work – one that loosens gender proscriptions and questions stereotypical masculine behaviour. Referring back to Gertrude Stein's comment on the sexually explicit nature of 'Up in Michigan', which made it – in terms of her art gallery metaphor – 'unhangable', Beegel comments that now: 'the *inaccrochable* is no longer *inaccrochable*; in fact, it is rather fashionable'.[5]

In this chapter I steer clear of psychoanalytic readings of Hemingway's life. I refer to such readings only as I show how previous critics have constructed 'Hemingway' as a writer. While accepting both the value of such approaches and their firm basis in the particular details of Hemingway's life, I prefer to consider the issue of gender as a cultural system that transcends individual intention and circumstance.[6] My interest is in the fiction and its representation of gender conflict in a modernist world rather than in the person himself. My analyses will consequently operate primarily at a textual level.

II

Before directly approaching Hemingway's fiction some brief comments on gender role and sexual difference are necessary. I would contend that the gender uncertainties foregrounded in the fiction are directly related to the historical changes that provide the larger horizon to Hemingway's work. His short stories and novels must be read in the context of a specific set of anxieties about masculinity, gender role and sexuality in American (and Western) society in the years on either side of, and including, the First World War.

My discussion of gender and sexuality is necessarily condensed.[7] 'Male' and 'female' are relatively stable terms as they relate to natural sexual difference. Notions of gender role, of what 'masculinity' and 'femininity' mean, are, however, culture-bound and change along with the economic and social order that underpins them. 'Masculinity' is a term generally used

> to refer to the set of images, values, interests, and activities held important to a successful achievement of male adulthood . . . it remains consistently opposed to the 'feminine,' those

characteristics that must be discarded in order to actualize masculinity.[8]

During Hemingway's adolescence and young manhood 'a perceived erosion of male dominance' occurred in American culture as social patterns – and gender roles – changed. This resulted in a male need either to adjust the set of images associated with 'manhood' to these changed conditions or to live according to the old images despite them. An established version of male adulthood as virile, autonomous and expansive now clashed with one emerging out of a new set of historical circumstances. In this new context man's 'control over his own condition' was radically diminished (as the modernisation process increased) and traditional notions of masculine authority were challenged by an apparent increase of social and political power on the part of American women. Michael Kimmel sums up the resulting 'crisis' in masculinity in America in the period 1880–1914 by saying that

> structural changes had transformed the structure of gender relations, and both men and women struggled to redefine the meanings of masculinity and femininity. . . . Men felt themselves besieged by social breakdown and crisis, as 'the familiar routes to manhood [became] either washed out or road-blocked'.

Teddy Roosevelt, Hemingway's boyhood hero, provided one response to this crisis with his robust masculinity. This was just one form of that 'compulsive reassertion of traditional masculinity'[9] which marked the turn-of-the-century years. Such a containment strategy – a way of 'managing' the contradictory positions available for the male subject within this social world by forcefully asserting the validity of an intense and apparently autonomous masculinity in order to meet the threat posed by fears of male diminishment[10] – could only temporarily defuse what was an ongoing problem. Indeed one might argue that the sense of crisis in masculinity only increased with, and after, the First World War. American entry into the war appeared to offer American men a solution to 'the crisis of their sex role'; a proving ground for masculinity and a test of strength and courage in vigorous action. Those who served in France found out the illusory nature of such a hope: 'the battleground had been not a proving ground for manly courage, but a site for the technological ferocity of military machinery. War had been an experience of impersonality . . . from which men emerged in diminished form'.[11] Sandra Gilbert in fact claims that 'male sexual anxiety' increased during the war.[12] The period after the war has equally been seen as a time of 'severe stress' for American men, when the 'task [of "being a man"] became even more baffling and frenzied'.[13] General post-war social and economic change meant that men had to make major readjustments to their sense of masculine identity, at precisely the time that further advances toward political, economic and sexual equality on the part of women (however illusory or limited these may have been[14]) led a majority of them to feel that the 'familiar balance of [gender] spheres' had gone awry. All of these things posed a further threat to the established sense of the male self.[15]

Hemingway's obsessive concern with sexuality and gender role must be seen in terms of these worries about masculinity. The inversion of sexual roles in his fiction, the uncertainty of his male protagonists' sense of their own manhood, and the divided and contradictory nature of his discourse of sexuality and gender in general are all markers of a deep concern about masculine identity and its relation to the feminine 'other' in a culture where gender roles are in transition and where traditional versions of masculinity are under acute threat. In the rest of this chapter I show how Hemingway – caught between various versions of maleness – foregrounds gender anxiety as an issue in his work. I briefly refer to his short fiction to show how different views of sexual politics are juxtaposed there. I take the prevalence of wounded male protagonists in Hemingway's fiction as a whole as indicating that traditional forms of male mastery are incompatible with the conditions of modernity. I see this as pointing in turn toward a new fluidity as far as categories of masculinity and femininity go, but a fluidity that is often viewed (at least in terms of the structure of male–female interactions) fearfully.

Hemingway is not radical in his sexual politics but his treatment of this area is fuller and more widely ranging than has usually been recognised. The peculiar set of paradoxes that occur in the two novels that deal most fully with the way in which couples interrelate – *A Farewell to Arms* and *The Garden of Eden* – help to show the complexity of his presentation of such issues. Romance itself is a key theme in both texts and is associated with emotional and sexual fulfilment. Such fulfilment stands in contrast to the realm of history, which is seen as 'unmanning' (Frederic Henry's experience illustrates as much). Romance, though, is also associated with androgyny and sexual role reversal, and with a move outside conventional social and gender roles. This proves disastrous to the male protagonists' sense of self. To abandon the world for romance and to realise the self in an emotional commitment to the female 'other' thus becomes, paradoxically, a different but equally dangerous threat to that same male identity; another form of 'unmanning'.

All sorts of contradictions are apparent here as my circular explanation suggests. The desire for a form of pre-social sexual wholeness and for a step outside history is denied by the knowledge of the actual impossibility of such a step – that to merge the self in a completely discrete but undifferentiated unit of two is a form of psychic and social suicide. The urge that androgyny suggests toward the exploration of new and improved forms of social and sexual relations turns out to be something quite different. For the historical conditions in which Hemingway writes leads him to present these new relations as merely a more threatening version of those that already operate. Androgyny is initiated by the female partner and is related (in *The Garden of Eden*) to the lack of power she holds in the actual social world. In both novels, androgyny, and the feminisation of the male protagonist that goes with it, operate to the diminishment of masculine authority – something that (in real historical terms) the majority of men feared. Hemingway 'manages' these contradictions of sexual ideology by presenting all these conflicting urges and positions in his fiction but only as prelude to closures that (safely) reassert traditional versions of male–female relations. Sexual inversion and social withdrawal then acts only as a prelude to the restoration of sexual normalcy and equilibrium and social re-entry at the texts' end as the (disastrous) death of masculine mastery is prevented.

Throughout his work Hemingway compulsively examines gender confusion and sexual ambiguity. Testing masculinity and its limits and writing out of gender anxiety, he recognises both the attractions and dangers of alternative constructions of sexual role. There is a clear and unusual recognition of the insufficiency of traditional forms of masculinity and of the need to renegotiate them – to 'feminise' aspects of the male self – in his work. This issue, though, can only be opened up once the threat of woman's intrusion into what are seen as male zones, or the worry that such 'feminisation' will lead to the loss of distinctive male difference, has been fictionally countered. If ultimately – at least in the cases of *A Farewell to Arms* and *The Garden of Eden* – Hemingway ends by reasserting conventional heterosexual gender norms, his representation of the ambiguous desires of the male subject mark him as a writer whose explorations of gender and sexuality are both central to his work and more complicated than has previously been allowed.

III

If sexual power relations were shifting in the pre- and post-war Western world, then Hemingway's handling of the problematics of gender identity and sexual authority illustrates the result-ing tensions. The representation of traditional forms of powerful masculinity runs alongside the questioning of the value of such forms and the presentation of male protagonists whose sexual authority is under threat. The diverse nature of the fictional versions of masculinity and gender relations that result led Sylvia O'Sullivan to remark of the main protagonists of *Across the River and into the Trees* and *The Garden of Eden*: 'it is difficult to believe that [Colonel Cantwell and David Bourne] are products of the same imagination and time frame'.[16]

Hemingway's texts show divided attitudes to matters of sexual politics. The formal techniques he uses in his shorter works leave the reader caught within single perspectives or between perspect-ives. 'Truth is always situational',[17] dependent on the position and viewpoint of the represented subjects. A certain intertextual fluidity results as Hemingway shifts perspective and experience to present different forms of gender positioning available to his various protagonists. The breadth of such explorations is wider than has generally been accepted. Thus, in stories such as 'Hills Like White Elephants', 'women's sensibilities' are certainly not ignored but rather highlighted in an extremely sensitive manner, while other short fictions assertively foreground 'hypermasculine' and 'strongly misogynist'[18] values. Hemingway's discourse of sexuality is not a fixed and coherent one.

'Hills Like White Elephants' is a Hemingway narrative that foregrounds a woman's point of view. This helps to explain the fact that it has begun to replace 'The Killers' as favourite anthology piece.[19] Jig, the female protagonist, is presented as the more sympathetic of the two main characters in this story, though in her assessment of reader responses to the text, Elizabeth Flynn shows how at least one male student was able to repress or silence such identification. His report on the text concluded: 'Finally after a lot of nagging she asked if he would do anything for her and he said yes. She then gave him the pretty please bit with a dozen pleases and asked him to quit bugging her and finish his drink.' A more typical response to the story was a general lack of comprehension with one student saying 'it left the reader blind'.[20] No doubt such a lack of understanding is due in part to its seeming lack of narrative focus. Jig's comment – 'That's all we do, isn't it – look at things and try new drinks?'(*MWW*, 45) – seems a self-referential pointer on the author's part to the apparent flatness and lack of obvious central subject that are a product of his paratactic and mimetic style. Such incomprehension may result also from the quality that so many Hemingway stories seem to have of being a fragment of a narrative torn from a missing larger whole, with no real beginning and certainly no firm conclusion to it. The refusal of internal and intertextual closure to the short fictions serves to highlight the fact that gender (and other) tensions are not subject to formal mastery; that further narrative possibilities and other subject positions remain available.

Perhaps that student left 'blind' by the text was in fact disconcerted by a story in which two ways of seeing are counterposed and which operates around a simile/metaphor that leads off in a number of different and contradictory directions. The text is usefully approached by examining focalisation – who sees what and when. For the most part, the narrative focuses on what Jig sees – particularly her repeated look to the hills that lie on the far side of the Ebro valley in the first stages of the story. Her viewpoint is thus implicitly linked to the apparently neutral narrative voice which calls attention to the same 'long and white' (*MWW*, 44) line of hills at the story's start. Jig's gaze shifts from the hills to the bead curtain of the bar doorway on which an advertisement, which her companion has to interpret, is painted. The range of her vision is further swiftly constricted when her partner brings up the matter of an 'awfully simple' operation. This immediately has her looking not at 'the lovely hills' just seen, but 'at the ground the table legs rested on' (*MWW*, 45); metaphorically a limited, dead-end view.

In the rest of the story her eyes start once more taking in the larger picture, from the bead curtain near at hand to the field of grain, trees, river and mountains that compose the Ebro Valley and its horizon.[21] She then looks at the hills on the dry side of the valley – the contrast between aridity and the prior fertility being of obvious relevance to the subject of abortion which hangs in the air between the couple. Finally we see her attention focused on the woman whose foreign language she cannot understand, who has served the drinks, smiling 'brightly' (*MWW*, 48) to thank her for the (translated) information about the soon-to-arrive train. This is then followed by her smiling at her companion, with the transferred suggestion that though in their case they speak the same language, real communication is no longer possible between them either, so wide is the gap between their different ways of reading and seeing the world.

In terms of the way the narrative operates, the man's range of vision is far more limited. He looks, as far as we are told or can deduce, at the bead curtain, at the girl and at the table, at their bags with the collection of hotel labels on them, up the tracks and at the people in the bar 'waiting reasonably for the train' (*MWW*, 48). As far as we are told, then, his eyes never leave the immediate environment of the station, apart from a look down the tracks. This latter act, like the detail about the bags, identifies him strongly with the movement and impermanence that Jig seems ready to reject. His use of the word 'reasonably' to describe those waiting for the train indicts him, for it assumes that Jig's upset about the idea of abortion is 'unreasonable'. This abortion is the unnamed central subject of the whole episode played out between the two of them.[22] The crass attempt of the unnamed male partner to present it as 'really not anything' – without affect and both 'simple' and 'perfectly natural' (*MWW*, 45) – undoubtedly reduces readerly sympathy for his position.

The 'hills like white elephants' figure to which Jig keeps returning leads, as a number of critics have pointed out, in several different directions. It describes the 'long' rather than rounded hills themselves, which become 'a metaphor for the early stages of pregnancy'[23] and so connect up with the vision of the fertile river valley that those hills frame. If the white elephant is to retain its own distinct identity in the comparison being made (simile), we are caught between at least two divergent meanings: a 'rarity in nature . . . considered sacred and precious' or 'an unwanted possession' now 'up for sale'. This last derives 'from the story of a Siamese king who "used to make a present of a white elephant to courtiers he wished to ruin"'.[24] Richard Godden considers the full implications of the moves and slippages between simile and metaphor in the story. It is enough for my purposes to point to the qualities of imagination and possibility associated with Jig's way of seeing in this story and the anxieties that are revealed in the tropes she uses. Such qualities are wholly absent from the male protagonist who, as far as we are actually told by the narration, never even looks at those hills to which Jig tries to draw his attention, and who, if he has doubts about the need for, or effects of, an abortion, certainly suppresses them remarkably well. His unsympathetic aspects are all too apparent. He refuses to share her way of seeing those hills, thus denying the exploration of their situation that her use of figurative language can inspire. He cuts such processes dead by his literalisation: '"They look like white elephants," she said. "I've never seen one," the man drank his beer' (*MWW*, 44). Then, when Jig finally comes out with her deeply felt plea for what we can interpret as pregnancy, stability and a meaningful relationship, 'And we could have all this. . . . And we could have everything and every day we make it more impossible', he either genuinely does not hear her or – if he does – pretends not to, for all he can reply is 'What did you say?' (*MWW*, 46–7).

'Hills Like White Elephants' is one of a sequence of stories about marriage/couples written around that time. It might be grouped with 'Out of Season', 'Cat in the Rain' and 'Up in Michigan' as showing Hemingway's ability to criticise the type of egocentric masculinity that considers the woman and her body as mere adjunct to his own desires, and to present the female sensibility from a sympathetic or potentially sympathetic perspective. Having said this, it is important to note that, if he here opens up a place where a woman's perspective can be given, the version of femininity he constructs is in its nurturing impulses entirely conventional. The masculine denial of the worth of such values is, though, the target here. If the sexual politics are not radical, neither are they misogynist. 'Compulsive masculinity' (*K*, 150), that type of masculinity which needs to position itself as fully as possible outside the domestic province, is judged harshly here. Kenneth Lynn's analysis of gender roles in 'The Short Happy Life of Francis Macomber' points in a similar interpretive direction when he suggests that Margot Macomber is treated sympathetically in the story and that what 'brings Macomber down [is] his own danger-ous aspiration to be recognized as intensely masculine'.[25]

Other Hemingway fictions, however, endorse such compulsive masculinity. Michael Kimmel, in writing of the period 1880–1914, sees men finding 'solutions to gender crisis in a vigorous reasser-tion of traditional masculinity' (*K*, 146). Misogyny was another response to what was seen by some men as 'the undoing of American masculinity' by women (*K*, 145). An analogous crisis mentality marked the post-war period. It is revealed in 'A Very Short Story', a text fuelled by a strong misogynist impulse. Grounded in sexual bias, the story is full of 'signs of anger and vengefulness' toward Luz, the female protagonist who damages her already (physically) wounded male lover. She narrows the boundaries of his life as she consigns him to home, work and sobriety; while the expression of her own independence and sexual freedom culminates in the casual disregard for his feelings that the letter with which she ends the relationship shows. The reversal of normative gender roles is judged harshly here. Examining the language and occurrences of the story (and of other related texts), Robert Scholes asks: 'Whose discourse is this, whose story, whose diegesis, whose world'? His answer is that

> it is Papa's, [of] course, who taught a whole generation of male readers to prepare for a world where men may be your friends but women are surely [punning on the story itself] the enema. . . . The story quite literally leaves its protagonist wounded in his sex by contact with a woman.[26]

The bullfight vignettes from *In Our Time* can be read as part of a 'promale backlash' to an American culture that was perceived as feminised (*K*, 146, 143). For how better to escape a culture where masculinity was in crisis than to position the fictional self in an apparently more 'primitive' culture where the challenge to gender relations did not apply and where exclusive male bonding and values and an active and heroic male individualism (in an arena from which women were excluded) were still available possibilities. Bruce Henricksen reads these vignettes within a biographical and political context to claim convincingly that their 'ideological subtext' can be discovered in the movement 'toward an identity with a masculine elite that has separated itself from everyday values and dedicated itself to a theatre of death'. He argues that the vignettes illustrate a move toward single-voicedness, the monologic: 'in the total story [the six pieces] a voice or a subjectivity is being born and launched out of a diversity of voices sequenced as a movement away from the mother country and toward identity with a cultural "other"'.[27] This process occurs in the shift from the voice of the keen and inexperienced American of the first vignette to the more 'authentic' voice of the later ones. There, the virtual disappearance of both youthfulness and Americanness coincides with an identification on the narrator's part with 'the values of a select, tightly codified . . . subculture'. He has become one who both understands and shares the perspective of the (male) bullfighting fraternity.

Having traced this movement, Hendricksen focuses on the 'reactionary' politics that he sees the text as 'unconsciously' speaking. He refers especially to the 'If it happened right down close in front of you' sequence where the now effaced narrator describes how Villalta becomes 'one with the bull' in killing it. Here the purity of style illustrated in the 'aesthetic ritual of the *corrida*'[28] connects up with Hemingway's conception of his own role as artist. For 'the bullfight story [is] an allegory of the growth of the artist' in its description of the use of what Hemingway would call in *The Dangerous Summer* 'absolute technical perfection' (*DS*, 17) to dominate the materials at hand with 'grace' (*DS*, 18) and skill. The problem here is that the aesthetic is being celebrated at the expense of the moral, a tactic that Henricksen associates with a typically modernist stress on 'objectivity' and on writerly craftsmanship. In Hemingway's accounts of bullfighting, an aesthetic will to power, a celebration of purity of style and of 'classic and beautiful' (*DS*, 157) performance, is linked to 'a civilized nostalgia for a barbaric world of triumph and tragedy'.

Such aestheticisation functions as 'an alibi for the violence that is being celebrated'.[29] Hendriksen sees in the subtext of the vignettes a closeness to what he calls 'fascist fantasies'. For this is a male-centred world in which 'blood and death' stand as the end of desire. The world of conventional social and sexual relations is displaced through this attention to a form of male power identified primarily with violence and death.

Henricksen is quick to point out that the form of fascist fantasy to which he refers has nothing to do with a Nazi political belief. Hemingway's conscious politics were anything but reactionary. He wrote for the Communist *New Masses* to condemn the bureaucratic mismanagement that had led, in his view, to the death in a hurricane of war veterans working in Florida for the Civilian Conservation Corps. He gave active support to the Loyalists in the Spanish civil war, both writing the script for, and narrating, the propaganda film *The Spanish Earth* (1937). He kitted out his boat for Nazi submarine hunting off the Cuban coast during the Second World War. Later, he would be supportive toward Castro's role in Cuba. The authorial self, however, Henricksen sees as being far from unified, and I would extend such an argument to take in Hemingway's body of textual production. His bullfight narratives are stories that interact dialogically with a series of others (like 'Hills Like White Elephants'). As Hemingway's conscious political decisions clash with the political unconscious that the bullfight texts evidence, so do the sense of a male subject and the sense of a world illustrated in the different (intertextual) parts of his fiction interact with and (to an extent) contradict one another. His discourse of sexuality and gender is a divided one.

IV

Masculinity in Hemingway is not always represented with the confidence that the bullfight vignettes suggest. The relation between masculinity and bullfighting traced there (and evidenced in the non-fiction generally) reasserts a traditional sexual politics where 'masculine' values and forms of behaviour operate in an exclusive gender zone. A contradictory and more ambiguous attitude toward masculinity becomes evident in examining the recurrent use of symbolic 'woundings' in his fictions. For the notion of untainted male integrity is, in Hemingway, often subject to slippage, and definitions of what constitutes masculinity and femininity are hard to fix firmly.

The metaphorical relationship between bullfighting and masculinity is a common one in modernist writing. Michel Leiris uses it, however, both to signify the fact of his manhood *and* to suggest that which threatens or diminishes that same manhood. He, too, links, though more explicitly than Hemingway, the activity of bullfighting with that of writing, and sees both as ways of stylistically authenticating the self. Leiris compares the dangers and engagement of writing one's 'manhood' to bullfighting in terms of the dangers involved – dangers that result from the attempt to introduce 'even the shadow of the bull's horn into a literary work'. The concern with 'authenticity' links such a writer to the *torero*. Both the former, who takes his own manhood as a subject, and the latter, are risking their own skin.[30] This analogy can be explained by seeing the gap between the *torero* and the bull as comparable to that between the artist and the 'truth'. As the *torero* coaxes the bull 'towards a union which is ultimately impossible', so the writer uses words as he 'enfolds' the material he engages 'closer and closer around his own body' without ever being able to close the gap between word and world.

This 'gap' can be seen to have a further significance and one that is crucial for my concerns here. For it is the subject of manhood that inspires the figurative play about authenticity and its dangers. Leiris's 'desire to be wholly phallic' is also 'ultimately impossible' – disrupted by 'the gap within [the] self'. For the bull and the bullfighter (both different versions of the masculine principle) can never be united, become one and the same. The gap between the *torero* and the bull 'signifies', moreover, 'that which threatens [the former's] manhood most: the female in himself'. Peter Schwenger explains this by describing André Masson's illustrations for Leiris's *Miroir de la Tauromachie*:

One illustration shows the *torero* evading a bull's horn that is patently phallic; and at the tip of the horn, in the space between bull and *torero*, is the 'wound' of the female genitals. In autobiography . . . that wound-like gap is actually a gap within one's self. In trying to close the gap, an autobiographer like

Leiris [writing his own manhood] is trying to exorcize his own female element. Like the classic Mexican *macho*, he abhors the idea of an opening in him. Any such gap has female connotations to one whose ideal of manhood is hard invulnerability.[31]

These comments bear obvious relevance to Hemingway, whose obsession with bullfighting echoes Leiris's. In *The Sun Also Rises* questions are raised about the contemporary value of the ritual of the bullfight and the definitions of masculinity it asserts. These relate to the novel's foregrounding of gender slippage in a post-war world where for instance – in terms of its use of bullfighting metaphor – Cohn and Jake are presented in the role of 'steers' to Brett's ungovernable and sexually powerful 'bull'. Concepts of natural sexual difference were chained to fixed forms of gender distinction by those resistant to woman's changing social role. To be 'truly' womanly was automatically to be passive, nurturing, docile and pure. The reversal of both poles of this nature–nurture link in the metaphoric identifications of the novel suggests a deep resistance to such ('unnatural' and thus socially damaging) change.

The threat to manhood that the bullfight wound signifies to Leiris is generally transferred in Hemingway to a more historically relevant version of the male wound. Conceptions of masculine force and mastery did not fit easily with twentieth-century social and historical conditions. And in Hemingway's fiction any traditional equation of masculinity with strong self-sufficiency is consistently challenged metaphorically through his repeated use of wounded male protagonists. The wound both denies the notion of manhood as hard invulnerability and further suggests, in Schwenger's terms, a 'female' (or feminine) element in man.

The wounds that Hemingway's protagonists suffer all point in the direction of sexual anxiety and dislocation. They all 'whatever their origin . . . cluster around the groin'.[32] Even when we are not told the exact location of the wound, as in Thomas Hudson's case in *Islands in the Stream*, the effect on the phallic region is made clear. Gil puts a tourniquet 'on his left leg as close to the crotch as he could tighten it'; Thomas's feeling of sickness after his wounding spreads 'into his bones and through his chest and his bowels and the ache went into his testicles' (*IS*, 390–1). Such wounds cause (or at least coincide with) an increased feminisation on the protagonists' part. So, in 'Big Two-Hearted River', Nick's 'cultivation of a traditionally female role . . . organiz[ing] and tend[ing] his "homelike" space'[33] follows the knowledge brought by injury in war that manliness and invulnerability are not one and the same thing. Likewise Frederic Henry's coldly rationalistic 'masculine' rejection of emotion just dissolves once he has been rendered passively 'feminine' by his wartime experiences – once he has had wounds 'inflicted' on him, and has been 'probed' (*FA*, 47–8) by the medical captain who works on him. The first time he sees Catherine after these events he is 'crazy in love' with her. 'When I saw her I was in love with her' (*FA*, 69–70), he reports, all his (masculine) reserve, at least temporarily, abandoned.

Inherited definitions of masculinity are being explored here. Hemingway 'severely disables the myth of the autonomous male individual'[34] with his constant focus on wounded men. The forms of feminisation that mark their consequent behaviour would seem to suggest the emergence of a different type of manhood in a modern age. Such new conceptions of masculinity are, however, forced from without – through the inflicted injury. If wounding is equated with a type of feminisation, the crossover from the physical to the cultural carries with it strong connotations of *damage*. Textual contradictions emerge here as the attraction of alternative versions of 'masculinity' (the domestic sensitivities of 'Big Two-Hearted River' and the emotional expressiveness of *A Farewell to Arms*) are automatically seen in the context of a type of crippling curse; something profoundly unnatural. Only in *The Garden of Eden* does this fail to apply. Changes in gender balance and alternative constructions of 'masculinity' and 'femininity' are explored in Hemingway's novels, but in these longer works any ambiguity of response is covered over in the containments that finally take place; in the reimpositions of new (though limited) forms of 'masculine' authority. Such processes will emerge as my argument continues.

V

In *The Sun Also Rises* anxieties about gender role and sexual identity are clearly focused around the motif of the (explicitly phallic) wound. There has been a great deal of speculation about the exact nature of Jake's wound, which is referred to in the text only in understated and/or indirect ways. This failure to name the wound typifies a text where so much remains unnamed or unsaid. The most powerful moment in the text where readerly attention is directed to Jake's sexual lack, occurs when he is undressing:

> Undressing, I looked at myself in the mirror of the big armoire beside the bed. That was a typically French way to furnish a room. Practical, too, I suppose. Of all the ways to be wounded. I suppose it was funny. I put on my pyjamas and got into bed. (*SAR*, 28)

It is at this point in the novel that Jake stops looking at others (the spectatorial role he assumes for much of the narrative) to focus, despite the initial diversionary tactics, reflexively on himself and it is here that the full extent of his loss is revealed. An alternative version of the novel's title was to be *Two Lie Together*, with the reference to Ecclesiastes: 'Again, if two lie together, then they have heat; but how can one be warm alone'.[35] Jake's pulling on of pyjamas and getting into bed is a natural conclusion to the described sequence of events, but it is also a revelation, if a downplayed one, of his fate: never to be warm and always to be alone.

Hemingway's jokey reference to his title in a letter to Fitzgerald, 'The Sun Also Rises (like your cock if you have one)' (*L*, 231), foregrounds the issue of sexuality in the text. From this and later comments it would seem that he envisioned Jake as having his 'prick shot off' (*L*, 764) but with 'his testicles and spermatic cord [still] intact'.[36] The lack of certainty about the exact nature of the injury has led to a number of speculations about whether Jake is capable of receiving sexual satisfaction, even if incapable of phallically giving it. Particular attention has been paid to the 'bedroom scene' with Brett where Jake is lying on his bed feeling 'rotten' and is joined by Brett who strokes his head and tells him she has sent the Count for champagne. Ellipsis then occurs, with the chronological linearity of the text continuing with 'Then later: "Do you feel better, darling?"' (*SAR*, 48). Brett's words, together with the explicit reference to a temporal gap, have led several critics to interpret the passage in terms of sexual relief given to Jake. Because of his condition it is a little difficult to imagine exactly the nature of this relief, so suggestions range from Brett

giving him 'perverted sexual satisfaction', to her leading him
through 'a sexual fantasy, perhaps including a phantom penis', to
Lynn's more explicit:

> the implication is fairly clear that . . . Jake remains capable of
> achieving a degree of satisfaction through oral sex, and that Brett
> has been a most willing mangeuse. Jake and Brett have appar-
> ently made love in a fashion often associated with lesbian as
> well as heterosexual intercourse.[37]

Time just might pass, of course, with Brett just sitting there.
Certainly, though, the ellipsis encourages speculation.

All the above interpretations cast Brett, in various ways, as
prime mover in this sexual episode, and certainly Jake's passivity
for much of the narrative appears tied to his damaged sexual
condition. Such a reversal of traditional gender roles does not just
apply here, but points to a concern that reveals itself throughout
the text. Conventional definitions of masculinity and femininity are
disrupted in the novel and such disruptions (in a novel where the
woundings of war provide the dominant metaphor) relate to recent
social change.

For Lacan, 'Phallus . . . because of its form, because of its erectile
power, because of its function of penetration . . . denies the
[female] lack . . . fills the empty space.[38] Such an assumption that
'gender distinction' is rooted in 'genital difference' with the penis
as 'prime *insignia* of maleness'[39] is common to Freudian psycho-
analysis. What are we then to make of a novel with a 'feminised'
central protagonist: with one whose 'wound' means that he is
denied erectile power and who cannot fill that (female) 'empty
space'; who indeed has only, so it seems, empty space where the
phallus would normally be?

Hemingway's use of an 'invalid' (in-valid?) main protagonist is
part of a more general upsetting of the relationship between
gender roles and sexual identity in the text. The types of gender
roles conventionally associated with natural sexual difference are
radically disrupted here. Referring to the 'sexualized power
structure' of modern Western society, Jon Stratton writes: 'In a
society determined by the phallus . . . he who becomes a
non-male . . . must therefore become in some senses female.'[40]
Gender codes are turned topsy-turvy in *The Sun Also Rises* as we

are given a main male protagonist with 'female' attributes and a main female protagonist with 'male' attributes. I have argued this case at some length in my *New Readings of the American Novel*[41] so just sketch briefly here the way I see such reversals as operating and to what end.

Themes of sexual play and display are first raised in the novel with Jake's pick-up of the prostitute Georgette and his introduction of her to his friends as his 'fiancée, Mademoiselle Georgette Leblanc' (*SAR*, 18). The latter was in reality 'the ex-mistress of Maeterlinck, an actress, singer, and . . . eccentric who regularly bicycled around Paris in a flowing medieval robe of gold-flowered velvet'. She was also, according to Kenneth Lynn, lesbian.[42] The textual and extratextual world interfuse here to signal an interest in gender issues, with the confusion of whore and actress and the immediate conjunction of themes of prostitution, illicit sexual liaison, lesbianism and impotence. Such signalling is also present with the focus on the theme of deceit as Jake raises expectations (on both Georgette and the reader's part) that cannot be fulfilled, and then goes on to parody heterosexual normality with his pretence of being engaged to 'Mme Leblanc'. Themes of dress codes and bicycling are also implicit here, both of which relate to the general sexual discourse of the novel as a whole. The shifting nature of this sexual world is quickly confirmed by the introduction of Brett and her companions. The homosexuality of the latter is first described in terms of the coding of external physical appearance – 'their hands and newly washed, wavy hair' (*SAR*, 19) – and affects by implication both Brett and Jake. Brett has a first name that connotes ambiguous sexuality. Jake's anger is triggered, and his awareness of his own 'non-male' condition made acute, by her choice as companions of those who can exercise the male heterosexual role but who do not choose to do so.

Traditional gender roles are in flux in the novel. The changing balance in sexual power in a post-war Western world is one of its main themes. Jake has many traditionally 'feminine' traits. He lacks the mastery normally associated with the male role. When Brett says she is going to San Sebastian and Jake asks 'Can't we go together?' (*SAR*, 49), traditional patterns of 'masculine' action and 'feminine' response/dependency are reversed. A similar role reversal is noticeable where Jake fails to recognise the ironic analogy between the A. E. W. Mason story about the bride waiting for the body of 'her true love' (*SAR*, 100) to emerge from the glacier into which it has been frozèn, and his own situation. In Jake and Brett's relation as a whole such patternings are subject to great fluctuation. Jake's tears, his pleas, his 'rotten' feelings which Brett soothes by stroking his head, the roses he is brought – all these are inversions of conventional male/female dualities in the novel.

This is even more obvious when we consider the role Brett plays. Conventional dominance and submission patterns are generally askew when applied to her behaviour. She does not inhabit the traditionally female domestic space; and when she is seen in a bedroom it is always someone else's. Brett is the active sexual force in the novel. She is, by and large, the one who calls the tune in its heterosexual relations. Brett's challenge to traditional definitions of a woman's role and thus to her socially given identity (what is defined as 'womanly') may not be thoroughgoing, but is clearly suggested in the elements of cross-dressing associated with her clothing and appearance. These can be linked to the general changes in women's fashion that accompanied social change in the war and post-war period. The cropped hair and military-cut leather coats of the women working in the war theatre and their self-assertive behaviour may well 'have infuriated men who felt that while they suffered and died, the war had become a "festival of female misrule"'.[43] Such a challenge may not be a consistently formulated one by Brett in this later post-war period. The line between play and ideological seriousness associated with cross-dressing (those for whom it is 'camp' activity versus those who use it as a deliberate ploy to question the social construction of sexuality) is unclear as far as we can know her motivations. The contradictions in her own (gendered) self-presentation are certainly evidence of a self-divided subject.

The Sun Also Rises thematically foregrounds the disruption of conventional gender and sexual roles. The use of first-person narration problematises the making of any straightforward value judgements on this subject. I would, however, argue that the emphasis placed on the movement across and between sexual and gender boundaries in the novel is seen more as a threat than as a promise of new and more satisfactory forms of gender relationship in a post-war world. The use of the 'You are all a lost generation' prefacing quote[44] seems enough to signal the distaste for such changes and instabilities. And if individual autonomy and male authority cannot be re-established in a post-war world, then some (limited) form of male authority can be. The threat of the dangerous woman appears to be contained at the text's end. The failed relation between Brett and Romero suggests two social orders which (in terms of sexual politics) cannot complement one another. The 'contamination' to traditional ways of doing things is checked. Jake's final note of verbal authority suggests that he can now go his separate way without Brett – capable now of greater control over his circumstances. The minimalist style he uses illustrates a 'masculine' repression of emotion that signals the success of such forms of control whatever the cost. If the tonal shifts between flat understatement, humour, desperation, irony, anger and self-pity that mark Jake's response to his condition are a sign of a web of contradictions and mixed emotions which an apparently seamless narrative covers over, then all those contradictions seem finally resolved in a dry irony that operates at the expense of the showing of emotion and vulnerability. Jake chooses – and so does the text – the assertion of the remaining available 'male' values (reason and a dry control), however limited and limiting these may be. This is presented as preferable to the opening of the self to any new scheme of social and gender relations and what that might possibly come to mean: a world perhaps where a close permanent relationship and phallic sexual union need not be conterminous.

VI

In *A Farewell to Arms* anxiety over gender role and sexual identity and the theme of androgyny to which it relates are connected up with the desire to retreat from the conditions of history (and the problematic social change it has brought). Such a desire is apparent in much of the earlier work; in the pastoral elements in 'Big Two-Hearted River' and *The Sun Also Rises*, and in the latter's stress on temporary bondings and geographical dislocations. William Adair's discussion of *A Farewell to Arms* in terms of its structural shifts between nightmare and erotic or romance dream[45] is a useful starting point here, particularly when considered in conjunction with Fredric Jameson's discussion of 'the salvational

logic of the romance narrative' as 'symbolic reaction' to a 'secular-
ized and reified' modern world.[46] For *A Farewell to Arms* and the
posthumous *The Garden of Eden* provide progressive explorations of
the romance dream. If the former illustrates the attraction and the
failure of such salvational logic, the latter goes further to rediscover such a logic, not in the original romance form, but in the
different narrative of (male) artistic accomplishment.

The assumption of both these novels is, however, that conditions
of public history diminish the self. The motif of disruption and
collapse is introduced early in *A Farewell to Arms* with the
repetitions and modulations of the word 'crack' in the conversation
between Catherine and Frederic about the war, where she shifts
from the theme of personal loss (the death of her fiancé) to the
larger historical picture:

> 'What's to stop [the war always going on]?'
> 'It will crack somewhere.'
> 'We'll crack. We'll crack in France. They can't go on doing things
> like the Somme and not crack.'
> 'They won't crack here,' I said . . .
> 'They may crack,' she said. 'Anybody may crack.'   (*FA*, 19)

Frederic is himself 'cracked' by the narrative's end, broken by
'the world' (*FA*, 178). The final stages of this process occur as a
result of Catherine's death, but his initial vulnerability to damage
is a corollary of his alienated position in an army world. Army life,
its secularisation and reification, becomes a paradigm for Hemingway of modernity. Such a paradigm and the related use of the First
World War to represent the condition of modernity should be
handled with great care. Hemingway's version of things, here, is a
highly subjective one.

The secular quality of army life in *A Farewell to Arms* has been
extensively discussed and needs little further commment. The
priest fits the army world uncomfortably. He is not 'in his own
country' (*FA*, 57), the highly traditional and hierarchical social
world of the Abruzzi, and his values have little relevance to those
around him. Frederic is attracted to his religious sensibility, but its
irrelevance to the conditions at hand (and to their historical end

results) is suggested by one of Hemingway's tentative endings for the novel which points to the anachronistic nature of religion in the modern nation state: 'I could tell how the priest in our mess lived to be a priest in Italy under Fascism.'[47]

Frederic's reification in an army world has been indicated in the previous chapter. He is caught in 'a broken and piecemeal world . . . out of control and threatening'.[48] The 'blunting of affect'[49] associated with him is both a product of his passive condition *vis-à-vis* the historical circumstances that fix him and a marker of his alienation from them. This can be clearly seen in his response as he talks and drinks in the mess at the start of the narrative: 'The priest was good but dull. . . . The King was good but dull. The wine was bad but not dull. It took the enamel off your teeth and left it on the roof of your mouth' (*FA*, 32).

Frederic's relationship with Catherine develops as a counter or 'symbolic reaction' to such a historical reality – a step outside all the problems of the modern world (*including*, it would at first seem, those that relate to gender relations). Adair sees the two sections of the novel in which Frederic and Catherine's relationship is allowed full and positive expression (the summmer of 1917, and winter 1917–18) as suggesting 'a continual present tense, an unchanging and erotic dreamworld wherein time and mutability have no power'.[50] When the two lovers are together the rest of the world tends to drop away, and Catherine's unpinning and letting down of her long hair, and their joint retreat inside it as 'inside a tent or behind a falls' (*FA*, 84), is a powerful image of their joint but temporary home-making – a deliberate but fragile curtaining off from a wider reality.

A Farewell to Arms has been described in terms of Edenic myth with Catherine as a 'prelapsarian Eve'.[51] This terminology is of interest in the way it points to the similarities in the presentation of sexual relationships in this novel and *The Garden of Eden*. What becomes particularly noticeable about the relationship between Frederic and Catherine, as it develops as a romantic counter to the historical nightmare that the war represents, is the highly ambiguous nature of its presentation. For the relationship points both to a new (and desirable) gender balance and sexual whole-ness and erotic play *and* to a loss of discrete personal identity (and thus a form of diminishment) at one and the same time. Frederic's particular 'unmanning' is here linked to the androgynous activity in which he engages. The gender discourse of the novel is divided and it is difficult to carve a clear way through it.

On the one hand, it is in the relationship with Catherine that Frederic discovers an emotional and sexual fulfilment previously denied. His affectlessness is cured as he finds meaning in their romance. Private feeling, as we have seen, flows as a direct consequence of his knowledge of his own physical vulnerability in the realm of public history, of war. From that time forward the two realms of romance and of social belonging and responsibility are more and more in tension, until the latter is symbolically cast off when Frederic crosses the Tagliamento to make his 'separate peace'. Thenceforth, his romantic union with Catherine is explicitly identified with a move away from full social and historical being: 'We could feel alone when we were together, alone against the others' (*FA*, 178). Such a giving over of the self to romance is a type of (temporary) 'symbolic closure',[52] a way of escaping real socio-historical problems by immersion in an idyllic private realm. Frederic's constant hesitations and comments of the 'I was awake for quite a long time thinking about things' (*FA*, 214) type suggest, though, his difficulty in shutting himself off completely in this way.[53] While Hemingway is able convincingly to represent and celebrate the intensity of feeling between the two lovers, he is also constantly suggesting its limitations and impermanency.

For the nature and price of that closure which occurs when romance becomes all-consuming is suggested in the loss of individual and social identity that then results. Life outside history is an impossibility. This is suggested in the fact that once Catherine and Frederic take off their uniforms they are left without a convincing social role to play. The consequent intensity of their turn to each other in the closed world of their romance brings with it a type of narcissistic collapse. The two lovers mirror one another to the point that their separate identities start to disappear. Sexual and emotional bliss occurs as Frederic and Catherine meld indistinguishably into one another, but such a melding has serious implications. The fact that Catherine is the one who is associated most clearly with the impetus for the move toward the loss of self should lead us to put aside any idea of her as code-hero(ine).[54] This collapse of personality is foregrounded in Catherine's 'There isn't any me. I'm you. Don't make up a separate me' (*FA*, 85) and 'We really are the same one' (*FA*, 102). By the time of the

Switzerland sequence Frederic too is beginning to echo, if in minor key, the stance she takes, when, to her 'I want to be you too', he replies, 'You are. We're the same one' (*FA*, 213).

Millicent Bell is exactly right in her comments on this 'flight from [that] selfhood . . . which depends on a recognition of the other' and her remarks are worth quoting:

> The regressive process, the withdrawal from reality, the surrender of complex personal being, the limitation of relationship to that with an other who is really only a mirror of self approaches more and more the dreamless sleep of apathy, the extremity of ennui. There is a suggestion of the pathologic in the 'I was deadly sleepy' with which . . . . chapter [26] ends.

Historical belonging and the full emotional and sexual fulfilment associated with the (separate) world of romance are in tension here. The utopian attractions of the latter clash with the knowledge of pragmatic reality. The 'drift toward death'[55] that occurs as Frederic and Catherine turn in on one another is a measure of the impossibility of the step outside history.

Such a drift is also suggested in the move toward the eradication of sexual difference that also takes place within the boundaries of their relationship. This is only touched on briefly in the novel but is apparent enough for Kenneth Lynn to say that Hemingway 'thought of [Frederic and Catherine] as the two halves of an androgynous whole'.[56] Such hints occur as otherness becomes oneness, and as Catherine suggests they alter their appearance accordingly: grow and cut their hair respectively so 'we'd both be alike' (*FA*, 213). So, too, she projects herself into Frederic's male sexual role – 'I wish I'd stayed with all your girls' (*FA*, 212) – in order to make their relationship even closer. Catherine's enthusiasm for a private androgynous union is logical given the lack of a permanent public role available to her (and other women) at the time. It is met though by a (passive) reluctance on Frederic's part. When, for instance, Catherine tells of her intent to cut her hair after the childbirth, to be 'a fine new and different girl for you', he just notes, 'I did not say anything' (*FA*, 216).

This pattern of female enthusiasm and male reluctance for androgynous experiment will be replayed in *The Garden of Eden* where the subject of androgyny becomes central, where David and (another) Catherine cut their hair the same way at the latter's prompting, and where David – with his 'I'd rather you didn't' (*GE*, 77) and his lack of response (*GE*, 45) – is the initially reluctant partner in the androgynous activities that take place.

The fear of male self-diminishment, of a form of unmanning, which the androgyny theme introduces, needs separating off from the romance theme. The lines between them, though, are blurred. The notion of a couple in mutual narcissistic retreat from history shades into that of a couple whose gender attributes, both in terms of physical appearance and role (who, for instance, is the protector and who the passive recipient of protection; who is strong and who weak), loosen. This then shades again into the notion of a single subject whose male difference is threatened by a female urge for equality and a lack of separateness. Contemporary concerns about gender balance seem to graft themselves uncomfortably onto the romance genre and its representation of new forms of socio-sexual relations. There are thematic contradictions present here that the text confuses. I will return to this issue of male reluctance to androgynous experiment in my discussion of *The Garden of Eden*.

In *A Farewell to Arms* the central thematic tension of the novel – that between history and romance – is finally resolved history's way, but not in any positive sense. The attraction of stepping out of the world of history is clear. Such a world (represented here by war) puts the identity and existence of the subject at risk. Frederic and Catherine counter the resulting sense of vulnerability and powerlessness by committing themselves to love. This leads to a renewal of emotional vigour on Frederic's part and opens up a type of regenerative and 'sacred' space (Count Greffi's 'love . . . is a religious feeling' – *FA*, 188) opposed to those unreasonable and uncontrollable threats to the self that constitute 'everyday' reality (history, time and action) in the novel. However, romance is presented as a merely imaginary answer to a real historical problem. The inability to escape time's demands is seen in that double death to which the 'lifegiving' relationship ironically leads. To lock oneself in a relationship of two is regressive. The references to androgyny suggest a negation of sexual difference; the references to the loss of separate identity, a negation of individual difference. In both cases the obliteration of difference spells death. The attraction of romance and of sexual fulfilment is confused here with the diminishment of the male self that accompanies it.

Frederic's desire must be repressed if his identity is to stay intact. The exploration of the blurring of sexual and gender role is ended with the reassertion of a traditionalist sexual politics implicit in the novel's closure. For Catherine, who has pulled Frederic toward an androgyny that signals the death of his masculine authority, is punished by death. Frederic can then, the assumption is, find again some diminished form of the 'masculine' balance that he has lost in the relation with her, and learn to find ways of going on and coping with the conditions of modernity alone.

Torn between history and romance, this novel evidences ambivalence and unease regarding both realms. To plumb the intimate, the world of erotic bliss and emotional expression, is to lose one's social identity and to discover a kind of wholeness – the completion in the other – which proves to be entirely hallucinatory: the other as merely the mirror of the self. Such a move ends in identity collapse, social alienation and either solitude or death. Yet to accept one's position in the 'monumental' world of history is to submit to a world of impersonality, violence and affectlessness. The very sense of masculine balance that Frederic is left to rediscover has already been shown as desperately compromised in the novel's beginnings. This is the Catch 22 of Hemingway's novel – indeed the Catch 22 of his whole fictional world. It is to be solved only by finding other forms by which history can be provisionally countered. Such forms though are never completely convincing.

In his later fictions Hemingway continues to sound variations on the above theme. In *For Whom the Bell Tolls*, for example, the romance motif is again introduced with the Robert–Maria relationship. Again the possibility of identity collapse is associated with intense romantic involvement. Again it is the female partner who presses in this direction, with Maria's 'we are different. . . . I would have us exactly the same' (*FWBT*, 234). Robert sees their relationship as an 'alliance against death' (*FWBT*, 235) and his insistent repetitions of the word 'love' at the point where he is sure that the blowing of the bridge will be going ahead – 'I love thee as I love what I love most in the world and I love thee more' (*FWBT*, 307) – is again the measure of the intensity and promise associated with the notion of completion in, and entire commitment to, inseparable romantic union. However, Maria, in this novel, is marginalised in a way that Catherine never is in *A Farewell to Arms*.

Robert retains his 'masculine' authority throughout. Gender roles within the Maria–Robert relationship remain more rigidly defined than in that previous novel too, perhaps because Pilar is intro duced in the role of the strong woman. Maria remains little more than a cipher in the text as Hemingway shifts tack to explore the ways in which the individual might in fact meaningfully engage with public history. The two worlds of history and romance remain, though, directly interconnected, as revealed in the fact that Maria can be put to one side by Robert as he engages in more meaningful work: 'She had no place in his life now' (*FWBT*, 237). In this respect the novel completely reverses the assumptions of *A Farewell to Arms*, and the secure and rigid masculinity of Robert Jordan may be seen as an inevitable concomitant of such a reversal.

VII

I will not examine all Hemingway's other texts to illustrate how the romance themes (and the associated issues of sexual identity and gender role) connect up with the examination of the status of the subject in his or her larger historical world. The previous chapter suggests that the nature of such discourse is in fact divided. Rather, I turn to *The Garden of Eden* as the Hemingway novel where gender roles are most clearly disrupted and where there is the most obvious reprise of the kind of romantic relationship found in *A Farewell to Arms*. My argument here is twofold. I see androgyny associated much more strongly with the assumption of female power and a consequent loss of male authority in the later novel than it is in *A Farewell to Arms*. And, secondly, I see a shift occurring from the presentation of romance as a (failed) symbolic counter to historical circumstance to a celebration of art (and the male artist) as successfully filling such a role. In art Hemingway finds the value that romance cannot provide.

In *The Garden of Eden*, Hemingway initially puts the public world to one side, removes his protagonists most fully from conventional social and historical restraint, as if to take it for granted that it is only in an area at one remove from such engagement that the subject can find full expression. Nothing presses in on them from without in the way it does, for example, on Frederic and Catherine. This lack of external pressure is reflected in the fact that the male protagonist bears no physical wound. David and Catherine have money and leisure, and their most unconventional behaviour is accepted without question by the various small European communities in which they live (perhaps as a result of their economic power). The responses of Madame Aurol, the patron's wife, to the complicated patterns of sexual and emotional exchange of the three main protagonists provide clear evidence of this (*GE*, 143, 254). The three central relationships are foregrounded to such an extent that the rest of the socio-historical world seems for the most part just to drop away or to act as comforting or scenic backdrop to their activities. This novel, to recall Adair, is more of a 'dreambook' than is *A Farewell to Arms*.

Romance and narcissistic intimacy, then, replace any sense of full social and historical interaction in *The Garden of Eden*. The static and timeless connotations of the title figuratively suggest such a move. The book starts in the Camargue with a description of Catherine and David's relaxed way of life as they cycle, swim, go fishing, drink aperitifs and, most insistently, just look – at the landscape; at the sea bass attacking mullet in the canal; at the sails of the mackerel fleet. Their activities are close to those of the couple in 'Hills Like White Elephants', looking at things and trying new drinks, but without their sense of dissatisfaction. The detailed presentation of the way David dices up his boiled eggs with a spoon, salts and peppers them and eats them with a pat of melted butter is a signal of the lack of conditioning pressure in their lives. The everyday has not become the mundane, or the trivial the empty. The keen pleasure that this (retrospective) description conveys suggests the immediate sensual delights shared by this couple in a world where, as we are straightaway informed, they 'don't have to worry about anything' (*GE*, 11). Even the way their eggs are cooked is 'an excitement' (*GE*, 10), for these two are intensely attuned to even the tiniest moments of their lives as they make meaning from them.

Our readerly attention is quickly focused, too, on David and Catherine's sexual life, obviously still keenly enjoyed. Right at the start of this narrative, in terms of the story time of the first day described, comes the couple, the double bed in their hotel room, and their lovemaking. 'Don't we have wonderful simple fun?'

(*GE*, 17) Catherine says as David catches a large sea bass to the applause of the villagers. The two of them are wrapped up together in an intense and inner-directed relationship that separates them from others.

The pervasive use of mirrors suggests the narcissistically closed nature of the love relationships in the text. 'Hallucinatory images of wholeness'[57] appear in these mirrors as the three central characters gaze at reflections of themselves and one another. The mirror stage in Lacanian theory is a necessary and key stage in what he calls the Imaginary order: 'In the other, in the mirror's image, in his mother, the child sees nothing but a fellow with whom he merges, with whom he identifies.' In this stage, and prior to the construction of a full social identity, one of two things happen. One is either locked into one's own self-image; sees only oneself and thus is armoured against the world in a way that has defensive, even paranoid implications if carried on into later life. Or one is swallowed up by the other, 'a fellow with whom he merges', taking on completely an identification with that reflected image and losing consequently the sense of self. As the move is made to the Symbolic order, toward social belonging – that state where self and other, language and the world are recognised as separate – the subject develops fluid boundaries, if all goes well, and is no longer caught within one limiting concept of identity. The characters in *The Garden of Eden*, as the stress on mirrors suggests, might be seen as still caught within (or regressed to) the initial stage: in 'a mirror relationship, a relationship of the merging of self and other' in which full social becoming and interaction is denied.[58] Thus, turning in on themselves, David and Catherine have from the first transformed the conditions of everyday normality and reality into a setting for their joint sexual play. Hermetically sealed in a (mirror) world of two, romance alone sustains them.

Hemingway returns here to the issues explored in *A Farewell to Arms*, but with a crucial difference. In the earlier novel 'history' is balanced against 'romance' and both are seen as leading to the loss of identity and selfhood. Now, the alienating public world is left out of the picture (except as David's successful writing provides access to it, and makes its mark in it). The study of what happens when male and female turn in on one another in excessive dependence on sexual and emotional intimacy is intensified, however, in this novel – though the nature of that study is complicated by introducing a third party into the original Edenic set-up (a second Eve in a story in which both Eves also function as serpents). In doing this, a crucial transfer can occur as one relationship of intense intimacy is replaced by another. The sexual and emotional permutations that occur when all three parties are present are all part of the study of androgyny and of the loss of psychological balance which occurs when the boundaries of sexual difference are crossed. Such transgressions again bring identity collapse.

Hemingway's interest in gender role and sexuality in *The Sun Also Rises* marks his awareness that traditional conceptions of the 'masterful male self' no longer accord with a changed social order. In the retreat from history to romance to rediscover a form of lost 'wholeness' which occurs in *A Farewell to Arms*, identity itself is, paradoxically, threatened. Such a threat is strengthened by the androgynous aspects of Frederic and Catherine's relationship, which suggest an obliteration of sexual difference. This is seen as potentially ruinous, most particularly as it affects the male subject. In both novels, the exploration of change in gender and sexual balance is related to the various forms of unmanning that occur. Both end by resisting, in their different ways, the implications of the changes which they present.

Sandra Gilbert discusses the themes of transvestism and androgyny in the work of Hemingway's female modernist contemporaries. She sees their presentation in a strongly positive light – as a way of looking towards a new and improved sexual and social order:

in the view of such women as [Virginia] Woolf and [Djuna] Barnes, [the fixed] social order is . . . fallen or at least misguided. Thus the only redemption that they can imagine from the dis-order and dis-ease of gender is in the symbolic chaos of transvestism, a symbolic chaos that is related not to the narrow power of male mastery but . . . to the androgynous wholeness and holiness of pre-history. For, as Mircea Eliade has noted, the ceremonial transvestism practiced in many non-Western societies is 'a coming out of one's self, a transcending of one's own historically controlled situation . . . in order to restore, if only for a brief moment, the initial completeness, the intact source of holiness and power . . . the undifferentiated unity that preceded the Creation'.[59]

This is an interesting quote even if we need to be wary of the Western reading of non-Western ritual it contains. In Hemingway, the recurring interest in themes of cross-dressing, bisexual experiment and androgyny evidence an awareness of the attractions but, more insistently, of the dangers of such 'undifferentiated unity'. Such a unity harks back, as Eliade's quote suggests, to a jump out of history and to a merger of self and other; to a collapse of difference. This is exactly what occurs in the Eden to which Hemingway introduces his reader in the late novel.

For if the closed world of two in *The Garden of Eden* is, briefly, an 'intact source of holiness', this is prior to androgyny. And the kinds of unity associated with the merger of self and other are finally, again, disastrous. In Hemingway's fiction, forms of sexual/gender relations which pre-date present social tensions ('the wholeness of pre-history') are presented as attractive but irrecuperable. The collapse of sexual difference is associated finally with madness, not with health, and traditional gender conventions are firmly re-established. Catherine's androgyny leads not to a new and improved gender order. She can rather be seen as one whose 'repudiation of conventional gender distinctions and restrictions'[60] destructively challenges David's *autho*rity as male and his authority as writer – both of which are interdependent. It is by means of David's writing that the public world is reintroduced in the text for, despite the threat it constitutes to the identity of the individual, such an identity cannot exist outside it. David can only function successfully, both in personal and public terms, by finally stepping back from that loss of self in the other and those sexual experimentations which are part of that process. In shunning identification with the female other, this Hemingway protagonist does not, however, return to a position of traditional male mastery (his behaviour is far from masterful throughout the text). Rather in both his occupation as writer and in the content of those writings he renegotiates traditional concepts of masculine behaviour.[61] Gender and sexual role and their meaning stand as the central subject of this novel. If it ends with David once more positioned within a traditional heterosexual marital relationship, the fact that one of the main strands of the novel concerns what happens when such a relationship is turned upside-down suggests the depths of the author's interest in, and anxiety about, this subject.

Traditional romance themes and themes of the loss of male mastery are again blurred in this text. The intensity of the closed love relationship, and the (disastrous) collapse of sexual difference associated with it, are the dominant motifs of the first stages of *The Garden of Eden*. As the novel progresses the related theme of what it means to be a writer becomes increasingly important. The dangers of intense romantic and sexual union, however, quickly become apparent. Right from the start Catherine speaks of her 'destructive' (*GE*, 11) nature and warns David of a 'dangerous' and 'complicated' surprise (*GE*, 18). She quickly takes the initiative in pushing the relationship in the direction of sexual role reversal and the erasure of difference in terms of clothes and appearance. Both practices point toward androgyny. This process is easily traced. Initially the couple are taken as brother and sister because of their deep suntans, sun and sea-streaked hair, and the French fishermen's shirts they both wear. The whole issue of gender distinction is then more radically foregrounded as Catherine has her hair cut short, like a boy's. This is the promised dangerous surprise. As she puts it, 'I'm a girl. But now I'm a boy too and I can do anything and anything and anything' (*GE*, 22). The romance theme (the intensity of the closed self-mirroring relationship of two) modulates into one of gender balance here, as this (symbolic) liberatory act promises her the (actual) assumption of 'male' power, freedom and confidence. Its consequence for David, however, will be his 'unmanning'.

Sexual difference blurs further as the couple come more and more to narcissistically reflect one another and to retreat into their separate shared world. Catherine wants them both to get as dark as they can in the sun so as to take them 'further away from other people' (*GE*, 38). At her instigation too they both, this time, have their hair cut and coloured alike. This blurring process is meanwhile acted out in their sexual relationship as Catherine starts playing the role of that boy she has now identified with:

he could feel the long light weight of her on him. . . . He lay there and felt . . . her hand . . . searching lower and . . . only felt the weight and the strangeness inside and she said, 'Now you

can't tell who is who can you? . . . You are changing . . . and
you're my girl Catherine.' (*GE*, 25)

It is difficult to know precisely what physically happens here.
Indeed, it is in the area of sexuality generally that Hemingway's
aesthetic commitment to the description of 'what really happened
in action' seems to get most compromised. There is a recurrent
evasiveness that marks his transformation of sex into language
which may speak an unease with the erotic and the force of desire
which is both cultural and personal. Whatever the reason, it
certainly leads to a certain confusion and vagueness at a crucial
moment of the text. What is clear, though, is that the boundaries
that conventionally define sexual roles have been breached, and
what seems likely is that some form of anal penetration occurs and
that 'by being penetrated, Bourne's identification with the feminine
is more complete than Catherine's verbal assertion that she is
"Peter" and Bourne is "Catherine"'.[62]

Here the unmanning of the central protagonist is foregrounded
much more forcefully than in *A Farewell to Arms*. We can see a
'relinquishment of masculine power' and authority, even the
(temporary) 'death of [David's] masculine identity' in the passive
sexual role that he now plays.[63] The loss of the sense of the
separate self – who is David and who is Catherine – is linked here
to the breach of sexual bounds, the step beyond 'everyone else's
rules' (*GE*, 23), to which David is the reluctant partner. For though
he recognises the attractions of such activity and the extent of his
own complicity in it (*GE*, 94), his first and strongest response is
one of alienation:

'Was it that bad?'
'No,' he lied. (*GE*, 80)

To him, such activity is bred of desperation and is fatal for the
relationship. The moves from one location to another and the
metaphoric resonances of his comment that 'There aren't many
more moves to make' (*GE*, 80) endorse such a sense of incipient
centripetal collapse.

The introduction of Marita provides a transition point in the
novel. Catherine, again the initiator, makes the twosome a three-
some. This develops its own tensions and dynamics as Marita

gradually comes to take Catherine's place as David's wife. First, though, conventional sexual roles are further collapsed. Marita and Catherine have a lesbian relationship. Marita and David also start sleeping together. Meanwhile Catherine and David once again switch sexual roles. Gender norms are in flux. Who plays what (active or passive) part in the traditional dynamics of sexual behaviour is likewise unstable.

David in effect has two wives at this point. He has nick-named Marita 'heiress' because of her money, but the word cuts two ways as Catherine speaks of Marita as inheriting the role of wife from her (*GE*, 159). The shift in wives that takes place is crucial, for each represents different possibilities. There is, in this section of the text, a reminder of what the breakdown of conventional gender roles on Catherine and David's part and the intensity of her need to merge her self in him has come to mean. When they switch roles and David answers Catherine's 'Are you really?' with a 'Yes if you want' (I take 'Catherine' to be the absent word), she continues: 'Oh I want so much and you are and I have' (*GE*, 185). The loss of certainty of meaning here points to a confusion of identity between them. Catherine's later 'I want us to be just the same' (*GE*, 194) suggests the obliteration of original difference that can only signal for David, when applied to the sexual realm, a type of death. For to be just the same means, for Catherine, to express forms of ('masculine') power and authority. And that, within the limits of the entirely private realm in which it is played out, is only possible at his expense. This whole thematic strand can be read as an implicit measure of the lack of opportunity open to Catherine (and women in general) in the public arena. But that is not the central issue here. Rather her need is shown as aberrant and as potentially fatal to both parties involved. Thus an increasing number of references to Catherine's 'craziness' – as when, for instance, she tears up the notebook in which one of David's African stories is written – indicate the dangerous impossibility of what she desires.

Indeed it is this latter action which signals the way that the development of the two heterosexual relationships are intimately connected to the theme of what it means to be a writer, an artist, in this highly self-reflexive text.[64] For the structural move of the novel from the one relationship (with Catherine) to the other (with Marita) is indicative of a vital thematic move – the construction of meaning not through love but through art. If both here and in *A*

Farewell to Arms romance loses its 'salvational logic' as the narrative develops, then it is art that takes on the salvational role in this later text. Max Weber saw 'authenticity' as internally sought in a 'disenchanted' public world. Art, he suggested, 'assumes the function . . . of a this-worldly *salvation* from everyday life'.[65] Through acts of artistic creativity the individual can stamp her or his personal sense of meaning on a world that would otherwise deny it, thus powerfully countering a reductive universe. In *The Garden of Eden*, Hemingway makes a classic modernist move in the belief implicit in the text that art (the writing of fiction) can act as field in which personal meaning, self-understanding, development and satisfaction can be realised in a world that otherwise denies it. In this way the artist can both enter history, by speaking publically to a potentially large audience, while retaining his identity apart from it, in terms of the personal nature of the values expressed.

It must be pointed out here that such a celebration of the role of the artist is open to a similar type of critique that can be levelled against the romance form. Fredric Jameson suggests as much in *The Political Unconscious* in his comments on Henry James. The stress on the artist as privileged subject can be seen as another kind of 'containment strategy' – a way of asserting the continued validity and sensitivity of the individual subject in a reified and systematised world.[66] For Hemingway, though, the celebration of the artist allowed for the existence and development of full and coherent subjectivity (however illusory such a notion might be) in contrast to his romances where the identity of the subject fragments and collapses.

In *The Garden of Eden* the romance form and the *Künstlerroman* (the narrative of individual artistic growth) compete with one another. For Catherine, David's creative identity as a writer cannot be allowed a separate existence apart from their intense 'romance'. David puts his work aside at the start of the novel in the first intensity of their marriage, and she encourages such a postpone-ment. Her response to the reviews of David's just-published first novel indicates the way his work threatens her conception of their joint identity: 'I'm frightened by them. . . . How can we be us . . . and you be this that's in the clippings?' (*GE*, 32). 'This' here might refer to 'artist'; it could equally refer to 'public figure'. By book two of the novel David is working again, but references to writing are brief and it is not until the third book that we find out that he is writing about their joint relationship. From Catherine's point of view, this might be seen as a validation of her importance and identity as her part in his life is given public recognition. In chapter 11, however, David leaves this narrative to work on an unrelated story and from that point distinguishes his work as a realm set aside from the complications of his relationships with the two women. More and more references to the writing process follow as he imaginatively translates the knowledge of his father and of an Africa gained as a child into a fiction that takes on a firm reality in the writing and reading of it: 'He could feel the weight of the heavy double-barreled rifle carried over his shoulder . . . and he tasted the pebble in his mouth' (*GE*, 141). This story about getting to know his father and about the 1905 native uprising in Tanganyika is only given in very partial form in the novel. All we find out concerning its 'horrible' and 'bestial' (*GE*, 172) aspects which lead Catherine to tear the notebook in two is in her later comment about 'the massacre in the crater' and the 'heartlessness' of David's father (*GE*, 241), a provocative clue to the story's fuller content.

The description of the composition of the story that David writes next is given in more detail. The story is about Africa again and his father's hunting of the bull elephant, Juma. It is also, though, about his own role (as a child) in this described event. The procreative aspects of artistic composition are stressed as David comes to an understanding both about himself and his relationship with his father as he writes. The descriptions here of the mental recovery of particular incidents and their conversion into narrative fiction make them some of the most interesting pieces about the writing process in all of Hemingway.

When Catherine reads these stories, she responds destructively. She claims a right to read the first one since it is her money that made it 'economically possible' (*GE*, 170–1). Her 'male' role as financial support gives her, in her mind, authority over David (and the art he produces). Catherine's verbal and physical attacks on the African stories can be seen as rejections of a part of David's life that she cannot share. She calls them 'dreary dismal little stories about your adolescence with your bogus drunken father' (*GE*, 227) and burns them all up since 'they were worthless and I hated them' (*GE*, 237). A clue to her motivation is given in her comment on (also) burning the reviews of his earlier book: 'I think he reads them by himself and is unfaithful to me with them' (*GE*, 233). She associates David's identity as an artist with a type of masturbatory activity which threatens their sexual and emotional engagement as a couple.

Catherine is happy so long as David is writing that narrative which narcissistically echoes their own closed relationship. She does not burn this – what he calls 'the stuff about her' (*GE*, 249). Locked in the intensity of her and David's relationship, Catherine cannot allow for difference – for the fact that there is a part of him writing and changing outside the scope of their 'romantic' union. To recall that earlier crucial quote, for Catherine 'we be[ing] us' is incompatible with 'you be[ing] this', a writer and an artist with his own separate existence. Catherine's love destroys itself as she reacts with hostility to David's self-expression as a writer. Her experiments with the changing of sexual role are part of a similar move to try and obliterate the differences between them; to pull them back to an original 'Edenic' state in which sameness and togetherness are one and the same thing. The unbalanced nature of such a desire to repress individual difference in a sexual and romantic focus on an other who is only allowed to mirror the self, is finally recognised by David when he says 'We've been burned out. . . . Crazy woman burned out the Bournes.'

The dialogue that follows this statement is also very significant. David is speaking here to Marita. He answers her next question 'Are we the Bournes?' with his 'Sure. We're the Bournes' (*GE*, 263). One couple replaces the other. Marita can, she tells David, do the things Catherine does when lovemaking (*GE*, 202) but we can assume that he does not wish her to do so. As Robert Jones says, 'Bourne's crisis of gender identification is resolved when he realizes "what a completely stupid thing he had permitted" and rejects Catherine's authority over his identity.'[67] With Marita, submissiveness replaces assertiveness. She takes the traditional female role that Catherine has rejected and is content to play satellite to David's star. She recognises the value of his work and 'loved and respected . . . his own country' (*GE*, 211), that of his artistic creation. David's discovery and realisation of the self that comes in writing finally stands as the most important thing in the novel[68] and this achievement and growth is encouraged by Marita. Her passive compliancy at the text's end is similar to Maria's in *For Whom the Bell Tolls*. The crazy 'woman', straining at the limitations of her gender role and ambitious for 'male' power and public reputation, has been replaced by a submissive 'girl': 'I'm your girl', Marita says in the dark, 'Your good girl who loves you' (GE, 265). With this assurance David returns successfully to his fiction, the threat to his male identity now safely contained.[69]

Hemingway ends the novel with traditional gender roles re-established, with the artist figure confirmed in his male identity and authority, his lost 'discipline' and 'control' (GE, 243) now restored. His ongoing fictional concern with sexual role ends with a reassertion of traditional norms which is linked to the ability to function as a writer. Once, though, a conventional heterosexual relationship is re-established and his manhood is no longer under threat, David is able in his writing to question the value of traditional concepts of masculinity. Militarist (Cantwell) and machismo (hunting, bullfighting, shooting) forms of male role model that are treated sympathetically in other fictions can now be opened up to criticism.

David's occupation as an artist is one often associated with shared gender attributes – a 'masculine' determination and confidence combined with 'feminine' intuition and sensitivity. The African tales he writes reject 'cliché masculine endeavors'. His father's 'masculine code' is presented as entirely unsatisfactory, and David in fact identifies with that which his father will destroy, the elephant Juma, 'object of the hunt, the victim of male pursuit'. David's words to his father, 'Fuck elephant hunting' (GE, 199), and his knowledge that full communication and trust between them is henceforth impossible, marks a turning away from male rituals of hunting and killing, and toward that role as artist which he is to adopt. As he rewrites his childhood, David rejects membership of 'the older, male order' which in 'Indian Camp' the young Nick Adams, in undergoing his rite of passage, appears provisionally to accept.[70]

Hemingway's exploration of gender role and sexuality in *The Garden of Eden* suggests deep anxieties on the subject. The stories David writes suggest the failings of traditional forms of masculinity. But in terms of the structure of the novel as a whole, it is as if this issue can only be safely explored when the traditional male–female balance has been, or is being, re-established; that only once the anxiety caused by female self-assertion has been eased can an exploration of the 'feminine' part of the male sensibility be calmly pursued and the flaws of an assertive masculinity revealed. The majority of Hemingway texts finally speak male mastery.

Catherine's presentation in *The Garden of Eden* does, however, begin to suggest an awareness of the damaging constrictions of the traditional female role. The narrative as it now stands supports John Updike's reading that, for Hemingway, 'Evil is, evidently, feminine in gender.' E. L. Doctorow, though, perceptively comments that Catherine's 'jealousy' (*GE*, 223) of David's artistic work may be that of 'a brilliant woman trapped into a vicarious participation in someone else's creativity'. This bears further consideration. The fact that it is David's focalisation that is primary in the narrative and that Catherine is denied interiority somewhat cuts against Doctorow's contention concerning the 'informed and delicate reading' Hemingway gives of her.[71] However, the centrality of Catherine's role in the novel and her knowledge of, and failure to understand, the disaster she has caused ('I knew I did it and I can't undo it. It's too awful to understand' – *GE*, 256) suggest that the compulsions which drive her cannot just be waved aside by categorising her as destructive bitch. We must remember that the Scribner's editor, Tom Jenks, pruned some 135,000 words to achieve the version of the novel that we now have. Critics who have studied the original manuscript speak of Catherine as one who 'struggles for independent creativity at all costs' and see her 'masculinization of herself, and her sun worship [as] ways she tries to deal with David's inability to beget a child'.[72] There is a suggestion of another story here, and one that comes from Catherine's point of view, though it has to be said that the sexual politics are hardly radical. Unable to have children and denied outlet for her creative impulses, she starts sexually experimenting, masculinises herself, and so destroys her relationship! Perhaps the fact that Hemingway could not complete the manuscript indicates that his view of gender issues was more ambiguous than this and too complex to be neatly resolved in the much simpler way taken by the posthumous edition.

To conclude then, Hemingway's constant dwelling on the subject of gender role and sexual identity, both in this novel and throughout his work, and his ability at times to shift sharply from the male perspective to represent an alternative female point of view, suggests his awareness of the uncertainty of traditional gender hierarchies. This can be related to the changes in gender relationships that provided the social and historical background to the work's production. Although his writing generally ends by validating male power and sexual authority, this does not mean that he is always sympathetic to the male perspective. The inversions of sexual and gender role and depth of the fictional explorations of this area both give evidence of ambiguous forms of desire and suggest deep anxieties about traditional binaries that could never quite be satisfactorily resolved. The fact that he never did formally 'close' *The Garden of Eden* would endorse such a view.

5

Geographies, Fictional and Non-fictional: America, Spain, Africa

---

An if you are goin to be a nacherlist // thass O/K/ but ef yew air goin to Afrik fer to annoy a tranquil family of man eatin lions etc // I reprobate you.

(Ezra Pound to Ernest Hemingway)[1]

And that is Hemingway, he looks like a modern and he smells of the museums.

(Gertrude Stein)[2]

Decadence – the threat of the city, civilization, machine – was stayed in the . . . art of taxidermy

(Donna Haraway)[3]

I

In this chapter I focus on the sense of geography in Hemingway's work, a sense that is inextricable from that of history, tradition and time. I restrict my scope mainly to the places indicated in my title because of the space available to me. Also, despite the importance of France, Italy and Cuba in Hemingway's work, it is his writerly moves between America and Spain and Africa that best illustrate

124

the quest for 'authenticity', for some type of 'original' source of value, which is central to my developing argument.

Richard Godden writes that 'taxidermy is implicit in much of [Hemingway's] fiction'. His hunting of animals for trophy and exhibition suggests that, if he smells of the museums, they are museums of natural history. 'Many of [his] privileged intensities involve sports, and particularly trophy-sports. Heads, horns, skins and fish are a common consequence of his moments of "maximum exposure".'[4] Maximum exposure for Hemingway, both in his life and in his fiction, was a way of countering the complications and restraints of a rapidly modernising world. The upper Michigan of his boyhood, Spain and Africa become, to borrow and alter the title of his unfinished story, last good countries, which can be inhabited or reinhabited by a protagonist – fictional or non-fictional – to attain a temporary state of grace.[5]

Such a condition, though, can never be more than provisional and uneasy, however much that fact might go unrecognised. Origins, in the form of an original place or state of grace, can never be recovered. The particular versions of Spain or Africa described in Hemingway's writings are not original paradisical spaces, but rather constructs of that modern American imagination which re-encounters them and products of that modern international and incorporated civilisation which inevitably alters them. My thesis in this chapter is that aspects of Hemingway's fiction clearly reveal such an understanding. In his non-fiction, however, and especially that published during the 1930s, Hemingway seems usually to repress or evade it.[6] The versions of Spain and Africa that Hemingway produces in *Death in the Afternoon* and *Green Hills of Africa* in particular are, metaphorically speaking, 'stuffed' versions of actual countries – artificial, static and idealised products of that quest for 'authenticity' and 'originality' which time and history in fact deny.

A contest between discourses of idyllic space and public history, of private feeling and social disenchantment, is pronounced in all areas of Hemingway's writing. There is a constant strand of his work that relates to the quest for an untainted area where the individual's deepest needs can be met. This quest shifts in direction and is linked to a sense of gradual diminishment. In the fiction, however, there is an awareness that to make of other countries or realms utopian spaces where one's private desires can be realised is radically to falsify the nature of history, of social reality and of cross-cultural interaction. This fictional awareness can be related to the narrative techniques Hemingway developed – techniques that reflected the fragmentary quality of experience and stemmed from a deep unease concerning the nature of subjectivity and its relation to objective reality. The non-fiction does not generally share this quality or show the same type of awareness.

There is a tension in Hemingway's work between notions of 'dwelling' and of 'mere circulation'. Some places are given strong and positive value. This is in contrast to the sense of homelessness suggested by the 'inconsequential randomness' and circular movements of so many of his protagonists.[7] This tension is crucial both to the fiction and to the non-fiction. To find home usually takes the shape of some kind of return: to some cultural and historical space where earlier forms of freedom, self-expression and oneness with the surroundings can be found; to some space where the pressured and confined world of 'everyday' reality does not yet operate.

Hemingway's vision of alternative space (a space that is both geographical and cultural) is essentially backward looking and always trembles on the edge of loss. The countries he chooses to inhabit, to call 'home', are imagined versions of a simpler world, which the protagonist can enter at his ease and where his presence causes no jarring note. As a general rule, it is the fiction again which evidences the awareness of the ambiguities and the dangers of that backward look which mark those versions of 'home' offered. In the non-fiction generally, even in the later Spanish and African writings where the utopian sense is diminished and where the narrator's position is to some degree problematised, such dangers and ambiguities usually go unrecognised.

II

Hemingway's idyllic notion of 'home', of sacred space, is associated first and foremost with a vanished and vanishing America, and especially, though not only, with the upper Michigan environment of his boyhood vacations. In 'Miss Mary's Lion', an article written about the 1953–4 safari (and unpublished until

1972), Hemingway writes of the 'homesickness' he felt for Africa after his first visit there. This is shortly followed by memories of his boyhood Michigan. The sensual qualities of his immediate African experience transport him nostalgically back to his earlier boyhood world. What is happening now and what happened in the Michigan of his childhood are linked in a Proustian way as the cider he is drinking in Africa and the smell of the balsam needles in the pillow on which he sleeps carry him back in memory to the tastes and smells of his Michigan past:

> It [the balsam smell] was the smell of Michigan when I was a boy. . . . The cider tasted like Michigan too, and I always remembered the cider mill . . . and the smell of the sacks used in the pressing and later spread to dry. . . . Below the dam of the cider mill there was a deep pool. . . . You could always catch trout if you fished there patiently. (*AJ*2, 39)

This strong and detailed passage about the remembered past speaks of a vanished and simpler rural American world now left far behind.

There is a nostalgic note to this passage that is never simply present in the fiction. In the non-fiction writing about America there is a straightforward and ever-increasing sense of diminished space, as places that might be called 'home' (where unspoiled 'country' can be found and where the self can rest content) disappear before the writer's very eyes. The 1935 *Esquire* article, 'Remembering Shooting-Flying: A Key West Letter', also describes a vanished and attractive earlier mid-western American world. Again memory is crucial here, one which recovers the sense of the past, the 'shooting and fishing and reading' that were such a 'pleasure' then:

> You can remember the miracle it seemed when you hit your first pheasant when he roared up from under your feet . . . and you can feel the bulk of him still inside your shirt . . . walking into town in the dark along the dirt road that is now North Avenue where the gipsy wagons used to camp when there was a prairie out to the Des Plaines river where Wallace Evans had a Game farm and the big woods ran along the river where the Indian mounds were.

The passage charts what has now disappeared. It leads the reader along from the presentation of alternative life modes unconstricted by convention (that of the gypsies), and beyond that (temporary) living space to open and unspoiled country, prairie and big woods. Here even the businesses that do operate (the game farm) are appropriate to the environment. Thence the reader is taken to historical first beginnings; to the Indian mounds which mark the traces of an earlier culture.

By the time Hemingway writes, though, all these things have gone. Their marks have been covered over by the signs of a commercial and faceless mass culture:

> I came by there five years ago and where I shot that pheasant there was a hot dog place and filling station and the north prairie . . . was all a subdivision of mean houses. . . . I was glad I went away from there as soon as I did. Because when you like to shoot and fish you have to move often and always further out and it doesn't make any difference what they do when you are gone. (*Byline*, 202–3)

It does, however, make a difference what they do when you are gone. If you have to move always further out, there is less and less chance of contentment and fewer and fewer places to which to come back. Thus Hemingway's sense of Spain and Africa as havens will, as I will show, also fade in the course of his career.

The loss of this first boyhood American world resonates throughout Hemingway's fiction, but there is a critical consciousness at work which acknowledges the impossibility of recapturing the idyllic moment. The romantic celebration of a return to nature and to the 'primitive' is treated generally in a self-conscious and ambivalent manner. The presence of the utopian moment disappears here in a sense of lost origins that can never be recovered.

In Hemingway's fiction, America – once boyhood is over – generally signifies not 'home', the place where private desire and communal codes can fall into comfortable alignment, but the alien. There is a recurrent sense of cultural failure in his American stories. To follow this through fully is beyond the scope of the present work,[8] but 'Wine of Wyoming' provides a brief and useful example. There is a passage in *Death in the Afternoon* in which the author compares the creature comforts of American life to the religious consciousness and ability to comprehend the centrality and importance of death which he finds in the people of Castilla (*DA*, 234). This comparison, which operates to America's discredit, is implicit too in his comment on the pleasures of wine as 'one of the most civilized things in the world and one of the natural things' (*DA*, 15) – a statement obviously intended to reflect back on the values of Prohibition America. In 'Wine of Wyoming', a similar comparison between cultural values operates.

'Wine of Wyoming' develops themes of aridity and betrayal. The story charts 'the dryness, [both] legal and spiritual' of America. Drink as 'symbolic act, drink as sign of life fully lived, drink as communion' is contrasted with 'Prohibition as closure, as hypocrisy, as denial of communion'.[9] The Fontans' home stands as a French enclave in arid America. While the Americans who come there do not know how to behave, putting whisky in their beer, and 'aussi une femme qui a vomis sur la table' (*WTN*, 139), the Fontans offer the narrator a place to sit in the shade away from the baking sun, to look at the yellow grain-fields and the snow on the distant mountains; invite him to join them inside at a dinner in which hospitality, communality and aesthetic/sensual appreciation combine: 'We ate in the dining-room. . . . We tried the new wine. It was very light and clear and good, and still tasted of the grapes' (*WTN*, 132).

The potential theme of the narrative is one of cultural possibility. Such possibility is linked to the notion of boundaries, where the values of different cultures can be tested out, with the prospect of new and positive combinations emerging. Here, though, the prospective vitality of such cultural combinations is swiftly suppressed. The dominant American culture overwhelms alternative value schemes and resists new and productive joint developments. The cultural combinations that do occur in fact only operate, in this American setting, in a one-sided way and to damaging effect. The Fontans are jailed and fined for their 'natural' activity – the selling of good wine and beer. Mme Fontan's son has married 'une américaine', but an American Indian whose own cultural displacement is suggested in her inactivity and conformity to the lax habits of a consumer culture: 'She don't work. She don't cook. She gives him beans en can' (*WTN*, 131). The anti-Catholicism of the dominant culture shows myths of democratic equal opportunity to be a sham, as the references to the Al Smith presidential campaign illustrate. If religious difference leads to bigotry in an American setting, so too does racial difference. The Fontans themselves are hostile to their Italian and Polish neighbours.

The possibility of new and rewarding cultural exchange in America is suggested in the easy mix of French and American English which formally composes the dialogue. But this finally collapses as Fontan fails to get from his (American?) neighbour the symbolic key that will allow for the 'fête' to take place before the narrator departs, and is reduced to 'swear[ing] in English . . . incoherent and crushed' (*WTN*, 144). The narrator, who normally lives in France, ruins the 'fête' (a term that 'means "feast" . . . in the religious sense . . . the resonance lingers') which is to centre around the drinking of the new wine, because he is 'too tired to go out' and because he does not 'want a foreign language' (*WTN*, 142), and the narrative ends in frustration and sadness. The similarity of the Wyoming country to Spain is mentioned twice at the narrative's end, but the comparison only 'underlies the radical disparity, the absence in Wisconsin of the rituals that made Spain and France the real old thing that Hemingway loved'. In a story of betrayal and bad faith, 'all things conspire against the slaking of thirst . . . It is "too late" for America, as Hemingway would explicitly assert in *Green Hills of Africa*, "too late" even for the very land, the spoiled country that had become a "bloody mess"'.[10]

What happens, then, when Hemingway returns from this contemporary American scene to that 'purer' boyhood world that he celebrates in the non-fiction? As I have suggested, the return to origins, to unspoiled nature, is never a simple or unqualified one in the fiction. Warner Berthoff's comment that Hemingway 'pivots his relentless narratives of disaster and defeat around ironic recollections of lost primal circumstance' is a useful one here. The 'purged and restorative "good country"'[11] of his fiction is never quite purged enough; never without its shadows, its looming sense of pressing historical presence, its sense of an origin beyond full reach or attainment. The notion of paradisical return is revealed here as a myth. However 'pure' such returns might seem to be, the original source of value is never reached. Nature is never presented as untainted but always remains linked in symbiotic relation to culture. In 'Big Two-Hearted River' repetition of action (the making of coffee according to Hopkins) and event (the return to waters once fished before) takes Nick finally back to a primal origin, the swamp that lies at the implicit end of his journey. But this end is also a beginning: the place to which he is returning is that from which he has first come. And this origin remains unexplored; the swamp is 'threatening and unfamiliar', profoundly unhomelike.[12] Entry to it remains deferred.

'The Last Good Country' is the Hemingway title that is most resonant in terms of the urge for return and recuperation, for exploration and the celebration of the 'primitive', those analogous urges that mark in their different ways both fiction and non-fiction. In this story, Nick Adams and his sister make their difficult way to a pastoral retreat, a type of sacred space where a step outside historical and cultural restraint appears available. As so often in Hemingway's American fiction, such a move is associated with the figure of the Native American. Their retreat to 'a very old place . . . [where] the firestones are Indian' (*NAS*, 91) is not, though, a return to origins (an impossibility) but rather a return to a trace of a previous presence (the Indians) who in their turn (as far as we know) originally settled the landscape. In other words, origins retreat before our quest for them.

Nick and Littless's journey constitutes a stripping away of the social self, in terms both of the nuclear family unit and of institutional law. The fact that Nick's flight takes place with his 'kid sister' (*NAS*, 97) alone marks a rejection of the fuller family. Both mother and father are associated with varying forms of absence: the latter literally away from home; the former (twice) described as retired to her bed with 'a sick headache' (*NAS*, 78), positioned behind a locked door. Littless's words, 'Haven't we seen enough fights in families?' (*NAS*, 85), imply a deep dissatisfaction with this basic social form. Nick has transgressed legal codes in killing a buck deer out of season, and his consequent movements constitute an escape from the figures of law and authority, those game wardens for whom Nick harbours only aggression: 'I'd like to . . . kill both of those bastards' (*NAS*, 74).[13]

Cultural prohibition, or at least disapproval, and its evasion, also figures in the references to miscegenation that occur at the edges of this story. Nick's relationship with his Indian girlfriend Trudy has previously (we are told) ended. Her 'natural' vitality has thus been subject to prior erasure. She is still, however, very much in his thoughts: 'None of it was her fault', he says, 'She's just built that way' (*NAS*, 100). Nick might here be referring to a change of

sexual partners on Trudy's part or he might be alluding to the fact
that she has become pregnant by him – a detail that has evidently
been edited out of the published text.[14] Whichever, her sexual
spontaneity cuts against dominant cultural norms (as her role in
'Fathers and Sons' confirms). Hemingway's fiction, like Faulkner's,
is full of doublings and redoublings, compulsive repetitions,
father–son obsessions. Here, for instance, Packard is the substitute
father figure of the story, whose preference for sex and 'good
bonded whisky' over culture and religion (*NAS*, 99) and relationship with the hired girl, Suzy, links him to Nick. In his case,
though, the relationship is a diminuendo version of Nick's: one
that transgresses conventional morality (the prohibition against
adultery) rather than crossing racial boundaries.

Nick and his sister appear to flee from culture to nature. If
cultural prohibition is apparently opposed to natural vitality, then
Nick's move here to the last good country and his self-
identification with the original inhabitants of that country ('you
should have been an Indian. . . . It would have saved you a lot of
trouble' – *NAS*, 111) also seem a regressive flight to unspoiled
nature and pre-social conditions. As such, it bears only positive
connotation. Littless, in such a reading, becomes a lesser, mirror
version of Nick's own self. To read this narrative in such a way, as
a straightforward celebration of the primitivist urge, certainly
seems possible. Between them, Nick and Littless spell out the
attractions of their retreat. The woods are like 'cathedrals' (*NAS*,
90). Their camp, a base for hunting and fishing almost magical in
its prodigality, is a 'beautiful, beautiful place' (*NAS*, 91). The last
good country is actually reached and with it idyll (wish fulfilment;
the end of that desire for a type of primal at-homeness) is realised
as nowhere else in Hemingway's American fiction.

As always in his fiction, however, things are not quite this
simple. Sexual difference cannot be abolished in this Eden despite
Littless's act of cutting short her hair to 'change me into a boy'
(*NAS*, 112). The threat of incest, as signalled both in the narrative
action and the playful conversations about marriage, signals the
fact that nature is only defined as such by human presence and
that immediately such presence occurs so the social, in the forms
of law and repression, is introduced. The prohibition against incest
has been described as the very first taboo to mark cultural and
historical belonging: 'the primal social repression which the

individual must accept, the anchoring prohibition in human history'.[15] A return to pure nature and to the presocial, to origins, is impossible.

Once, too, the 'secret place' for which Nick and Littless aim is reached, there is still something beyond, and, as in 'Big Two-Hearted River', it is the swamp: 'Bad swamp that you can't get through' (*NAS*, 88). The threat of the unfamiliar is never finally cancelled out. Another barrier always remains to be penetrated (dangerously) before the (receding) origin can be recovered. The story, as it stands, ends with Nick about to read *Wuthering Heights*, one of the books they have brought with them (along with *Swiss Family Robinson*). Both these texts have as their subject the inextricability of nature and culture. Nick ends the narrative with the reading of a text, an act that signals his own inevitable failure to return to pure natural source.

This very interesting story remained unfinished by Hemingway. This might be due to the fact that the text moves between two worlds: parents, game wardens, culture, religion, reform school and penitentiary on one side; desire, the retreat from history and culture into nature, the merger of self and other in some kind of tensionless pre-sexual/pre-social condition on the other. The illusory nature of setting up binary oppositions of this type, the impossibility too of reaching back to a source of pure value, is then revealed in the details of Nick and Littless's conversations, thoughts and actions once this 'last good country' is apparently reached. If such tensions can explain Hemingway's lack of formal resolution to this text, they also point to the fact that the 'primitive' strain in his fiction is never uncomplicated. The pressures of social and historical reality and the force of individual desire remain in complex and entangled coexistence here. The same is not always true of his non-fiction work.

III

Spain also serves as idyllic and 'homelike' space in Hemingway's writing. The sense of unspoiled country – a crucial element in his spatial utopics – returns in this different context. Driving from

Seville to Madrid in *The Dangerous Summer* the narrator reports, 'I loved this country in all seasons' (*DS*, 49). Of his return to bullfighting he says 'I had been away for fourteen years. A lot of that time . . . was like being in jail except that I was locked out; not locked in' (*DS*, 13). The return to Spain, synonymous here with a return to bullfighting, is associated both with being set free and with being allowed back home from exile. The attraction of Spain, its geographical conditions and cultural traditions, had been a recurrent Hemingway theme. His July 1925 letter to Scott Fitzgerald suggests such an enthusiasm: 'God, it has been wonderful country. . . . To me heaven would be a big bull ring with me holding two barrera seats and a trout stream outside' (*L*, 165). Similarly his comment in a letter to Gertrude Stein and Alice B. Toklas in the same month, 'Spaniards are the only people' (*L*, 168), endorses this sense that place, people and cultural value are all intimately connected in Hemingway's consciousness.

The narrative of *The Spanish Earth*, the documentary film made in 1937 by the Dutch director, Joris Ivens, to promote the Republican cause, was both written and spoken by Hemingway. Near the start of the film, when he is speaking of the village of Fuentedueña and the need to irrigate the land there, he says 'For fifty years we've wanted to irrigate but they held us back.' The film then focuses on the simple culture of the village people: the bread-making, the use of primitive wooden agricultural implements and the ploughing by hand behind two horses. This version of Spain, which first concentrates on its rural and undeveloped aspects, takes the form of a celebration of a set of primitive values with which the author explicitly identifies himself. The use of the first-person plural may be for rhetorical and propagandist effect but it none the less reveals his deep identification with the country and its people.

For reasons of space, I will mainly bypass Hemingway's political involvement in the Civil War, and his reporting, the stories and the novel which used that war as their subject. It is worth pointing out, however, that his move from professional journalism to the fictional representation of this war corresponded with a shift from exemplary vignette and/or report and analysis of a specific military event, and from a reportage necessarily affected by the writer's ideological commitment,[16] to a fictional construction (*For Whom the Bell Tolls*) that uses the direct experience of its central protagonist to develop a complex treatment of issues of political action and morality and individual ethical responsibility[17] that moves considerably beyond those initial narrow limits.

Hemingway's extended non-fictional writing on Spain centres on the bullfight. Indeed this event, which for Hemingway defined the essence of Spanish culture, provides the still, ritualistic moment which – in textual terms – literally contains the process of Spanish history. For the two books on bullfighting, *Death in the Afternoon* and *The Dangerous Summer*, both focus on the repeated ceremony of the bullfight; on *torero* as what Allen Josephs calls 'the still center of sacred time'.[18] Repeated studies of sacred ritual thus effectively contain (and cancel out?) 'profane time', the realm of history. For *Whom the Bell Tolls*, the book that represents the particular disruptive historical event of the Civil War, is placed, in time of writing, between the two others. Recurrent analysis of a (repeated) 'sacred' ceremony thus frames (his fictional version of) messy historical reality.

In both Hemingway's non-fiction and fiction the bullfight is represented as a source of value. It is an art form: 'There is absolutely no comparison in art between Joyce and Maera – Maera by a mile' (*L*, 119). It is an activity in which heroic behaviour is manifest at a physical level. Writing of his search for 'people that by their actual physical conduct gave you a real feeling of admiration', he enthuses, 'Well I have got ahold of it in bull-fighting. Jesus Christ yes' (*L*, 117). It is, as suggested above, also a ritual. Thus Josephs explains the centrality of the bullfight in *The Sun Also Rises* as a step out of 'profane time', that historical period associated with the moral and spiritual dislocations of the Lost Generation, to return to the ritual ceremony of the 'sacred world' of the bullfight. The bullfight, he suggests, 'recapitulates as spectacle and as rite the oldest myths of the Western world'. This reading concurs with Michel Leiris's description of the *corrida*:

as a kind of mythical drama, whose subject is as follows: the Beast mastered, then killed, by the Hero. The moments when the divine is present . . . are those moments when the *torero* plays with death, escaping it only miraculously, charming it; thereby he becomes the hero, incarnating the crowd which attains through him to immortality.

Pedro Romero's 'perfect sacrifice of the bull' in *The Sun Also Rises* becomes accordingly the 'precise centre and climactic moment' of the text; the recapitulation of a ritual that goes back to archetypal ceremony and sacrifice and beyond. For this is a step beyond history to 'fiesta . . . time . . . sacred time, original time, primal time'.[19]

Such a reading of the bullfight suggests a primitivist impulse. 'Spain', Hemingway writes in a letter to Howell Jenkins, 'is the real old stuff' (*L*, 131). Stanley Diamond asserts that the 'sickness of [modern] civilization consists . . . in its failure to incorporate . . . the primitive'.[20] In *Death in the Afternoon* and *The Dangerous Summer*, Hemingway turns his back on (a sick) modern civilisation to celebrate a pre-modern culture. This culture (and the books themselves) have the 'well ordered . . . tragedy and ritual' (*DA*, 13–14) of the bullfight at their centre – a ritual that involves both violence and death. At the centre of *Death in the Afternoon*, Hemingway inserts a story, 'A Natural History of the Dead', with death at its core, a story that appears to have little connection with anything else in the book. This 'amusing yet instructive' (*DA*, 120) tale, told apparently to 'break the flow of fact' that composes the main part of the book, is described by Ronald Weber as 'dropped [in] . . . as a way of closing out a section on the breeding of fighting bulls, one of the least inspired in the book'.[21]

On the contrary, 'A Natural History of the Dead' is crucial in terms of the structure and intention of the larger text. Its narrator takes the role of dispassionate naturalist, ironically commenting on those anthropocentric versions of the natural universe which would stress the intimate relationship between divine plan (as revealed in nature) and human fate. The main subject of the tale is the First World War. The case histories concerning human and animal nature that the narrator observes in the different named settings of Greece and Italy contradict the versions of that world offered by 'any self-called Humanist' (*DA*, 125). This epithet seems to extend beyond a particular literary school (the New Humanists) to refer more widely to anyone who believes in man's innate nobility and in a world that proceeds according to a (humanity-centred) divine plan. What war in fact reveals is violence and death in extreme, undignified and random form: broken-legged mules pushed into a harbour to drown; fragments of female bodies blasted by high explosives; the swollen bodies of dead and rotting soldiers, their bodies positioned according to the looting that has taken place and their colour changing from 'white to yellow, to yellow-green, to black' (*DA*, 123) with the passing of time. The story ends with two 'humane' men quarrelling over how best to deal with a dying soldier, his 'head . . . broken as a flowerpot may be broken' (*DA*, 126). They give way to insult and also, in their turn, to violence, under such stress.

This story forms one of the two bases from which Hemingway conducts his study of bullfighting. It is a study of death and violence in the modern world, where 'men die like animals' (*DA*, 124) without dignity, where human corpses become grotesque objects and where the distinction between the human and the non-human becomes blurred: 'a half-pint of maggots working where their mouths have been' (*DA*, 125). The random workings of the object world are here echoed in their effect on the human subject, defamiliarised by their force, 'blown into pieces which exploded along no anatomical lines' (*DA*, 123).

Bullfighting then, in *Death in the Afternoon*, can be seen in terms of a return to, and continuation of, cultural forms that pre-date, and can be measured against, the random violence and grotesque deaths which mark modern warfare. Hemingway's textual starting point, the indefensibility of the killing of the horses in the ring from 'a modern moral point of view, that is, a Christian point of view' (*DA*, 7), takes on, in retrospect, an ironical ring in this light. I would argue that Hemingway uses the war here, and throughout his work, to figure the condition of modernity.

The other base from which Hemingway conducts his study is that of the American culture which composes his own point of origin and to whose representatives (the book's audience) he speaks as 'translator' of Spain and its culture. Part of Hemingway's intention in the book is to criticise contemporary American culture and its 'pragmatic' repression of any knowledge of, and any 'intelligent interest in' (*DA*, 234), the 'taboo' subject of death.[22] Certainly American modernity is, often implicitly but sometimes explicitly, compared unfavourably with Spanish traditionalism throughout the book. This opposition is not architectural or even demographic: Madrid is a modern city but contains 'the essence' (*DA*, 50) of Spain with the Prado, the bullfight, and the country around. The 'malady of specialization' (*DA*, 79) may have affected bullfighting, but the term points us back to American culture just as surely as does the reference to the 'civilized' aspects of wine drinking. The concern with death and religion in Spain is contrasted with the shallow materialism of America ('a bath-tub in every American home'); the stress on spectacle and community activity that attends the bullfight with the private culture of technology ('the radio') (*DA*, 234). 'Integral' is a key word in the text and in the final chapter the bullfight comes to stand as central subject pointing in the direction of a total celebration of the Spanish landscape and its culture. Although this is the book where Hemingway develops his 'iceberg' theory of art, paradoxically the reader finds, in this chapter, passages of considerable lyric intensity where the writer points toward the idea of an impossible wholeness: the desire to get it all in – all of Spain and what it means to him. This forms a powerful hymn to Spain. Throughout the text the sense is of a geography that offers what America has lost – an integral culture focused round the ritual spectacle at its centre.

This is not to say that Hemingway sees Spanish culture, or bullfighting itself as an art, in static terms. Far from it, the golden age is now over, though as Hemingway does here point out, origins tend to recede before us: 'bullfighting has always been considered by contemporary chroniclers to be in a period of decadence' (*DA*, 212). However, what can still be found in 'the sculpture of modern bullfighting' (*DA*, 90) is, first of all, the presence of a major art form, though one that must of its very nature be temporary. The 'ecstasy' that can come from watching a complete *faena* 'while momentary, [is] as profound as any religious ecstasy' (*DA*, 183). The artist-bullfighter can even seem to slow or stop time (*DA*, 18) in a purer traditional realm where art is not separate from life, but where physical action, aesthetic achievement and spiritual satisfaction can merge. The bullfighter is the subject who is neither fragmented (as those subjects literally are in the example from 'A Natural History of the Dead') nor passive. He is, rather, the powerful individual who enters the arena with courage, grace and skill, to risk his very life against the brute force and violence of the bull. This arena, in Hemingway's reading of Spain, stands at the very centre of its culture, with the bullfighter thus placed as culture hero. Hubert Zapf calls the bullfights in *The Sun Also Rises* 'an idealized mythical counter world', which is set against 'the totally deritualized and incoherent life of the foreign group of bourgeois bohemians'. In *Death in the Afternoon,* a non-fictional text, this counter-world is fully realised. Myth becomes historical fact and cultural practice. Life in Spain has the type of 'ritualized coherence'[23] lacking elsewhere.

The good bullfighter dominates the bull with grace (*DA,* 24). At the heart of bullfighting and of Spanish culture lies the notion of honour or *pundonor:* 'it means honour, probity, courage, self-respect and pride in one word. Pride is the strongest characteristic of the [Spanish] race. . . . Honour in the bullfighter is as necessary to a bullfight as good bulls' (*DA,* 84–5). The killing of the bull, along with other forms of killing, gives 'aesthetic pleasure and pride' when done 'cleanly'. In 'rebellion against death', man – according to Hemingway's text – 'has pleasure in taking to himself one of the Godlike attributes; that of giving [death]' (*DA,* 205–6). If bullfighting is associated with the return to mythic origins, and the realisation of that myth in contemporary practice, then in the figure of the bullfighter Hemingway gives his reader a culture hero who is also a model of grace, power and supreme authority: at his best a Godlike figure – killer, artist and magician all in one.

This is clearly a version of Spain, and of the bullfighter as archetypal hero, that is a product more of personal or cultural need than of objective reality. Spain here becomes a form of desired 'other', marginal to that mainstream of modern history shown in paradigmatic terms in the broken and senseless world of 'A Natural History of the Dead', and valuable exactly because of that fact. Spain becomes another version of Hemingway's 'real thing'; a restorative good country where 'authenticity' marks the heroic masculine figure who stars in that repeated ritual which signifies 'true' cultural value. Again, words like 'true' and 'authentic', as used here, are subject to question. It is Hemingway's nostalgia and desire for an environment where nature is still a redemptive presence, where cultural practice is coherent and organic (centred on the primary ritual of the bullfight), and where individual autonomy and action are powerfully represented, that triggers this version of Spain he has constructed.

This Spain, then, acts as desired other to the modernised (American) world from which Hemingway is in full retreat. There is no information in *Death in the Afternoon* about those aspects of Spain that would contradict such a representation: about the problems of Spanish agriculture ('the central sore which radiated throughout

the country'[24]) and of working-class violence. There is almost no
mention – except briefly in the final chapter – of the political and
social difficulties that were to result in Civil War four years after
the book's publication. It is, it must be said, possible to read the
final chapter as Hemingway's acceptance that the book has not
'Spain in it' (*DA*, 240), and that it is after all a book about
bullfighting alone, not about the historical condition of the country.
I would claim otherwise: that in widening his scope to Spain as a
whole at this point, the author is suggesting that the country has to
be read as an integral whole with bullfighting at its very centre. If
this is so, it is a highly subjective, not to say dubious, cultural
reading.

Fredric Jameson is useful in suggesting why the figure of the
bullfighter was so attractive to Hemingway. I am extracting from
comments in *Marxism and Form* to apply them only to this realm
rather than relating them also, as he does, to Hemingway's style.
Jameson sees the 'Hemingway cult of *machismo*' as an attempt 'to
come to terms with the great industrial transformation after World
War I . . . it reconciles the deepest and most life-giving impulses
toward wholeness with a status quo in which only sports allow
you to feel alive and undamaged'. Bullfighting can thus be seen as
projecting an 'image of man's active and all-absorbing . . .
participation in the outside world'.[25] The bullfighter plays a
godlike role at the centre of cultural life in a way that, here,
because of its ritualistic aspects, goes beyond the mere category of
'sports' (used by Jameson). The bullfight in *Death in the Afternoon*
provides an example of meaningful individual action. This is a
life-giving activity and the figure at its centre is whole, alive and
undamaged; exactly, in other words, the opposite of the figures
described so graphically in 'The Natural History of the Dead'. In
depicting Spain as 'good country' in *Death in the Afternoon*, with
the bullfighter as its hero, Hemingway is constructing a version of
authentic manhood operating in a predominantly rural environment. Although he does not ignore the facts of modernisation, he
puts their details to one side as he focuses on those pastoral
aspects of the country that have, for him, more appeal.

The Dangerous Summer is revealing in this respect. Returning to
the 'unspoiled' country outside Pamplona, the narrator says, 'I was
as happy as I had ever been and all the overcrowding and the
modernisations at Pamplona meant nothing' (*DS*, 100). This

version of things entirely suits the needs of one writing against the dehumanising and reifying effects of a modernised post-war world. That Spain constructed in the non-fiction is one which mirrors first and foremost the author's own deepest needs. Spain signifies for Hemingway what America no longer is.

I now wish to turn from the non-fiction about Spain to the fiction. I have argued earlier that Hemingway's fiction is not one dimensional: that he plays with points of view and uses material in different ways as he moves between texts, and in so doing prevents any simple categorisations of his final authorial position. This play with point of view might be illustrated with regard to 'The Undefeated', one of his short stories about bullfighting. My larger point here is that the multiplicity of perspective in this single story about a bullfight illustrates a tactic that informs the fiction about bullfighting as a whole. When we move to this higher level and look at the whole range of his fiction on this subject, such a multiplicity of perspectives and presentations prevents the construction of any satisfactory single 'ideological' reading of the authorial attitude to it.

'The Undefeated' poses problems of interpretation. Is it about a matador who is also a code hero – one who, to quote Philip Young, 'dares, and sticks to the rules, and will not quit when he is licked. He is undefeated, he endures, and his loss therefore, in the manner of it, is itself a victory'? Or is the title ironic, with Manuel depicted as an incompetent, 'a middle-aged man . . . engaged in a stubborn fight from the simple fact that he is too old to be a matador'?[26] Is it perhaps Zurito, the picador, to whom the title refers? Hemingway's technique of using an apparently neutral narrative voice to present a series of focalisations and of allowing that voice to take on the shadings of that particular perspective being represented at any one point, makes any final verdict difficult. Does Zurito go to cut off Manuel's coleta because he hasn't 'go[ne] big' (*MWW*, 17) and it has been agreed that, in this event, he should retire? Or is it because Manuel, with his jerky movements and faulty technique at the moment of killing (launching himself at the bull), has shown himself unworthy to wear it? Is Manuel's failure one of luck ('the man must have the good luck that the sword point should not strike [bone]' – *DA*, 208) or of talent? Does his perseverance and refusal to give up, even when gored, compensate for any failure of skill? At the point when the audience and the matador are furthest apart, with Manuel equating both bull and crowd as his enemy ('dirty bastards . . . lousy bastard' – *MWW*, 35), Zurito – the one figure associated with knowledge and authority throughout the text – is absent. Thus neither the audience nor the matador's perspective can be validated. Has Zurito left because of his nervousness or because Manuel is disgracing himself? Can we trust the crowd and the critic's responses? Does the crowd lack knowledge and act arbitrarily in terms of its responses ('If it was Belmonte . . . they'd go crazy')? Or is it Retana's man, who makes this latter comment, who lacks knowledge ('Zurito said nothing' – *MWW*, 31)? I would suggest that the reader is left finally uncertain here, caught between multiple perspectives.

Such a tactic can be seen to operate in a slightly different way in *The Sun Also Rises*; but here the effect is to undercut any simple or single ideological reading of bullfighting. This fiction introduces the type of complications and indeterminacies that the non-fiction generally avoids, and acts also as a counter to the version of the bullfight revealed in the *In Our Time* vignettes. As I suggest earlier, the bullfight is depicted in *The Sun Also Rises* as a type of sacred ritual with Romero as its potent high priest, but it is here juxtaposed with the foreign 'other'; the 'strangely eccentric and out of place' expatriate group. It is the presence of this counter-world that complicates any response to the bullfight materials. Romero is, for Jake, undoubtedly a heroic figure, 'the natural man of action . . . an example of that original beauty and vitality of life from which he himself is forever separated'.[27] The phrase 'forever separated', however, suggests an unbridgeable gap between two realms: that of the modern (expatriate rootlessness) and that of the traditional (Spanish culture). Things are not quite this simple. My point is, though, that no such gap or separation occurs in the non-fiction about Spain.

For there, the narrator becomes one with the culture of which he tells. For example, he joins the 'brotherhood' (*DS*, 103) of bull-fighting as a type of honorary member in *The Dangerous Summer*. In the non-fiction, Hemingway's status as tourist and his effect on those he visits, is never fully recognised. His representation of himself as an honorary Spaniard prevents it. When, in *The Danger-ous Summer*, he says 'I've written Pamplona once and for keeps. It is all there as it always was except forty thousand tourists have been added. There were not twenty tourists when I first went there nearly four decades ago' (*DS*, 97), his own status (as tourist or not) remains ill-defined. There certainly does not seem to be a recognition of the fact that it is he who bears major responsibility for the increase in numbers he so regrets. Spain is described, in *Death in the Afternoon*, as a place apart, resistant to foreign influence and culturally self-sufficient: 'The bullfight is a Spanish institution; it has not existed because of the foreigners and tourists, but always in spite of them' (*DA*, 13). It was Hemingway, though, who in visiting Spain, and able to do so because of the strength of the dollar, began to transform it to a tourist venue, catering to exactly that foreign influence which could earlier be so easily contained. In the fiction (*The Sun Also Rises*) something of this process of cultural interaction, and its larger meaning, is recognised. In *Death in the Afternoon* it is not. This difference is a matter of focalisation, of narration, and of generic form. Once you have a first-person authorial figure as narrator, the possibilities of irony and of multiple perspective automatically diminish.

There is a passage in *The Dangerous Summer* that is suggestive of the way one culture inevitably affects another in its role as consumer. For the working of the *banderillas* is described in terms of American shopping metaphor: 'He put in four pairs of banderillas; not the very expensive kind he had placed in his first bull but good ones from Macy's' (*DA*, 80). The way experience is described and conceptualised is automatically subject to change once cultural translation and exchange occurs. In *The Sun Also Rises*, however, the reference to commercial transaction and patterns of dependency are much more self-consciously introduced.[28] The discourse of buying and selling dominates the whole text. The Pamplona merchants raise their prices one hundred per cent during the Fiesta (once the tourists and the peasants are in town). Bill spends his money there conspicuously, senselessly, and in a manner that demeans its local recipients – with the eleven shoeshines he buys Mike at a single sitting. Jake, relatively sober, has the grace to be 'a little uncomfortable about all this shoe-shining' (*SAR*, 144).

Tourists inevitably alter the territory they tread. Romero sits at the table next to the shoe-shining. He too becomes a target for tourist need as Brett gets herself 'a beautiful, bloody bull-fighter' (*SAR*, 172). He, however, is already adapting to the demands of the (international) market, and speaks English – culturally unacceptable in a *torero* (*SAR*, 155). Spanish culture is up for sale and in process of change. The importance of the exchange rate in what is now an international market has cultural as well as financial implications. Thus, again, in his fiction Hemingway opens up the kind of issues which in his non-fiction remain unexplored.

In *Death in the Afternoon*, the celebration of bullfighting is straightforward. In *The Sun Also Rises*, the text foregrounds the (irreconcilable) disparities between the expatriate, tourist world and that of traditional Spanish life. It also foregrounds disparities between the code of the bullring and the activities that take place there and the 'everyday' fabric of community existence. Differences and tensions mark the relationships between the two areas, inside and outside the ring, which are never apparent in *Death in the Afternoon*. The waiter's comment on the useless death of Vicente Girones, killed 'All for sport. All for pleasure. . . . All for fun' while running the bulls, leaving a wife and orphaned children behind him, together with his comment on bulls as just 'Animals. Brute animals' (*SAR*, 164), opens up an alternative reading of bull-fighting, even within the context of Spanish culture. Bullfighting for the waiter becomes a form of 'sport' only; not an organic and integral part of the rituals of Spanish life but a circumscribed form of activity peripheral and damaging to the business of that life. His reactions work to effect a questioning of the relationship of this 'sport' to Spanish life and culture as a whole.

Moreover, throughout the book, this gap between what occurs and is represented inside the bullring and what occurs outside, is highlighted. In the ring Romero is a heroic performer; outside he is a 'boy' (*SAR*, 135) who gets caught up in the messy emotional relationships of the 'foreign' group, and gets badly beaten because of it, unable to hold his physical own with the more powerful Cohn. His affair with Brett may be the first signal of the ruination of his career inside the ring if Montoya's warning (*SAR*, 143) and his own attraction for things foreign are to be taken seriously. If the 'ritual' of bullfighting still signifies positively in the text, other readings of it are also available. Action occurring in its arena does not necessarily bear significance outside that (limited) province. And in the gulf that lies between this ritual and the broken world of Barnes and company, and in the suggestion that no return to prior 'wholeness' is finally available for the latter, we get in the fiction the type of awareness, both of historical process and of the difficulties of combining the needs and distractions of one (financially dominant) culture with the continued smooth and meaningful operations of the cultural other on which it would feed, that the non-fiction work would generally repress.

In his book on Hemingway and Spain, *Hemingway's Spanish Tragedy*, Lawrence Broer discusses the Civil War in terms of 'the disquieting insights [Hemingway] had . . . receiv[ed] into the soul of his adopted country'. Broer is suggesting here that Hemingway saw certain flaws in the Spanish character as having 'predetermined the tragic consequences of the war'.[29] While the accuracy of this verdict is open to question, it is certainly true that the war temporarily undermined his sense of Spain as an 'adopted country'. Perhaps more simply, in the light of my previous argument, the political complexities of that war and the knowledge that Spain could no longer be represented simply in terms of bullfighting and the pastoral idyll, led Hemingway to look elsewhere for images of 'home'. Warner Berthoff's comment on the Spain of *For Whom the Bell Tolls* as having become 'the "good country" being ravaged and betrayed in the amoral violence of war'[30] certainly points to such a conclusion.

It is revealing, too, that when Hemingway did finally return to Spain after the war and came to write about it, it should again be in terms of bullfighting. But this time it was in a book with few of the wider socio-cultural reverberations of *Death in the Afternoon*. For *The Dangerous Summer* focuses specifically on the 1959 Ordonez-Dominguin 'mano a mano' contests, described revealingly as a type of civil war (*DS*, 75). This 'war' is not the messy affair of the 1930s, though, but a struggle between two individual heroic figures in the controlled arena of the bullring, where the described actions are charged with aesthetic and emotional meaning. By focusing so narrowly on this one contest, the author can partially recover what had been feared lost: the sense of Spain's 'value' for him.[31]

Discussing Conrad, Jameson speaks of 'the feudal ideology of honour' as a social value alien to the capitalist mode of production.[32] In Hemingway's non-fiction on the bullfight, stress is put on the crucial importance of *pundator* to the Spaniards and, here, the charismatic and heroic figures of the two bullfighters are (implicit) representatives of this quality. This can be seen as a rejection of complex socio-political contemporary realities in favour of a nostalgic recapturing of a set of irrelevant and out-moded values – values that in fact find their last expression inside the very limited confines of the bullring, *at one remove* from daily existence. Hemingway wrote to his son, Patrick, concerning some land he was buying in the Conil area: 'It is like everything was in the old days before they spoiled everything. Wonderful beach, fine people, real Arab town and good fishermen . . . on this trip . . . I have had the best time I ever had' (*L*, 895). This part of Spain represents a recovered paradise. Similarly, to write of the attrac-tions of the bullfight is, in both *Death in the Afternoon* and *The Dangerous Summer*, an attempt to recover a lost and simpler world ('like everything was in the old days'); to tap back into a source of value and vitality which was illusory – part of a feudal world that had, in Hemingway's lifetime, already lost its original meaning and relevance.

IV

With Hemingway's African trip of 1933–4, which took place the year after publication of *Death in the Afternoon*, East Africa joined the short list of places associated with personal fulfilment, a sense of belonging; with 'home'. In *Green Hills of Africa* he reports that, 'smelling the good smell of Africa, I was altogether happy' (*GH*, 15). Positive values are strongly identified with this territory. The emotional force that prompts Hemingway's celebration of this African landscape reminds me of Donna Haraway's comments on Carl Akeley and his visits to Africa from 1921 onward. Her analysis of the version of Africa created in the diorama of the gorilla group in the African Hall in the American Museum of Natural History (planned by Akeley) is particularly relevant here. She describes the representation of Africa portrayed there as a 'lush green garden . . . outside the Fall' and comments: 'This is the scene that Akeley longed to return to. It is where he died, feeling he was at home as in no other place on earth'.

Hemingway's Africa is similarly, I would suggest, an imagined Africa and one constructed according to the psychological and cultural needs of an American profoundly uneasy about modern civilisation and its effects. Haraway's comments on the way Americans from the turn of the century through to the end of the 1920s 'read' Africa can be usefully extended to take in Hemingway:

> From 1890 to 1930, the 'Nature Movement' was at its height in the United States. Ambivalence about 'civilization' is an old theme in US history, and this ambivalence was never higher than after the Civil War, and during the early decades of monopoly capital formation. Civilization, obviously, refers to a complex pattern of domination of people and everybody (everything) else, often ascribed to technology – fantasized as 'the Machine.' Nature is such a potent symbol of innocence partly because 'she' is imagined to be without technology, to be the object of vision, and so a source of both health and purity.

Hemingway wished both to enter the vision and to objectify it, but otherwise the analogy stands (though by the time he returned to Africa in the 1950s such a construct was no longer so easily available). Indeed the idea of health and purity can be extended in his case to take in not just Africa, but also the Spain and those earlier versions of America to which I have already referred; all rural landscapes where the presence of simpler, more 'primitive' forms of society offered the apparent 'promise of restored manhood'.[33] Hemingway's focus on hunting and fishing, and on physical confrontation with the natural world, fit such a conceptual frame.

In a letter written soon after the end of the Spanish Civil War, Hemingway wrote to Patrick:

> Ben Finney was out in Africa and is absolutely crazy about it. . . . He says that your slogan 'Papa, if Africa is like you say it is we are fools to be here.' is his motto now. He says we ought to all go out there and I think he is probably right. (*L*, 487)

In terms of my argument, Africa is similar to the version of Spain offered in the bullfighting texts, in that it was not like Hemingway said it was. If Africa is one more version of 'home' in his writing, it can be so precisely because he is able to domesticate and contain his representation of its space and culture in a way that suits his personal needs. Africa becomes a limited province of the (white) American imagination in which dreams of autonomous manhood and of communion with nature can be acted out in an unspoiled (that is, pre-industrial) setting:

> Hemingway's Africa was clearly as much a territory of the mind and spirit and imagination as it was geographical reality; it was the Africa of myth . . . that of the collective imagination of the Western world . . . the Africa of wonder.[34]

Hemingway's first and most interesting book about Africa is the much underrated *Green Hills of Africa*. He claims in the Foreword to have tried to write an 'absolutely true' book which might compete with 'a work of the imagination'. In its highly crafted nature, in its shaping and patterning of a country and a life, this 'formally ambitious work'[35] extends the limits of the conventional non-fictional travelogue; it becomes a type of experiment in what would now be called 'new journalism'. The narrative is shaped both artistically and imaginatively to clear ends, and charts an initiation ritual. This is a physical and spiritual journey: a discovery of the value of Africa for a protagonist who continues to stumble in the movement toward renewal and cleansing that his experience there offers, but whose move in that direction is clear. Africa functions as an unspoiled territory where 'decadence . . . decay's contagion, the germ of civilization' can be combated by a narrator who 'restor[es] manhood in the healthy activity of sportsmanlike hunting'.[36]

The need for such a restorative is raised as an issue in the narrative in several forms. Illness is a condition shared by both the narrator and, metaphorically, the country from which he comes. The former is physically weak at the start of the narrative (in terms of its story time), having been ill with dysentery back in Nairobi (*GH*, 44). He gains strength and attains a 'feeling of well being' (*GH*, 50) while hunting. He is still, however, ill at the narrative's end, but the form of this (different) illness deserves comment. For the disease he has caught, not in Africa but on the dirty boat from Marseilles in coming there, necessitates 'washing a three-inch bit of my large intestine . . . and tucking it back where it belonged an unnumbered amount of times a day' (*GH*, 213). I do not wish to indulge in fanciful interpretation, but the detailing of such an

unusual(!) physical condition is striking in such a carefully pat-
terned text. Connotative networks of meaning appear evident on
returning to the earlier powerful image of the hyena, which
represents the worst aspects of the wilderness (as scavenger and
'potential biter-off of your face at night while you slept'). The
hyena, when shot, circles crazily about, 'tearing at himself' until
finally he jerks out 'his own intestines . . . and eat[s] them with
relish' (*GH*, 37). The narrator's washing and tuckings back of his
intestines have cleansing and reparative weight in comparison
with this 'stinking, foul . . . camp-follower'. If the hyena can be
read as nature tainted by culture's contagions ('camp-follower'),
then the narrator moves in the opposite direction, purified by
contact with nature in the form of the beneficent African landscape.[37]

The use of sickness as a metaphor in the text relates to national
well-being as well as personal. Thirties America is in Depression. It
is the place where, according to Pop, 'No one knows how to
behave' (*GH*, 40). In the last chapter of the narrative, the
description of Africa as 'good country', as one of the 'good places
to go' is contrasted with America, a country made by its people 'a
bloody mess' (*GH*, 214–15).

The movement of *Green Hills of Africa* is away from 'the germ of
civilization' toward solitary immersion in a restorative landscape.
The narrator travels, in the course of the text, away from the traces
of civilisation. In the book's final section, unaccompanied by any
other whites – though not, note, hunting 'alone' as he and Pop
assume (*GH*, 160) – he follows a cattle track to reach 'a virgin
country, an un-hunted pocket in the million miles of . . . Africa'
(*GH*, 168). From there, clearly a type of last good place, the
narrator finally proceeds to shoot that kudu – 'the miracle' (*GH*,
177) of a kudu – which has been the primary object of his quest
right from the narrative's start. The lyric celebration of the dead
kudu that follows the finding of its body is the book's epiphany.
The stress on the aesthetic and sensual quality of the experience
(with references to sight, colour, smell, even by implication texture
and taste) and the shift toward the sentimental at the passage's end
seem out of kilter with the fact that it is a corpse that is being
described:

It was a huge, beautiful kudu bull, stone-dead. . . . I looked

at . . . the great, curling, sweeping horns, brown as walnut meat,
and ivory pointed, at . . . the great, lovely heavy-maned neck . . .
and I stooped over and touched him to try and believe it . . . he
smelled sweet and lovely like the breath of cattle and the odor of
thyme after rain. (*GH*, 176–7)

It is at this point that the natives signal by the form of their
handshakes a relationship with the narrator 'on the order of blood
brotherhood but a little less formal' (*GH*, 220). The fact that this
information is given right at the end of the narrative reinforces its
importance: 'it is . . . as though the narrator has truly moved as far
into the clean new world as he can go and where the Romans
[natives with 'ancient characteristics'] and Masai now accept him
as an equal';[38] where he and they have moved beyond 'the bar of
language' (*GH*, 192). In capturing, through hunting, the essence of
the beauty at the heart of the wilderness, the narrator has moved
beyond speech to become one with that 'primitive' native world
seen as a source of health and physical and psychic vitality. The
apparent paradox remains, however, that it is in death (of the
kudu) that the narrator finds life.
The fact that the description of the dead kudu figures so
crucially in the text relates obviously to the centrality of hunting
and killing in the book. To recall the discussion of killing in *Death
in the Afternoon*, the giving of death is seen as man 'taking to
himself one of the Godlike attributes'. Hunting cleanly, Hemingway wrote, 'has always been one of the greatest enjoyments of a
part of the human race'. It is associated 'with the 'best elation of
all, of certain action to come . . . in which you can kill and come
out of it'.[39] Hunting as desired activity is directly compared early
in the text with being in the Prado (*GH*, 28). Both involve the
appreciation of different forms of aesthetic activity. In the former,
action and aesthetics combine as 'the pursuit of animals and the
act of killing them [translates] into a pursuit of beautiful images
and an act that arrests them so that they can be visually
appreciated'.[40] The problem with this (if we take it as an accurate
representation of Hemingway's attitude) is, of course, that arrest
and appreciation are synonymous with rigidification and the
life-denying. The admiration of the 'trophy' might recall, but it also
replaces, the vital grace of the creature as it freely moves in nature.
I am reminded of the frozen leopard in 'The Snows of Kilimanjaro',

a symbol of the eternal qualities of grace, beauty and vitality fixed, paradoxically, in absolutely rigid form.

While hunting in Africa, the narrator gains power. To hunt and to kill is to function as an autonomous individual exercising 'Godlike' authority. The narrative of *Green Hills of Africa* functions in a more complicated way than this suggests but does, nevertheless, tend in such a direction. To borrow from Donna Haraway's comments on Roosevelt (one of Hemingway's boyhood heroes): 'it is in the craft of killing that life is constructed'. The African scene becomes, in *Green Hills of Africa*, an imagined and unspoiled geography in which (white) manhood can be tested and proved. Any alternative (African) version of events is either marginalised or forgotten. Thus the fact that the road being travelled at the start of the book is marked by a native migration away from 'famine country' (*GH*, 17) bears no narrative weight, deserves no further explanation or development in a text that centres on the meaning of the white protagonist's final encounter with virgin landscape, handsome 'savage' and noble beast. Haraway discusses safari literature in which 'Africans were imagined as either "spoiled" or "unspoiled", like the nature they signified'.[41] That statement rings particularly true in reference to this text where there is a clearly traced move from the hyena to the kudu and, in its final stages, from the Wanderobo with the 'depraved-looking face' (*GH*, 159) and the theatrical 'bastard' whom the narrator nicknames 'Garrick', to the Masai, 'the tallest, best-built, handsomest people I had ever seen' (*GH*, 168).

As I have suggested, my brief analysis of this text does not do it full justice. For example, in its final hunting sections, the narrator reverts to earlier type, shooting badly at a sable bull and consequently engaging in a frustratingly comic/mysterious search for the wounded but vanished animal. Any notion of final triumph or of positive and enduring change is thus undercut. The move toward full integration with this landscape remains incomplete. The journey to Africa has, however, been one away from a complex (and self-diminishing) society to 'good country' where the self can become more whole, restored in its energy and effectiveness: 'I loved this country and I felt at home and where a man feels at home . . . is where he's meant to go' (*GH*, 213–14).

As time passed, however, Hemingway's favoured (home-like) spots gradually lost their value. Perhaps this was due to the fact that history cannot be stayed, because repetition (in the form of return visits) involved acknowledgement of socio-political and personal difference: in sum, that he had changed together with the country he was visiting. Hemingway returned to Africa in 1953. The published sections of *African Journal* (released posthumously) that describe this return commence with the words: 'Things were not too simple in this safari because things had changed very much in East Africa' (*AJ1*, 44). [42]

The idea of an African 'homecoming' has by this historical point become problematic. The narrator now recognises his status as an alien, a 'stranger', in Africa. The second part of *African Journal* starts with a list of his accoutrements as a hunter, all products of the international market: mosquito boots from Hong Kong, pyjamas from Idaho, whisky (presumably) from Scotland. There seems to be a recognition here that his own composite status (one who has moved between countries and who has bought in a market worldwide in scope) bars him from easy return to any one home. This particular unease, though temporarily dissolved by the whisky, is symptomatic of a more general unease. For, in writing up this trip, he comments on the way Africa has served as just another setting for Western moral failure, 'just been another place for more ample bitchery or fuller drunkenness' (*AJ2*, 28). The 'Fast International Sporting House Set' with which he (ironically?) identifies himself (*Byline*, 446–7) operates its own social codes and hierarchies with no regard for native culture. Tribal life too has changed, affected both by anti-colonial political activity and by international commercial influences. When he discusses the Masai, noble warriors in *Green Hills of Africa*, it is in terms of those of them who have

> unfortunately . . . taken up the habit of drinking due to their wealth and the inactivity of the men, who do not now kill the marauding lion nor engage in war. The warriors have generally, in this area, become addicted to a beverage manufactured in South Africa and shipped into the colony, which is known as Golden Jeep sherry. (*Byline*, 459)

An awareness of the impossibility now of constructing a version of Africa as 'pure' place unaffected by Western cultural forms, and of the increasing impact of modernisation and the commercial activity that tourism has bred, are implicit in the description of the 'rescue' that takes place after the Hemingways' plane crash at Murchison Falls. The boat that picks them up has been chartered as a pleasure outing (a golden wedding celebration) for British colonists, and the boat itself is that allegedly 'used in the motion picture called *The African Queen,* which starred two intrepid African characters called Katherine Hepburn . . . and Humphrey Bogart' (*Byline,* 440).

Of course, the safari that Hemingway had described in *Green Hills of Africa* had also been a form of tourist activity, deeply affecting the lives of those Africans who served the needs of the 'white hunter' and his clients. The economics of the enterprise are briefly hinted at in a passing comment by Pop on the cheapness of porters in comparison to petrol (*GH,* 98). The narrator's feeding of the dregs of his beer to the old man and giving of empty beer bottles, their labels and bottle caps, to the Masai all point in the direction of that cultural change which inevitably accompanied both tourist activity and the colonial enterprise.

However, the safari is still associated with the salvational in the writing about the 1950s visit; with a move back into the wilderness and to simpler forms of social relationships than those found in Nairobi or Laitokitok. Although aware of the changes that have occurred in Africa and the political tensions there, the narrator can only choose to evade their full implications by shifting attention to the safari. Here, despite changes in racial interactions and in the conditions of hunting, old hierarchies and relationships still generally prevail and the larger problems of colonialism can be put to one side in the step back into nature and in the activity of the chase.

The Wakamba head scout on the safari described in 'Miss Mary's Lion' is 'very soldierly'. G.C., in charge of the group, jokingly refers to the narrator as 'the brusque, semi-heroic, outmoded miracle type who brings them down like the bowmen at Crécy' (*AJ2,* 33–4). Simpler and truer forms of manliness, based on the 'warrior' type, can – the suggestion is – still find outlet for active self-expression on safari. The word 'outmoded' becomes one of praise here rather than one that points to any form of critical self-awareness.

There is, though, in these excerpts, a much more equivocal attitude to killing than that found generally in *Green Hills of Africa.*

For Hemingway writes that 'the time of shooting beasts for trophies was long past with me' (*AJ1*, 60). Referring to a coat made from the hides of cheetah shot on the first Africa trip, he goes on to say that he does not want to disturb a cheetah he now sees; that 'their skins belonged on their own backs and not across any woman's shoulders' (*AJ3*, 27). The hunt, however, is still the centre of the narrative: the 'rogue' status of the lion, in the case of 'Miss Mary's Lion', making its killing acceptable and necessary. Once the lion's roar is heard, a certain unease about hunting is replaced by its celebration:

> it was the start of that wonderful thing: the hunt . . . hunting . . .
> is something that is probably much older than religion. . . .
> Mary . . . [was] trained . . . into the purity and virtue of killing a
> lion by Pop who had made her his last pupil.

A laying-on of the hands takes place here as Pop hands on his (sacred) knowledge to Mary. Hunting is equated with both grace ('purity and virtue') and happiness: 'Probably no one is as happy as hunters with the always new, fresh, unknowing day ahead' (*AJ2*, 36).

On safari, virgin territory can be recovered: 'you and your disreputable companions made what tracks there are and you can make a few new ones' (*AJ1*, 45). The safari provides an escape from historical disturbance. The Mau Mau, in fact, paradoxically protect the sense of harmony between self and landscape; they are 'owed . . . a considerable debt' for discouraging tourist intruders from a 'world where bores can now move from place to place so rapidly' (*AJ3*, 25). On safari, pure country and innocent recovery of idyll are realised: 'There are always mystical countries that are a part of one's childhood. . . . In Africa . . . we had such countries' (*AJ1*, 47). The process and complications of history, though recognised by Hemingway in these later writings, are still resisted in favour of the attempt to recapture original rapture outside or on the margins of its province.

Politics do intrude, if minimally, into these narratives. For Africa is not just an idyllic garden where true manhood (or exceptionally – in Mary's case – womanhood) can be effected and displayed in the hunt. It is also in political turmoil: this is southern Kenya during the Mau Mau uprising. When Harry Steele, a Kenyan police officer arrives in camp, reference is made to the trouble and to the man Steele has just lost: 'the sergeant chopped into pieces and mutilated in the last week' (*AJ*2, 38). We have two different narratives here, which are in fact irreconcilable: one of the testing of manhood in a (by and large) stress-free pastoral realm; the other of historical strife. Both here in 'Miss Mary's Lion' and at the start of 'The Christmas Gift', where another reference to the 'war' taking place occurs, a shift swiftly occurs to other subject matter with no attempt at all to explain the causes for, or develop the details of, the political situation. I would suggest that this is precisely because Africa for Hemingway had been constructed as a type of 'pure' landscape where man and nature could interact without the pressures of history and politics. Although he cannot help but be aware of the problems now emerging in those latter areas and does in fact refer to them in these writings, their intrusion cannot be contained by his version of Africa as idyll – as home. 'The Christmas Gift' is not set on safari. In it, contemporary problems and changes are alluded to, though never fully explored. But generally its fragmented and uneasy status as a narrative contrasts strongly with the overall power and coherence of the writing about safari.[43]

This reading of the African material is tentative. One theme of *African Journal* was evidently to be 'bloody and topical, involving the Mau Mau, the police and the weakening of British colonial rule in Kenya',[44] and it may be that in the 200,000 word unpublished manuscript Hemingway does this subject full justice. In the published material that I have been able to obtain, however, the references to contemporary African history are not fully developed or integrated in a coherent narrative frame. Thus 'The Christmas Gift' lacks formal control and covers a wide and at times almost incoherent range of subject matter. There is a very uneasy tone to the piece as it moves between the serious, the ironic, the satiric, the whimsical and the nostalgic. There are very few of the kind of descriptions of nature as sanctuary found elsewhere in the African writing and the focus on the two air crashes that occurred at this time – and from which it would seem that Hemingway never fully recovered[45] – not only points toward a desperate decline in the author's physical and mental powers, but also gives the article the only narrative coherence it seems to have: a move from disaster to disaster. Modern Africa may be the location of this article, but his focus on personal catastrophe suggests both his artistic unease with contemporary political materials (he says that 'Africa is very complicated' in 'Miss Mary's Lion' – *AJ*2, 38) and his sense of having reached some kind of an end of the road there: an ending given symbolic form in the air crashes. The release of more of the African materials may modify such an analysis.

I end this section by looking at one of Hemingway's best African stories, 'The Short Happy Life of Francis Macomber'. Again the form of his fiction encourages an engagement with complexities and ambiguities which by and large the non-fiction either does not recognise, avoids or fails satisfactorily (in both formal and thematic terms) to pursue. This is all to do with narrative viewpoint. In the non-fiction the controlling voice of the central author-protagonist means, in *Green Hills of Africa* anyway, that despite the narrator's attraction to, and acceptances of the difference of, African culture, we are still left finally with an ethnocentric version of the African 'other'. The text is scattered with references to 'niggers' (*GH*, 69), 'black Chinaman' – a joke on the narrator's part directed at M'Cola (*GH*, 208) – 'niggery legs' (*GH*, 190) and 'savage' (*GH*, 200).

'The Short Happy Life of Francis Macomber' is, in contrast, a fiction that works to deny any definitive single reading. Because the issue of point of view (focalisation) is raised as crucial in the text and because the narrative voice is predominantly unobtrusive, so generally neutral in its presentation of information, the reader is left between versions (of a story; of a country; of ways of seeing and being). My contention is that generally, and whatever the authorial intention, Hemingway's fictional texts resist closure. The formal techniques he developed early in his career to represent an unease about subjectivity and its relationship to the objective world and to reflect his sense of the broken and fragmentary nature of existence, never let him down; rather, they kept him more open-minded than he sometimes knew.

In this story, a series of voices and points of view are represented. The one voice, however, given little to say is the African voice. We are told, when Macomber shoots the lion and it has run into the tall grass, that the gun-bearers beside him 'were . . . chattering, in Wakamba' (*WTN*, 19), but what they say is left untranslated. Later, after the shooting of the two buffalo, one of the gun-bearers calls out to Wilson in Swahili, and this is translated on Margot's request: 'He says the first bull got up and went into the bush' (*WTN*, 33). The same gun-bearer speaks to

Wilson while they are tracking the wounded animal, and his words are presumably rendered in translation by Wilson's, 'He's dead in there' (*WTN*, 37). This as it happens is inaccurate and helps to cause Macomber's death. Malicious intent is presumably absent, given that the bearer puts his own life at risk by running forward toward the animal. Apart from that, the only words said by the Africans are 'Yes, Bwana' (*WTN*, 20), the reply the driver gives to Robert Wilson when, presumably, he is given some command. Given Hemingway's general technique where the silences of the text speak as loudly as what is actually said, I would suggest that it is impossible to ignore the issue of race in this short story: that it is not only about the relationships between the three central white characters but also about the relationship between the colonial master class (as represented by the white hunter, Robert Wilson, and his clients) and the native 'other'.

In terms of focalisation, the native point of view is also fairly comprehensively suppressed; represented in much less detail overall, for instance, than that of the lion at which Macomber shoots. The two lengthy passages that describes what the lion sees and feels (*WTN*, 18, 22) can be set against the few brief sequences where the native perspective is given. This perspective can sometimes be implied through external description of expression: the gloomy looks of the gun-bearers when it comes to finishing off the lion (*WTN*, 22); the gloom and disgust on one of their faces when he reports that one of the buffaloes is still alive (*WTN*, 33). It is given on one occasion, mediated through Wilson, in the form of those details necessary to explain the wounded buffalo's action: the gun-bearer's view of the bull's partial recovery after it had first been shot down (*WTN*, 34). In another instance, Wilson sees 'Macomber's personal boy looking curiously at his master' (*WTN*, 10): the black perspective again mediated through the white character. Only once are we given internal focalisation, and directly told by the narrator what the black character is feeling: the two bearers looking at Macomber 'in contempt' (*WTN*, 23) when he shows his cowardice; in this they are at one with their white 'master'. For the most part, however, the black perspective is marginalised.

This is true also in terms of black identity, which is entirely in terms of function or status in the safari hierarchy. We are given headman, mess boy, personal boy, cook, skinner, porter, driver and

gun-bearer, rather than name, thought or feeling. Names are given
on three occasions, Kongoni (twice) and Abdulla. They convey no
clear sense of individual identity, however, especially when contrasted with the almost constant use of the names of the three
central (white) characters. For the most part the Africans are
referred to in terms of function or as 'boys'. In her discussion of
the safaris undertaken by the Akeleys over a thirty-year period,
Donna Haraway refers to the photographs taken of 'usually
solemn African people in a semi-circle around the core of white
personnel, with the cars, cameras, and abundant baggage in the
background' as 'eloquent about race, sex, and colonialism'. Many
of the details of this story speak eloquently on the same subjects.
The very epithet 'boys', for example, is part of that 'casual and
institutional racism' (again to use Haraway) which marks the
behaviour of Wilson in particular, and which Macomber goes
along with. Wilson's words that 'in Africa no woman ever misses
her lion and no white man ever bolts' (*WTN*, 11) puts the meeting
of 'the singular man and animal' at the centre of the stage of action
and meaning. 'Nature' in such a scenario becomes a 'worthy foil to
his [the white man's] manhood', with white woman 'empowered
by race and class . . . stand[ing] in a similar moral position as
white man –a hunter, an adult'.[46]

Although the narrative voice in this story echoes Wilson's
'casual racism' in its use of the word 'boys' to describe the
Africans, it might be argued that this voice functions as an
extension of the dominant viewpoint, merely reflecting the conceptual focalisation of the central characters – a common tactic in
Hemingway. The point must remain unresolved. It is, however,
interesting that Hemingway should comment on precisely this
issue in the later non-fiction, identifying himself with a position in
the 1930s similar, in this respect at least, to that associated with
Wilson in the fiction: 'Once they had been "the boys". . . . Twenty
years ago . . . neither they nor I had any thought that I had no
right to [call them boys]. . . . But the way things were now you did
not do it' (*AJ1*, 45–6). There seems here to be a case of trust the tale
not the teller, in that Hemingway's argument about accepted
norms – that the term 'boys' was a 'natural' one at that time and
no one thought twice about it – is contradicted by the fictional text,
where it is exactly this that becomes, if briefly, a point of issue.

For it is noticeable in this narrative that Mrs Macomber resists

Wilson's way of viewing the world. After the lion has been killed and Wilson has said that 'Boys will skin him out', we move to Margot's focalisation as she looks at 'the black men flesh[ing] away the skin'. Again, though the relation between the narrative voice and character focalisation is problematic here, the former appears to signal a resistance on Margot's part to the use of the term 'boys' for 'men' that is part, I would argue, of a more general resistance to the white male reading of Africa (a dominant reading that the black servant may have come to accept, as the shared contempt for Macomber's 'cowardice' may indicate). It is clear that Margot questions Wilson's version of vital virility. Her irony, as she tells her husband that 'I want *so* to see you perform again. You were lovely this morning. That is if blowing things' heads off is lovely' (*WTN*, 12), acts to combat that view of hunting as a cure for decadence and a mark of true manhood which her husband comes to share with Wilson. Her comment about, and question to, Wilson have the same effect: 'Mr Wilson is really very impressive killing anything. You do kill anything, don't you?' (*WTN*, 12). Kenneth Lynn has questioned traditional readings of this story as miso-gynist. His reading points to the narrative statement that 'Mrs Macomber . . . had shot at the buffalo . . . as it seemed about to gore Macomber' (*WTN*, 38) as clear evidence of her innocent intent. And he sees Wilson's accusations of murder as a counter against the knowledge that she can ruin his career by exposing his breaking of the law governing methods of hunting (a law that accords in fact with the generally accepted codes of the sport) by 'chasing those big helpless things in a motor car' (*WTN*, 32).

I would suggest that, as in so many of Hemingway's stories, the narrative tactics result in the reader being left uncomfortably stranded between positions. Macomber's finding of courage and thus 'manhood' certainly cannot be dismissed nor can Wilson's own bravery in the face of danger. But Margot's perspective is equally valid, and presented as such by the text. Lynn's description of the negative version of Wilson is a convincing one:

the Englishman's face is red; indeed, it is very red; indeed, it is baked red. The emphasis hints at his bloodymindedness – at his British colonial bloodymindedness, for in the thirties carto-graphers were still coloring the British Empire red. 'Flat, blue, machine-gunner's eyes' . . . are further indications of Wilson's coarse and unappetizing nature, and they are confirmed beyond doubt by his reaction to the mess boy [threatened with an illegal lashing, for an apparently disrespectful look, on the callous grounds that 'they prefer it to . . . fines'].[47]

The fact that Wilson responds to Mrs Macomber's comment that his face is 'always red' with the retort 'Must be racial' (*WTN*, 9) backs up the first part of this reading.

The narrative also strands us between the position of the white 'master' race and that of the powerless black colonial 'servant'. The issue of authority is foregrounded in the story. 'They govern, of course' (*WTN*, 13), Wilson notes of Margot as paradigm of American womanhood, but the gender issue raised here (who governs whom and how) can equally be transferred to the area of race. Wilson governs by command and threat. The Africa to which Margot and Francis come is one constructed imaginatively for the psychic and emotional needs of the white visitors, as the society columnist's report of their trip as a romantic adventure emphasises (*WTN*, 25). If Wilson makes his living by 'the international, fast, sporting set' whom he 'despised' in their absence (*WTN*, 29), so the blacks in this story make their living in turn from Wilson and his clients. We do not see their perspective fully enough to know their attitude to their employer/'master'. The problem of translation is one suggested in the constant references to the Macombers' ignorance and Wilson's knowledge of the native languages. The fact that the black voice is marginalised, filtered almost entirely through Wilson, points to the absence of a different side to this story: an absence highlighted by an almost constant black physical presence. This other story is one of colonial exploitation, cruel authority, the denial of the worth of the black subject.

I am claiming here, once more, that in Hemingway's fiction we find a far more open-ended and ambiguous version of the relation between the tourist and the visited cultural space than we find in the non-fiction. This is not to say that the non-fiction is completely unaware of the problems foregrounded in the fiction nor that it is one-dimensional. The fiction, though, explores – in a way that his writings in the non-fiction mode never quite do – the problems involved in the construction of a different culture and landscape as a 'primitive' arena where he who is alienated from his own modernised country can find a 'home'; where self-expression and satisfaction are potentially attainable in ways denied elsewhere.

V

Philip Young writes in *Byline* that 'many of [Hemingway's] favourite places were by [his last years] permanently spoiled for him', and goes on to quote Hemingway's question, 'Where the hell does a man go now?', and answer: 'the sea is still ok. And the unpopular mountains' (*Byline*, 408). The move here is beyond society (and history) to 'pure nature' and in particular to the sea: 'It's the last free place there is, the sea. Even Africa's about gone.'[48] Referring to the sea in Conrad's *Lord Jim*, Jameson calls it a 'non-place' which is also 'the space of the degraded language of romance and daydream'. This could be reapplied to Hemingway, with his stress on the pleasure of deep-sea fishing in a location at one remove from social pressure and complexity. Such activity becomes, again to nod in the direction of Jameson, an expression of private feeling and of 'sensory intensity'; a last ditch (and asocial) form of defence against, and attempt to avoid, the networks of a modernised and systematised world, which are in fact unavoidable.[49] It is the sea that becomes the last pure space for Hemingway; the last version of 'home'.

In a famous sequence in *Green Hills of Africa*, Hemingway sets the purity and permanence of nature against the dross of civilisation. The Gulf Stream, he writes, 'has moved, as it moves, since before man', and, despite all the 'garbage' dumped into it, remains 'as clear and blue and unimpressed as it ever was . . . one single, lasting thing – the stream (*GH*, 116–17). This powerfully romantic vision posits nature as separate from man; as a 'pure' space, unable to be contaminated by him. As Gregory, Hemingway's son, would caustically note in his later description of the polluted Gulf Stream: 'even the sea can endure only so much'.[50] The inevitability of this final spoilage was never recognised or reported by Hemingway. The sea – a type of romantic non-place (nature in untainted form) – was where Hemingway found his very last good country and the only one in which he never lost belief. The processes of history, as Gregory recognised, proved such a belief illusory.

There are a whole series of paradoxes in Hemingway's position as represented in the non-fictional material examined here. His delight in bullfighting, fishing and hunting relates to their status as forms of repetitive diversion. They provide an apparent step outside the controls of a dominant and self-diminishing modernised culture to a 'free' space where 'unique selfhood'[51] can be expressed in acts of skilful domination over nature. Such free space is, however, illusory. The realisation of self through the 'isolated consumption' of what the ocean, Spain or Africa can offer, and the avoidance of 'social complexity' that this entails, becomes a mere indicator of what others (the majority) necessarily lack and will, once financial resources are available, come to share and thus alter. It is only through wealth or privilege that a constricting social reality can be temporarily countered. But such an apparent counter is only an indicator of the further spread of the dominant system; a pointer toward exactly that social complexity that would be avoided. For this form of consumption predicts the opening up of a leisure and tourist market for others who seek (temporary) self-gratification; who wish to take 'extended holidays to "primitive" places',[52] and who will, in so doing, inevitably affect the cultural and commercial forms of the place that they visit (Pamplona with its forty thousand tourists).

Such forms are in constant process of alteration. The individual tourist only mirrors what occurs at a larger economic level. In the modernised world, 'empty' markets are constantly bought into and colonised. The larger forms of international commercial activity simultaneously exploit (for money rather than for pleasure) those places where the wages are cheap, as well as the living. Mary Hemingway says that to reach 'Fig Tree Camp', one of the stages on the 1953 safari, they had to pass through 'the ugly, treeless town of Magadi, where the Imperial Chemical Industries Company runs a soda factory'.[53] The quest for 'free' space in a modernised world is a futile one.

A further paradox in the non-fiction (and in the details of Hemingway's life) lies in the fact that if selfhood is expressed through acts of violence in nature, such a 'proclaiming of his own uniqueness also necessitated a destruction or diminishment of the natural world which [Hemingway] loved and revered'.[54] This does get explicit treatment in the non-fiction, if only briefly. The later fictions, though, explore this particular issue more fully and show clear awareness of the paradox involved. This is most noticeable in *The Old Man and the Sea* where action and dream are in tension with one another. The old man's struggle with the marlin and its destruction consequent on his act of prideful overreaching ('I went out too far' – *OMS*, 104) is positioned in oppositional relation to the image of the 'long, golden beaches [of Africa] and the white beaches, so white they hurt your eyes' with 'the lions . . . play[ing] like young cats in the dusk' there (*OMS*, 18–19), which comes to him as he sleeps. Two versions of nature and man's relation to it exist in unreconciled tension here, placed in the separate realms of doing and dreaming.

In the story about Africa which is partly told toward the end of *The Garden of Eden*, the father's shooting of the elephant and removal of its tusks is linked to his replacement as 'hero' (*GE*, 218–19) in his son's mind by that elephant he has slaughtered. It is this 'great elephant' (*GE*, 197) that David 'betrays' to his father. In this father–son conflict and its basis in the destruction of nature versus the love and respect for its forms, we get a picture of those internal conflicts that went largely undeveloped in the author's life (as represented in the non-fiction). The fact that the final resolution that does occur is in the direction of reverence rather than violence may point in the direction of a final 'change of sensibility' on Hemingway's part.[55]

6
Coda: *A Moveable Feast*

Jackson Benson speaks of the 'posthumous cosmetology' carried out on *The Dangerous Summer* and *The Garden of Eden*, two of the books published since Hemingway's death. He calls them 'open casket literature' in the trimmings and pastings that make up their eventual composition.[1] Such a description seems overly harsh. I prefer Roger Asselineau's comparison of the posthumous work to 'mutilated statues whose pieces have been put carefully together, but many fragments are missing and the statues we have before us do not correspond to exactly what Hemingway had in mind'.[2]

The extent of the piecing together that has been involved is still under review. What has become clear, however, is that the process has been more extensive than was first realised and includes texts like *A Moveable Feast*.[3] A mutilated statue, however, is better than nothing (though Benson would not agree) and, unlike the marble busts that Frederic Henry notices in Catherine Barkley's hospital, these (literary) remainders certainly do not have the 'quality of all looking alike' (*FA*, 25). Instead, they provide an extra and revealing dimension to our knowledge of the author's work.

A Moveable Feast was the first of the works to be published posthumously and, like *Green Hills of Africa*, it provides us with a version of the writer as protagonist which we must be wary of taking too literally. The book commences with such a recognition (*MF*, 9). Statues appear in this text, too, when Hemingway takes Fitzgerald over to the Louvre to check out the size of his penis (Zelda has made disparaging comments on his sexual build) against 'the people in the statues' (*MF*, 126). This incident follows fast on the 'Hawks Do Not Share' chapter, ostensibly about Zelda, but which also discusses the writing of *The Sun Also Rises*. Issues of sexuality and writing come together here when we remember that letter to Fitzgerald where he followed the title of the book with the (playful) words: 'like your cock if you have one . . . a greater Gatsby' (*L*, 231). Hemingway also shows himself as a hawk who does not share; a man alone in his artistic integrity and creativity. For he says of Fitzgerald's anxiousness to help him with the novel, 'Scott did not see it until after the . . . manuscript had been sent to Scribner's. . . . I did not want his help while I was rewriting' (*L*, 123).

Just as the myth of Hemingway's acute poverty in Paris, so central to *A Moveable Feast*, has been revealed as untrue,[4] so this version of literary production is flawed. Fitzgerald both read and commented on *The Sun Also Rises* and it was on his advice that Hemingway cut two chapters before publication.[5] What presents itself as literal autobiography is in fact the construction of the myth of a self. Stories about comparative penis measurements and about the process of writing have a powerful joint metaphoric weight. Fitzgerald's failure to influence Hemingway artistically and his lack of confidence in his own masculinity both act to endorse Hemingway's (mythical) sense of his own status as independent artist and self-assured man.[6]

A Moveable Feast, then, uses prior experience to build, retrospectively, a preferred version of the writerly self. The book, however, also 'unconsciously tracks' Hemingway's 'literary . . . physical and psychological decline'.[7] Echoes of loss run through the book, connected primarily with his relationship with his first wife, Hadley. The story of the making of the writer is also that of his unmaking. Hemingway returns to his Paris youth in this text, in his desire to recover 'a past paradisal scene of writing'; to recapture his artistic life before the fall. Louis Renza makes a convincing case for such a reading and suggests that the nature of this fall was away from his 'original project [of] . . . writing "truly"' toward a catering for public (rather than private) demand: a writing 'subject to public consumption, evaluation, influence'.[8] Renza's argument is complex and contains (recognised) ambiguities. What I wish to focus on here, though, is the twin impulse both to recall an original (and impossible) state of writerly grace (associated with the early work) and to attempt in some form to repeat it at the end of Hemingway's literary career.

This ties in with my comments on the role of the artist in my

chapter on gender role, and with those on the geography of
Hemingway's fiction in my last chapter. In the latter, I suggested
that a desire is evident in Hemingway for a return to a rural or
'primitive' space where the self might function autonomously in a
way denied by the conditions of modernity. Such a desire I saw as
wholly illusory. The same kind of backward glance toward earlier
forms of wholeness and self-completion is also evident in *A
Moveable Feast*. The difference here, though, is that it is the self as
fiction writer that finds its completion – even its perfection – in the
remembered past. Paris becomes the place where, 'in those days',
Hemingway the hunger artist 'worked better than [he] had ever
done' (*MF*, 68).

A *Moveable Feast* represents the writer in a state of original grace.
Writerly style had – and would continue to have – utopian connotations for Hemingway. Through it a concrete world could be
created that could outdo and replace the actual historical world. In
A Moveable Feast, however, both worlds were complementary. In
Paris, nothing could (at first) stand in the way of Hemingway's
expression of his artistic self. Standing within history, he is at the
same time unaffected by it – a figure whose vocation and privileged point of view act as an index of an (illusory) full and
autonomous subjectivity. In the expression of this self, though,
Hemingway as artist could further create a separate world: an
authentic version of 'essential' reality that would then survive
always, in its tactile physicality, outside of historical process. This is
a highly romantic version of what the artist can do.

For Hemingway, to write 'purely enough' was to step outside or
beyond history and create something that 'would be . . . valid . . .
in ten years or, with luck . . . always' (*DA*, 8). Although he would
pursue this artistic intent throughout his career, it is noticeable that
he associates such 'pure' writing, both here – and in 'On Writing'[9]
and *The Garden of Eden*, two of the fictions in which he treats the
same subject – with the figure of the young artist. 'Pure' writing
carried you away from the actual historical world into an alternative and equally real sensory world: 'you would . . . sharpen the
pencil carefully . . . then . . . feel the pine needles under your
moccasins as you started down for the lake'. Such an artistic
project acted as a form of utopian activity. To rewrite the world in
terms of perception and sensation was to create an ahistorical other
world of *eternal* worth and validity that could be entered at will.

You could actually 'make the country so that you could walk into it' (*MF*, 64) and continue always to do so. No writing can remove spatial–temporal boundaries or elide the gap between word and world. Hemingway's portrayal of his attempt to do so, and of its success, is sheer utopian fantasy; one of a return to a lost (and impossible) unity between word and world and between real, concrete thing and aesthetic and 'eternal' art object. The presence he seeks/says that he recovers is mediated by writing, and that mediation and the difference it represents cannot be transcended.

What we have in *A Moveable Feast,* then, is a text written in Hemingway's final years in which he returns to the time of his writerly beginnings. These beginnings are associated in turn with the practice of a 'true' and original form of writing uninfluenced by market pressures and able to bridge the word/world divide. The possibility of practising such an original form of writing is, however, subject to doubt from the first. Renza claims that this is revealed in displaced and metaphoric form throughout *In Our Time,* and especially in 'Big Two-Hearted River'. There, he sees Hemingway as equating fishing and writing, both of which are associated with pleasure, skill, private satisfaction and achievement. Nick acts in the story as his 'surrogate Adamic (or original) writer . . . fish[ing] or writ[ing] in his own private camp or scene of writing'. However, Hemingway's doubts about the very possibility of writing in a radically new way, in a context where audience, market and critics are a fact of literary life, are suggested by the displacement (and sense of difference) that his use of the fishing metaphor introduces (for fishing is identified *also* with an '*escape* from the demand to write'). Such doubts emerge too in the gulf that lies within the story between private camp and public space and the restriction of Nick's fishing to the former realm. To translate metaphorically, writing for private pleasure can have a kind of purity to it that writing for the market lacks. To bring the work to public attention is inevitably to compromise that purity.[10]

The original and essentially 'true' writing that Hemingway sought to practice was, in fact, unrealisable. Both the limits of language itself and the fact of prior literary influence and audience expectation worked against it. This is, however, in *A Moveable Feast,* never recognised. Instead, the text seeks to recapture the idyllic writerly past, returning to the Paris so artistically precious to him and recalling both how he felt at that time and the actual process of composition of the text, *In Our Time*, then being written (but still, at that point, unfinished). In repeating this past, Hemingway puts himself back into his former shoes and writes again of the scenes that were so important to him then. The text thus comes to read as a type of autobiographical supplement to *In Our Time*.

In 'On Writing', Nick Adams is presented as a writer and one who seems responsible for the stories in which he acts as protagonist. As a writer, however, Nick insists on the difference between life and art, as the former's materials are subjected to the power of what Hemingway (who insisted similarly) would call invention. Thus he writes: 'Nick in the stories was never himself. He made him up. Of course he'd never seen an Indian woman having a baby. That was what made it good. . . . He'd seen a woman have a baby on the road to Karagatch and tried to help her. That was the way it was' (*NAS*, 238). Hemingway here creates as fictional protagonist a writer whose experiences bear a (sometimes close) relationship to his own. This writer creates, in his turn, a fictional persona (with his own name) whose experiences similarly relate to his own. Voices differ but voices merge.

So also, in writing *A Moveable Feast*, Hemingway's voice merges, at the end of his career, with the voice he had used in his early fiction. When he writes in *A Moveable Feast*

> The waiter brought me a *café crème* and I . . . left it on the table while I wrote. When I stopped writing I did not want to leave the river where I could see the trout in the pool. . . . The story was about coming back from the war but there was no mention of the war in it (*MF*, 56)

he could easily be Nick discoursing 'On Writing'. In *A Moveable Feast*, memory transports the author back to 'the early days' (*MF*, 140) and invests the whole text with a quality of nostalgic desire. This in turn allows Hemingway to repeat some of his best writerly effects, capture his best prose rhythms, as he takes the reader with him into the clean, sharp and idyllic world of the past. The following reads like a first-person retrospective supplement to 'Cross-Country Snow':

> I remember the trails up through . . . the fields of the hillside farms above the village. . . . I remember the smell of the

pines . . . and the skiing through the forests following the tracks of hares and of foxes. . . . I remember following the track of a fox until I came in sight of him and watching him stand with his right forefoot raised and then go carefully to stop and then pounce, and the whiteness and the clutter of a ptarmigan bursting out of the snow and flying away and over the ridge. (*MF*, 133, 136)

Hemingway returns here to the past for present inspiration. He also signals this past as an area still to write about. He will return in the future to fill in what is still left unsaid about it. Writing that, though he has begun 'many stories' about 'bicycle racing', he has never 'written one that is as good as the races are', he continues:

But I will get the Vélodrome d'Hiver with the smoky light of the afternoon and the high-banked wooden track and the whirring sound the tyres made on the wood as the riders passed. . . . I will get the . . . noise of the motors with their rollers set out behind them. (*MF*, 48)

A curious sense of circularity comes, then, to mark this text. Returning to his writerly origins, Hemingway reworks the subject matter and repeats the stylistic nuances of that former period. The sentences used now are longer – a product, it seems, of the lyric intensity of the voice – but the sequential chains and the concentration on hard sensual detail remain the same. Writing at that moment, and intending to write in the future, about the past, the narrative he tells is one of inevitable loss and personal and artistic decline. But this narrative, which charts a fall from writerly grace and a loss of radical originality, comes to repeat something of that former grace and originality. The paradox is that this is not an original act but a later retraced version of it, and not the fiction of that original but autobiography. Hemingway ends up in this, the text he was writing in his last years,[11] coming back on himself, compulsively returning to scenes of past literary and personal meaning to find (again) the kind of emotional and artistic sustenance he was formerly able to find.

His ability to do this in *A Moveable Feast* is a double-edged sword. His powerful song of the past is at the same time a recognition both of that past's disappearance and of a loss of writerly promise that accompanied it. The irony lies in the fact that this original writing project was utopian and unrealisable. A private writing that collapses word/world distinctions just cannot be done. Hemingway's achievements were considerable. That his original intentions failed him marked out their impossibility rather than his lack. *A Moveable Feast*'s return to the subject of writerly origins and its story of decline is, at one and the same time, in its prose rhythms, its metaphoric shaping of its materials and the power of much of its writing, a striking illustration of just how successful and distinctive an artist he still remained at his life's end.

Notes

Chapter 1 Introduction

1. Anthony Burgess, 'Papa in Decline', *Observer*, 23 June 1985, p. 22.
2. Ihab Hassan, 'The Silence of Ernest Hemingway', in Melvin J. Friedman and John B. Vickery (eds), *The Shaken Realist: Essays in Modern Literature in Honor of Frederick J. Hoffman* (Baton Rouge: Louisiana State University Press, 1970) p. 14.
3. Robert Scholes, *Textual Power: Literary Theory and the Teaching of English* (New Haven, Conn.: Yale University Press, 1985) p. 38.
4. John Raeburn, 'Skirting the Hemingway Legend', *American Literary History*, vol. 1 (Spring 1989) no. 1, p. 206.
5. Quoted in John Raeburn, *Fame Became of Him: Hemingway as Public Writer* (Bloomington: Indiana University Press, 1984) pp. 138 and 153.
6. Peter Griffin, *Along With Youth: Hemingway, The Early Years* (New York and Oxford: Oxford University Press, 1985) p. 74.
7. Diane Johnson, 'Mama and Papa', *New York Times Book Review*, 19 July 1987, p. 3.
8. Raeburn, *Fame Became of Him*, p. 72. Diane Johnson, in 'Mama and Papa', points out that the version of manhood which Hemingway proposed was 'the received version of his time (for women too)' (p. 3). Carlos Baker's biography (1969) was the first to undercut the 'public' and heroic image of Hemingway. Biographies by Jeffrey Meyers (1985) and Kenneth S. Lynn (1987) completed the process. See bibliography for full details.
9. Kenneth S. Lynn, *Hemingway* (London: Simon and Schuster, 1989 [1987]).
10. Raeburn, *Fame Became of Him*, pp. 1, 11 and *passim*.
11. Michael Reynolds, *The Young Hemingway* (Oxford: Basil Blackwell, 1986) p. 5.
12. Scott Donaldson, *By Force of Will: The Life and Art of Ernest Hemingway* (New York: Viking, 1977) p. xiii.
13. T. J. Jackson Lears, *No Place of Grace: Antimodernism and the Transformation of American Culture, 1880–1920* (New York: Pantheon, 1981).

Chapter 2 Style: Personal Impressions

1. Georg Lukacs, 'Narrate or Describe?' [1936], in *Writer and Critic and Other Essays*, ed. and trans. by Arthur Kahn (London: Merlin, 1978) pp. 110–48. This quote pp. 132–3. Page references will be given in the text from henceforth, where appropriate.
2. Alfred Kazin, 'Hemingway the Painter', in Harold Bloom (ed.), *Modern Critical Views: Ernest Hemingway* (New York: Chelsea House, 1985) p. 206.
3. Paul Goodman, *Speaking and Language: Defence of Poetry* (New York: Random House, 1971) p. 181.
4. The majority of Hemingway's central protagonists are male. I therefore choose to use the male pronoun throughout.
5. Lukacs, 'Narrate or Describe?', pp. 144, 131.
6. Cecelia Tichi, *Shifting Gears: Technology, Literature, Culture in Modernist America* (Chapel Hill: North Carolina University Press, 1986) p. 229.
7. Lukacs, 'Narrate or Describe?', p. 134. Although Lukacs does not use the word 'impressionist' here, it is implicit in his argument. It is important to note that Hemingway's style varies greatly in the course of his career, so any generalisations I make must be treated with reservation. I restrict myself by and large here to Hemingway's early work as this is recognised as most typical in terms of his development of a distinctive stylistic signature.
8. Kazin, 'Hemingway the Painter', p. 206.
9. I follow, throughout this book, the distinction between modernisation (which I tend to equate here with modernity) and modernism made by Marshall Berman in his *All That is Solid Melts into Air: The Experience of Modernity* (London: Verso, 1983 [1982]). Modernisation refers to the process of late nineteenth-century and twentieth-century socio-historical change – urban and technological growth, increasing bureaucratisation, the development of a capitalist world market and so on. Modernism is in dialectic relationship to this: the 'visions and values' (p. 16) associated with those human subjects responding to this fast changing world. Modernism is a hetero-geneous movement and consists of a whole range of such visions and values. Hemingway's version of it is one resistant to modernisation (unlike, say, the Futurists). He describes, not modernity, but a version of it which threatens and inevitably diminishes the human subject. This version is not one that Lukacs would share; nor need we.
10. 'A style like Impressionism . . . discards even the operative fiction of some interest in the constituted objects of the natural world, and offers the exercise of perception and the perceptual recombination of sense data as an end in itself', Fredric Jameson, *The Political Unconscious: Narrative as a Socially Symbolic Act* (London: Methuen, 1983 [1981]) pp. 229–30. I acknowledge my overall debt to Jameson

and his critical terminology. I see the extreme nature of his statement here, though, as open to serious challenge.

11. Kazin, 'Hemingway the Painter', p. 206.
12. See Jameson on Conrad in *The Political Unconscious*, p. 236 for instance.
13. Robert Scholes discusses the processes of reading, interpretation and criticism, and applies them to interchapter vii of *In Our Time*, in *Textual Power* (New Haven, Conn.: Yale University Press, 1985) pp. 21–38. I have found his approach most helpful, though my arguments move in a different direction.
14. Quoted in Christopher Wilson, 'Containing Multitudes: Realism, Historicism, American Studies', *American Quarterly*, vol. 41 (1989) no. 3, p. 466.
15. Peter Schwenger, *Phallic Critiques: Masculinity and Twentieth-Century Literature* (London: Routledge and Kegan Paul, 1984) p. 39.
16. This connects with Lukacs, where naturalism and modernism are linked, not seen as alternatives. Both (determinism and subjectivism) are, for him, inadequate responses and malformations; evading what it means to function as a fully social being.
17. Jameson, *The Political Unconscious*, p. 221. I make his 'myths of the self' singular.
18. Ibid., pp. 239 and 221.
19. David Seed, '"The Picture of the Whole": *In Our Time*', in A. Robert Lee (ed.), *Ernest Hemingway: New Critical Essays* (London: Vision Press, 1983) p. 20. Seed's application of the phrase can be extended beyond his title text.
20. Michael Reynolds, *Hemingway: The Paris Years* (Oxford: Basil Blackwell, 1989) p. 39. For Hemingway's acknowledgement of his literary forebears, see *Writers at Work: The Paris Review Interviews*, selected by Kay Dick (Harmondsworth, Middx.: Penguin, 1972) p. 185. The argument I pursue in this chapter suggests Hemingway's particular close artistic relationship to Stephen Crane.
21. Jacob Korg, *Language in Modern Literature: Innovation and Experiment* (Sussex: Harvester, 1979) p. 37.
22. Quoted in Janice L. Doane, *Silence and Narrative: The Early Novels of Gertrude Stein* (Westport, Conn.: Greenwood Press, 1986) p. xii.
23. See Sara Mills, 'No Poetry for Ladies: Gertrude Stein, Julia Kristeva and Modernism', in David Murray (ed.), *Literary Theory and Poetry: Extending the Canon* (London: Batsford, 1989) pp. 85–107; especially p. 101.
24. It should be noted that Stein's prose work is diverse. Although much of it shares the qualities I have described, other parts of it do have a more secure narrative coherence and are less syntactically ruptured than I here imply.
25. Quoted in Laszlo Gefin, *Ideogram: History of a Poetic Method* (Austin: University of Texas Press, 1982) pp. 38–9.
26. Korg, *Language in Modern Literature*, pp. 9–10.
27. Quoted in ibid., p. 43.

28. Quoted in Linda Welshimer Wagner, *Hemingway and Faulkner: Inventors/Masters* (Metuchen, NJ: Scarecrow Press, 1975) p. 18.

29. See Jacqueline Tavernier-Courbin, 'Ernest Hemingway and Ezra Pound', in James Nagel (ed.), *Ernest Hemingway: The Writer in Context* (Madison: University of Wisconsin Press, 1984) p. 181.

30. Quoted in Gefin, *Ideogram*, p. 8.

31. Ibid., p. 8.

32. Kenneth S. Lynn, *Hemingway* (London: Simon and Schuster, 1989) pp. 197–8. Reynolds, *Hemingway: The Paris Years*, pp. 115–16.

33. Emily Stipes Watts, *Ernest Hemingway and the Arts* (Urbana: University of Illinois Press, 1971) p. 58. She suggests here the parallels between Hemingway's technique and that used by Goya in his 'The Disasters of War' etchings (1808–13): 'The attention of the viewer is forced upon the image of horror and suffering because of the very simplicity of the conception and design, or because of the few figures, the minimized background, and the clarity of action or scene.'

34. E. R. Hagemann argues otherwise in '"Only Let the Story End as Soon as Possible": Time-and-History in Ernest Hemingway's *In Our Time*', *Modern Fiction Studies*, vol. 26 (Summer 1980) no. 2, pp. 255–62. Putting in what Hemingway discards, he reinscribes the individual incident into a larger historical narrative, claiming that the vignettes (interchapters) 'become an entity when re-arranged chronologically . . . for what Hemingway has done is to reconstruct a decade, 1914–23' (p. 255). This, to my mind, is wishful thinking. It is exactly such historical detail that Hemingway chooses to omit.

35. Carlos Baker, 'The Way It Was', in Bloom (ed.), *Modern Critical Views: Ernest Hemingway*, pp. 95–6.

36. Quoted in Tavernier-Courbin, 'Ernest Hemingway and Ezra Pound', p. 183.

37. Quoted in Korg, *Language in Modern Literature*, p. 46.

38. See Gérard Genette, *Narrative Discourse*, trans. Jane E. Lewin (Oxford: Basil Blackwell, 1986 [1972]) pp. 48–9. 'First narrative' is a term that causes difficulty. It is best approached pragmatically, and Schlomith Rimmon-Kenan, glossing Genette, gives as good a definition as any: 'Both analepsis [flashback; 'a narration of a story-event at a point in the text after later events have been told'] and prolepsis [anticipation; 'narration of a story-event at a point before earlier events have been mentioned'] constitute a temporally second narrative in relation to the narrative onto which they are grafted, and which Genette calls "first narrative". The "first narrative", then, is – somewhat circularly – "the temporal level of narrative with respect to which an anachrony [a temporal disjunction] is defined as such"'. See *Narrative Fiction: Contemporary Poetics* (London: Methuen, 1983) pp. 46–7.

39. It is possible to trace all the chronological moves of the narrative, as Genette does with sections of Proust in his *Narrative Discourse*. I choose not to do so here for reasons of space. I will, however, make

some general points about the way in which these patternings work and will focus on one particular section of the text for more extended analysis.

40. 'How brilliant his spots were colored and how bright the edges of his fins . . . the lovely golden sunset color of his belly' ('The Last Good Country' – *NAS*, 110).
41. See Schlomith Rimmon-Kenan, 'The Paradoxical Status of Repetition', *Poetics Today*, vol. 1 (Summer 1980) no. 4, pp. 151–9.
42. Henry David Thoreau, *Walden or Life in the Woods* (London: J. M. Dent, 1912 [1854]) p. 58.
43. The text I am working from (the Grafton paperback) has 'normalised' this sequence by shifting the present back to the past tense – thus cancelling out the transgression (p. 127). All other texts I have consulted, however, use the present tense. I take my text as corrupt here.
44. David Wyatt, *Prodigal Sons: A Study in Authorship and Authority* (Baltimore, Md.: John Hopkins University Press, 1980) p. 54.
45. Michel Foucault, *The Order of Things: An Archeology of the Human Sciences* (London: Tavistock, 1982 [1966]) p. 310.
46. Quoted in Wagner, *Hemingway and Faulkner*, p. 47.
47. Kenneth G. Johnston, *The Tip of the Iceberg: Hemingway and the Short Story* (Greenwood, Fla.: Penkevill, 1987) p. 139.
48. David Lodge, *The Modes of Modern Writing: Metaphor, Metonymy and the Typology of Modern Literature* (Ithaca, NY: Cornell University Press, 1977) p. 159.
49. Jameson, *The Political Unconscious*, p. 221
50. Louis Althusser, quoted in June Howard, *Form and History in American Literary Naturalism* (Chapel Hill: University of North Carolina Press, 1985) p. 27. Howard's general discussion of realism in her first chapter is an extremely useful one.
51. The 'existentialist' ethic associated with his protagonists as they become 'strong at the broken places' (*FA*, 178) would form such a counter. Jameson discusses 'the problematic of existentialism' in *The Political Unconscious*, p. 217 and *passim*.
52. See Baker, 'The Way It Was', p. 99.
53. Quoted in Richard Godden, *Fictions of Capital: The American Novel from James to Mailer* (Cambridge: Cambridge University Press, 1990) pp. 44–5. Godden's work has been a particularly stimulating influence on my thinking about Hemingway.
54. Sam Girgus, *Desire and the Political Unconscious in American Literature* (Basingstoke and London: Macmillan, 1990) p. 212.

Chapter 3 The Status of the Subject

1. Harold Bloom (ed.), *Modern Critical Interpretations: Ernest Hemingway's The Sun Also Rises* (New York: Chelsea House, 1987) p. 3.

2. Quoted in Bruce Henricksen, 'The Bullfight Story and Critical Theory', in Susan F. Beegel (ed.), *Hemingway's Neglected Short Fiction: New Perspectives* (Ann Arbor, Mich.: UMI Research Press, 1989) p. 111. I acknowledge my critical debt to Henricksen's brief article.

3. Michel Leiris, *Manhood*, preceded by 'The Autobiographer as Torero' (London: Jonathan Cape, 1968 [1946]) p. 118.

4. Henricksen, 'The Bullfight Story and Critical Theory', pp. 111–12.

5. Thomas Strychacz, 'Dramatizations of Manhood in Hemingway's *In Our Time* and *The Sun Also Rises*', *American Literature*, vol. 61 (1989) p. 254.

6. T. J. Jackson Lears, *No Place of Grace: Antimodernism and the Transformation of American Culture, 1880–1920* (New York: Pantheon, 1981).

7. Henricksen, 'The Bullfight Story and Critical Theory', p. 112. Henricksen claims that the stories about Nick Adams in *In Our Time* do, in fact, obey the law of the novel of growth. I would challenge this.

8. Strychacz, 'Dramatizations of Manhood', p. 255.

9. Hubert Zapf discusses Jake's perspective in *The Sun Also Rises* and suggests how it is the 'irredeemable "break" between self and reality, consciousness and life which . . . determines the structure of the novel'. I reapply his argument here. See 'Reflection vs. Daydream: Two Types of the Implied Reader in Hemingway's Fiction', *College Literature*, vol. 15 (1988) no. 3, p. 297.

10. Paul Smith points out that the 'locust' lecture contains a 'kind of "rhetoric of sanity"' and suggests that an 'ironic analogy' is being drawn by Nick between the locust's colour and that of 'the uniform upon which he tells them to fix their eyes'. This may be so, though how conscious Nick is of the analogy remains moot. It is still, though, the lack of immediate rational connection between the extent and nature of Nick's discourse on the locust and the context for it which disturbs both the audience to whom he speaks and the reader. See *A Reader's Guide to the Short Stories of Ernest Hemingway* (Boston, Mass.: G. K. Hall, 1989) p. 275.

11. Sandra M. Gilbert, 'Costumes of the Mind: Transvestism as Metaphor in Modern Literature', *Critical Inquiry*, vol. 7 (Winter 1980) no. 2, p. 394.

12. Steven K. Hoffman, '*Nada* and the Clean, Well-Lighted Place: The Unity of Hemingway's Short Fiction', in Harold Bloom (ed.), *Modern Critical Views: Ernest Hemingway* (New York: Chelsea House, 1985) p. 182.

13. Kenneth G. Johnson, *The Tip of the Iceberg: Hemingway and the Short Story* (Greenwood, Fla.: Penkevill, 1987) p. 173.

14. Hoffman, '*Nada* and the Clean, Well-Lighted Place', p. 181.

15. Henricksen, 'The Bullfight Story and Critical Theory', p. 115.

16. Quoted in Claire Johnston, 'Double Indemnity', in E. Ann Kaplan (ed.), *Women in Film Noir* (London: British Film Institute, 1980) p. 102.

17. Paul Smith, 'The Tenth Indian and the Thing Left Out', in James Nagel (ed.), *Ernest Hemingway: The Writer in Context* (Madison: University of Wisconsin Press, 1984) p. 68.
18. David Seed, '"The Picture of the Whole": *In Our Time*', in A. Robert Lee (ed.), *Ernest Hemingway: New Critical Essays* (London: Vision Press, 1983) p. 22.
19. David Wyatt, *Prodigal Sons: A Study in Authorship and Authority* (Baltimore, Md.: Johns Hopkins University Press, 1980) p. 54.
20. Ibid., p. 55.
21. Catherine Belsey, *Critical Practice* (London: Methuen, 1980) p. 86.
22. Marshall Berman, *All That is Solid Melts into Air: The Experience of Modernity* (London: Verso, 1983 [1982]) back cover and p. 27.
23. Robert Elbaz, 'The Mechanics of Repetition in the Discourse of Ernest Hemingway', *Zagadnienia Rodzajow Literackich*, vol. 27 (1984) no. 1, pp. 84–5.
24. Zapf, 'Reflection vs. Daydream', p. 295.
25. Henricksen, 'The Bullfight Story and Critical Theory', p. 109.
26. Rosalind Rosenberg, quoted in Daniel J. Singal, 'Towards a New Definition of American Modernism', *American Quarterly*, vol. 39 (Spring 1987) no. 1, p. 10; and see my *New Readings of the American Novel* (Basingstoke and London: Macmillan, 1990) p. 128.
27. Scott Donaldson, *By Force of Will* (New York: Viking, 1977) pp. 152–3.
28. Michael Reynolds, *Hemingway's First War: The Making of A Farewell to Arms* (Princeton, NJ: Princeton University Press, 1976) p. 255.
29. Robert E. Gajdusek, '*A Farewell to Arms*: The Psychodynamics of Integrity', *The Hemingway Review*, vol. 9 (Fall 1989) no. 1, p. 29. Although Gajdusek takes a different approach than mine, he, too, is concerned with 'the lost Self, the perjured Self and the Not Self' (p. 27) in the novel. He is rather more optimistic about the possibility of the realisation of identity and integrity in it than I would be.
30. Ibid., p. 27.
31. Scott Donaldson, 'Frederic Henry's Escape and the Pose of Passivity', in Harold Bloom (ed.), *Modern Critical Interpretations: Ernest Hemingway's A Farewell to Arms* (New York: Chelsea House, 1987) p. 107. Donaldson's stress on the way in which Henry's sense of guilt over his 'separate peace' influences the telling of his narrative is particularly interesting.
32. Reynolds, *Hemingway's First War*, p. 257.
33. Donaldson, 'Frederic Henry's Escape and the Pose of Passivity', p. 103.
34. This is where existentialism becomes an issue and the related problems concerning the nature of the gap between 'free' subject and determining world. See Fredric Jameson, *The Political Unconscious: Narrative as a Socially Symbolic Act* (London: Methuen, 1983 [1981]) pp. 216, 258–62.
35. Harold Bloom, Introduction to *Modern Critical Interpretations: Ernest Hemingway's A Farewell to Arms*, p. 7.

36. William Adair, '*A Farewell to Arms*: A Dream Book', in Bloom (ed.), *Modern Critical Interpretations: Ernest Hemingway's A Farewell to Arms*, p. 33

37. This can be read as a rewriting of that opposition between the Spanish natives and the expatriates in *The Sun Also Rises* from the viewpoint of the economic inferior.

38. The edition I use differs in terms of chapter numbering from the American edition consulted (Scribner's, 1953). The chapters to which I have referred run as follows in the latter – 15, 24, 10 and 18.

39. The word 'fucking' is omitted in the paperback edition I use. I take the Scribner's edition quoted above as authoritative. See p. 225.

40. Donaldson, *By Force of Will*, pp. 109–10.

41. Richard Godden, *Fictions of Capital: The American Novel from James to Mailer* (Cambridge: Cambridge University Press, 1990) p. 62.

42. James L. Kastely, 'Toward a Politically Responsible Ethical Criticism: Narrative in *The Political Unconscious* and *For Whom the Bell Tolls*', *Style*, vol. 22 (Winter 1988) no 4, p. 544.

43. Wyatt, *Prodigal Sons*, p. 67.

44. Kastely, 'Toward a Politically Responsible Ethical Criticism', p. 550.

45. Linda Wagner calls the novel 'nearly apolitical' in *Hemingway and Faulkner: Inventors/Masters* (Metuchen, NJ: Scarecrow, 1975) p. 92. Lynn calls Hemingway's political judgements about the war, 'crude', in *Hemingway* (London: Simon and Schuster, 1989) p. 494. Raeburn, in refuting the latter, calls the book 'one of the best ever [political novels] written by an American' – 'Skirting the Hemingway Legend', *American Literary History*, vol. 1 (Spring 1989) no. 1, p. 215.

46. I take my term here from Henricksen ('The Bullfight Story and Critical Theory') who discusses the bourgeois novel in terms of its tacit devaluation of history 'by positing the transcendental sanctity and stability of the subject' (pp. 111–12). In the tension that he develops between the status of the subject and constraining external circumstances, Hemingway does not exactly devalue history. He does in the novels I have just discussed, however, resist recognition of its full effect on the subject. See also my first chapter.

47. Gerry Brenner suggests, for instance, that he 'fabricates' Renata as a 'dream maiden'. See *Concealments in Hemingway's Work* (Columbus: Ohio State University Press, 1983) p. 160.

48. Ibid., pp. 155–6.

49. Brenner, in his revisionary analysis of the novel in *Concealments in Hemingway's Work*, sees Cantwell as a divided figure, 'incurably split. His excursions into paranoia and estheticism, jargon and poetry, history and fantasy, vindictiveness and confessions, obscenity and tenderness portray him at best as schizophrenic' (p. 162). I would argue that Cantwell contains contradictions within one unified self, successful as warrior *and* lover, man of action and art lover, and so on.

50. Quoted in Kenneth Lynn, *Hemingway*, p. 565.

51. David Timms, 'Contrasts in Form: Hemingway's *The Old Man and*

the Sea and Faulkner's "The Bear"', in A. Robert Lee (ed.), *The American Novella* (London: Vision Press, 1989) p. 106.

52. Quoted in Richard B. Hovey, '*Islands in the Stream*: Death and the Artist', in Donald R. Noble (ed.), *Hemingway: A Revaluation* (Troy, NY: Whitston, 1983) p. 246.

53. For useful comment on the theme of the artist in this text see Evelyn J. Hinz and John J. Teunissen, '*Islands in the Stream* as Hemingway's *Laocoon*', *Contemporary Literature*, vol. 29 (1988) no. 1, pp. 26–48, and Stephen Mathewson, 'Against the Stream: Thomas Hudson and Painting', *North Dakota Quarterly* (Fall 1989) pp. 140–5.

54. Gerry Brenner's discussion of the novel in terms of the theme of the 'filicidal father' offers a stimulating example of one such interpretation. See *Concealments in Hemingway's Work*, pp. 188–206.

Chapter 4 Gender Role and Sexuality

1. Judith Fetterley, *The Resisting Reader: A Feminist Approach to American Fiction* (Bloomington: Indiana University Press, 1978); Faith Pullin, 'Hemingway and the Secret Language of Hate', in A. Robert Lee (ed.), *Ernest Hemingway: New Critical Essays* (London: Vision Press, 1983) pp. 172–92.

2. See John Raeburn, *Fame Became of Him* (Bloomington: Indiana University Press, 1984) pp. 55 and 64.

3. Diane Johnson, 'Mama and Papa', *New York Times Book Review*, 19 July 1987, p. 3.

4. John Raeburn, 'Skirting the Hemingway Legend', *American Literary History*, vol. 1 (Spring 1989) no. 1, p. 208.

5. Introduction to Susan F. Beegel (ed.), *Hemingway's Neglected Short Fiction: New Perspectives* (Ann Arbor, Mich.: UMI Research Press, 1989) pp. 10, 12, 13. I give a condensed version of Beegel's argument here.

6. Mark Spilka writes of the situation of the 'maturing middle-class boys' of Hemingway's generation: 'changing conditions made for changing assumptions . . . the sheer possibilities for adventure by which masculine identity might be defined . . . had been sharply reduced. Indeed, they had virtually disappeared with the disappearing frontier, with the triumphant spread of commercial sameness, and with the conversion of wartime gallantry into random slaughter. It was these radical changes, and not the Victorian feminine impress, that would destroy "masculine authority and power" in modern times . . . the real problem [which Hemingway's 'satiric portrait of genteel Christian mothers' concealed] lay in changing conditions in a rapidly changing world' – *Hemingway's Quarrel with Androgyny* (Lincoln: University of Nebraska Press, 1989) pp. 63–4.

7. A useful brief analysis of the difficulties surrounding these terms

can be found in the Introduction to Laura Claridge and Elizabeth Langland (eds), *Out of Bounds: Male Writers and Gender(ed) Criticism* (Amherst: University of Massachussets Press, 1990) pp. 3–21.

8. Susan Jeffords, *The Remasculinization of America: Gender and the Vietnam War* (Bloomington: Indiana University Press, 1989) p. xii.

9. Michael S. Kimmel, 'The Contemporary "Crisis" of Masculinity in Historical Perspective', in Harry Brod (ed.), *The Making of Masculinities: The New Men's Studies* (Boston, Mass.: Allen and Unwin, 1987) pp. 143, 139, 142, 147. Quotes from this source will, where appropriate, appear in the text from henceforth, with the abbreviation *K* used to signal source, when necessary.

10. My approach here is loosely based on Fredric Jameson, *The Political Unconscious: Narrative as a Socially Symbolic Act* (London: Methuen, 1983 [1981]). See especially pp. 94–5, 266–7.

11. Peter Gabriel Filene, *Him/Her/Self: Sex Roles in Modern America* (New York and London: Harcourt Brace Jovanovich, 1974) pp. 107, 157.

12. Sandra Gilbert, 'Costumes of the Mind: Transvestism as Metaphor in Modern Literature', *Critical Inquiry*, vol. 7 (Winter 1980) no. 2, p. 408.

13. Joe L. Dubbert, *A Man's Place: Masculinity in Transition* (Englewood Cliffs, NJ: Prentice Hall, 1979) p. 192; and Filene, *Him/Her/Self*, p. 156.

14. Glenda Riley, in *Inventing the American Woman: A Perspective on Women's History* (Arlington Heights, Ill.: Harlan Davidson, 1986), shows how limited political advance was during this period. See ch. 7, pp. 183–208.

15. See Dubbert, *A Man's Place*, p. 204, and Filene, *Him/Her/Self*, p. 164. It is clear from my comments in this section that men felt similar feelings of threat and loss of balance throughout the period 1890–1930, though the precise socio-historical causes for such feelings changed. The impact of modernisation and its developing effects can perhaps serve as a general explanation. Equally, women consistently saw what had been achieved in their struggle for equality in terms of the failures and limitations of that movement. For the way in which the conditions of the 1930s, too, 'rendered obsolete many of the old symbols and standards of virile masculinity', see Dubbert, *A Man's Place*, p. 209. Although Hemingway wrote through to the post Second World War period, I would suggest that his social attitudes and values were formed in this earlier period.

16. Sylvia O'Sullivan, *Hemingway vs Hemingway: Femininity and Masculinity in the Major Works* (Ann Arbor, Mich.: University Microfilm International, 1987) p. 146. I am indebted to the author for permission to quote from her valuable, but as yet unpublished, dissertation.

17. Lawrence Broer, 'Hemingway's "On Writing": A Portrait of the Artist as Nick Adams', in Beegel (ed.), *Hemingway's Neglected Short Fiction*, p. 135. Broer is referring specifically to 'On Writing'.

18. I take my terms from Michael Kimmel who discusses the vigorous reassertion of traditional masculinity in the face of 'social and political trends of which feminism was but a sympton, not a cause' – 'The Contemporary "Crisis" of Masculinity', p. 143.

19. Raeburn, 'Skirting the Hemingway Legend', p. 208.

20. Elizabeth A. Flynn, 'Gender and Reading', in Elizabeth A. Flynn and Patrocinio P. Schweickart (eds), *Gender and Reading: Essays on Readers, Texts, and Contexts* (Baltimore, Md.: Johns Hopkins University Press, 1986) pp. 278, 277.

21. There is a fluctuation here between narrative voice and character focalisation. It helps, though, to confirm a reading of the story that would be sympathetic to Jig's perspective. The narrative voice would seem to describe this view. It is only at the paragraph end that what is seen is tied to Jig's perspective (*MWW*, 46). Her focalisation is, thus, retrospectively pinned to what has been described.

22. David Bleich in his reader response study of the text claims that 'women regularly "see" an abortion much more quickly and with much more certainty than men do' when asked what 'operation' is being discussed. See 'Gender Interests in Reading and Language', in Flynn and Schweickart (eds), *Gender and Reading*, p. 258.

23. Richard Godden, *Fictions of Capital: The American Novel from James to Mailer* (Cambridge: Cambridge University Press, 1990) p. 67.

24. Paul Smith quotes the first two interpetations (from Lewis Weeks and John Hollander) in his *A Reader's Guide to the Short Stories of Ernest Hemingway* (Boston, Mass.: G. K. Hall, 1989) p. 208. Godden adds the crucial detail concerning the notion of the market (*Fictions of Capital*, p. 67).

25. Kenneth Lynn, *Hemingway* (London: Simon and Schuster, 1989) pp. 431–6. For an earlier, brief, 'misogynistic' interpretation of the story see Leslie Fiedler, *Love and Death in the American Novel* (New York: Stein and Day, 1975 [1960]) pp. 318–19.

26. Robert Scholes, *Semiotics and Interpretation* (New Haven, Conn.: Yale University Press, 1982) ch. 7. For quotes, see pp. 121, 119. Scholes's sharp analysis reveals the misogynist underpinnings of the text in some detail. Rather than repeat his argument, I would direct my reader to his book.

27. All quotes in this section of my argument, unless otherwise noted, are taken from Bruce Henricksen, 'The Bullfight Story and Critical Theory', in Beegel (ed.), *Hemingway's Neglected Short Fiction*, pp. 107–21. Henricksen uses Bakhtin, Jameson and Lacan in his approach to this text. I would query Henricksen's use of the word 'reactionary' to describe Hemingway's position. The 'fascist' mentality he describes is a thoroughly modern(ist) phenomenon.

28. Robert Scholes, *Textual Power: Literary Theory and the Teaching of English* (New Haven, Con.: Yale University Press, 1985) p. 70. Henricksen leans heavily on Scholes's prior analysis, as he acknowledges.

29. Scholes, *Textual Power*, p. 72.
30. Michel Leiris, 'The Autobiographer as Torero', in *Manhood* (London: Jonathan Cape, 1968) pp. 14, 16.
31. Peter Schwenger, *Phallic Critiques* (London: Routledge and Kegan Paul, 1984) p. 137. I have paraphrased Schwenger's arguments in this part of my text. For a deconstructionist reading of gender roles and the bullfight ritual in *The Sun Also Rises*, see Nina Schwartz, 'Lovers' Discourse in *The Sun Also Rises*: A Cock and Bull Story', *Criticism*, vol. 26 (1984) no. 1, pp. 49–69.
32. Godden, *Fictions of Capital*, p. 62.
33. Thomas Strychacz, 'Dramatizations of Manhood in Hemingway's *In Our Time* and *The Sun Also Rises*', *American Literature*, vol. 61 (Spring 1989) no. 2, p. 253.
34. Ibid., p. 260.
35. Michael S. Reynolds, 'False Dawn: *The Sun Also Rises* Manuscript', in Harold Bloom (ed.), *Modern Critical Interpretations: Ernest Hemingway's The Sun Also Rises* (New York: Chelsea House, 1987) p. 118.
36. See Wolfgang Rudat, 'Jacob Barnes and Onan: Sexual Response in *The Sun Also Rises* and *For Whom the Bell Tolls*', *Journal of Evolutionary Psychology*, vol. 9 (1989) nos 1–2, p. 50.
37. See ibid., pp. 51, 54; Lynn, *Hemingway*, p. 324.
38. Anika Lemaire, *Jacques Lacan*, trans. David Macey (London: Routledge and Kegan Paul, 1977 [1970]) p. 59.
39. Caroll Smith-Rosenberg, *Disorderly Conduct: Visions of Gender in Victorian America* (New York: Alfred A. Knopf, 1985) p. 287; Robert Stoller, quoted in Gilbert, 'Costumes of the Mind', p. 398 footnote.
40. Jon Stratton, *The Virgin Text: Fiction, Sexuality and Ideology* (Brighton: Harvester, 1987) pp. 45, 62.
41. Peter Messent, *New Readings of the American Novel* (Basingstoke and London: Macmillan, 1990). I reach different conclusions this time round.
42. James Hinkle, 'What's Funny in *The Sun Also Rises*', in Bloom (ed.), *Modern Critical Interpretations: Ernest Hemingway's The Sun Also Rises*, p. 146; Lynn, *Hemingway*, p. 320.
43. Virginia Scharff, *Women and the Coming of the Motor Age* (New York: The Free Press, 1991) p. 94.
44. The prefacing quotes are (inexcusably) omitted from the Grafton edition I am using. See Scribner's paperback edition.
45. William Adair, '*A Farewell to Arms*: A Dream Book', in Harold Bloom (ed.), *Modern Critical Interpretations: Ernest Hemingway's A Farewell to Arms* (New York: Chelsea House, 1987) pp. 33–48.
46. I am condensing Jameson's argument considerably here. See *The Political Unconscious*, pp. 132, 148, 135.
47. Michael S. Reynolds, *Hemingway's First War: The Making of A Farewell to Arms* (Princeton, NJ: Princeton University Press, 1976) p. 46.
48. Adair, '*A Farewell to Arms*: A Dream Book', p. 38.
49. Millicent Bell, '*A Farewell to Arms*: Pseudoautobiography and

Personal Metaphor', in James Nagel (ed.), *Ernest Hemingway: The Writer in Context* (Madison: The University of Wisconsin Press, 1984) p. 112.

50. Adair, '*A Farewell to Arms*: A Dream Book', p. 37.
51. Carol H. Smith, 'Women and the Loss of Eden in Hemingway's Mythology', in Nagel (ed.), *Ernest Hemingway: The Writer in Context*, p. 130.
52. Jameson, *The Political Unconscious*, p. 112.
53. Scott Donaldson writes that 'they haven't ['gotten away from the war'], nor will they ever, despite the oblivion-inducing therapy she administers' – 'Frederic Henry's Escape and the Pose of Passivity', in Bloom (ed.), *Modern Critical Interpretations: Ernest Hemingway's A Farewell to Arms*, p. 106.
54. See Sandra Whipple Spanier, 'Catherine Barkley and the Hemingway Code: Ritual and Survival in *A Farewell to Arms*', in Bloom (ed.), *Modern Critical Interpretations: Ernest Hemingway's A Farewell to Arms*, pp. 131–48, and Ernest Lockridge, 'Faithful in Her Fashion: Catherine Barkley, the Invisible Hemingway Heroine', *Journal of Narrative Technique*, vol. 18 (1988) no. 2, pp. 170–8.
55. Bell, '*A Farewell to Arms*: Pseudoautobiography and Personal Metaphor', pp. 114, 116, 118.
56. Lynn, *Hemingway*, p. 389. Mark Spilka writes of 'the androgynous nature of their fusion' and pays particular attention to Frederic's 'feminization' in the sexual arena; to Catherine's 'mounting' of the 'receptive. . . supine' Frederic (*Hemingway's Quarrel with Androgyny*, pp. 212–4). While accepting that an androgynous move takes place, Sylvia O'Sullivan argues that Catherine's pregnancy acts as 'a gender distancing phenomenon' in the final section of the novel and that Frederic learns 'how to reenter the male world now that biology has curtailed his involvement with the female world' (*Hemingway vs Hemingway*, ch. 3, see pp. 86–7).
57. I take this phrase from Tony Tanner, in *Adultery and the Novel: Contract and Transgression* (Baltimore, Md.: Johns Hopkins University Press, 1979) p. 309.
58. Lemaire, *Jacques Lacan*, pp. 78–9. To enter the Symbolic order means the repression of desire and rule by Law. It is by no means wholly positive.
59. Gilbert, 'Costumes of the Mind', p. 415.
60. Smith-Rosenberg, *Disorderly Conduct*, p. 288. Smith-Rosenberg is not referring to the novel. She is showing how, in America, the New Women of the 1920s used a symbolic androgynous discourse in their effort for self-definition. This, she claims, constituted an (unfortunate) shift from the constructions of the female self of the previous generation, and one which contributed to their 'increasing marginality'. See 'The New Woman as Androgyne', pp. 245–96.
61. See O'Sullivan, *Hemingway vs Hemingway*. Her discussion of gender roles in *Across the River and into the Trees* and *The Garden of Eden* is particularly interesting. She, too, notes how Bourne's writing

challenges 'the chains of [constricting] gendered behaviour' (pp. 152–3).

62. Ibid., p. 149. Catherine's taking of the name 'Peter' is interesting here as suggesting an attempt, as sexual role is exchanged, to construct an identity in some way outside the scan of her and David's narcissistic union.

63. Warren Bennett, 'Sexual Identity in "The Sea Change"', in Beegel (ed.), *Hemingway's Neglected Short Fiction*, p. 226. I apply Bennett's remarks on the short story to this novel. His comments on the description of Thomas Hudson in *Islands in the Stream*, who 'felt weak and destroyed inside himself' when he acts as his wife's 'girl' in bed, are also relevant here. See Bennett, p. 232.

64. Robert B. Jones develops this theme in 'Mimesis and Metafiction in Hemingway's *The Garden of Eden*', *Hemingway Review*, vol. 7 (Fall 1987) no. 1, pp. 2–13.

65. *From Max Weber: Essays in Sociology*, trans. and ed. H. H. Gerth and C. Wright Mills (London: Kegan Paul, Trench, Trubner, 1947) pp. 155, 342.

66. Jameson, *The Political Unconscious*, p. 221.

67. Jones, 'Mimesis and Metafiction in Hemingway's *The Garden of Eden*', p. 6.

68. James Nagel writes that 'For David, it is art that is the forbidden fruit that leads to knowledge of oneself and the way out of the Garden of Eden.' Nagel's analysis of the way in which the betrayals and disillusions of the present relationship with Catherine connect up with David's ability to write that story of betrayal and disillusion of his childhood is a useful one. See 'The Hunting Story in *The Garden of Eden*', in Beegel (ed.), *Hemingway's Neglected Short Fiction*, pp. 329–338.

69. Robert E. Fleming, in 'The Endings of Hemingway's *Garden of Eden*', *American Literature*, vol. 61 (May 1989) no. 2, pp. 261–70, convincingly argues that the version of the novel as it now stands, edited by Tom Jenks of Scribner's, betrays Hemingway's intentions regarding the novel's ending. Fleming argues for a version of the ending where, following a temporal ellipsis, we see Catherine and David together again in the South of France, with David tending a wife who is mentally disturbed and with dialogue that raises the possibility of a joint suicide pact. He argues too that Hemingway did not write the passage about David's successful rewritings of the stories destroyed by Catherine as the ending to the novel. Such claims certainly would affect my reading and other readings of the novel as it stands, which stress Marita's final importance as, in Fleming's words, 'a new supportive mate' (p. 270). Spilka puts an interesting twist in the tale of even this ending when he says that the manuscript shows that 'signs of [Marita's] own . . . obsession with androgyny burgeon in the late chapters' (*Hemingway's Quarrel with Androgyny*, p. 290). Readings of this novel have to be tentative because of its status as posthumously published novel, neither

sanctioned nor edited by the author himself. Any reading too has to acknowledge that, because of its edited state, there are elements in the text that operate against any firmly consistent critical analysis.
70. I am here condensing arguments from Sylvia O'Sullivan. For quotes, see *Hemingway vs Hemingway*, pp. 134, 153, 154–5.
71. John Updike, 'The Sinister Sex', *New Yorker*, 20 June 1986, p. 87; and E. L. Doctorow, quoted in Robert B. Jones, 'Mimesis and Metafiction in Hemingway's *The Garden of Eden*', p. 4.
72. See Mark Spilka, *Hemingway's Quarrel with Androgyny*, p. 310; and Robert E. Gajdusek, '"An Alpine Idyll": The Sun-Struck Mountain Vision and the Necessary Valley Journey', in Beegel (ed.), *Hemingway's Neglected Short Fiction*, p. 177.

Chapter 5   Geographies, Fictional and Non-fictional

1. Quoted in Jacqueline Tavernier-Courbin, 'Ernest Hemingway and Ezra Pound', in James Nagel (ed.), *Ernest Hemingway: The Writer in Context* (Madison: University of Wisconsin Press, 1984) p. 188.
2. Gertrude Stein, *The Autobiography of Alice B. Toklas* (Harmondsworth, Middx.: Penguin, 1966 [1933]) p. 234.
3. Donna Haraway, 'Teddy Bear Patriarchy: Taxidermy in the Garden of Eden, New York City, 1908–1936', *Social Text* (Winter 1985) p. 21.
4. Richard Godden, *Fictions of Capital: The American Novel from James to Mailer* (Cambridge: Cambridge University Press, 1990) p. 73.
5. My use of the term 'authenticity' and the related concept of 'grace' are taken from T. J. Jackson Lears's study of late nineteenth- and early twentieth-century American culture, *No Place of Grace: Antimodernism and the Transformation of American Culture, 1880–1920* (New York: Pantheon, 1981). He charts the 'antimodernist' quest for '"authentic" alternatives to the apparent unreality of modern existence' (p. 5) and links Henry Adams, for instance, to Ezra Pound in their pursuit of such a quest.
6. Hemingway crosses generic boundaries as he writes on America, Spain and Africa. In this chapter I use a mixture of types of material – fiction, autobiographical and journalistic commentary, and his longer non-fiction. I see such a critical tactic as both valid and useful in a situation where the fictional materials must 'be seen as . . . text[s] among a particular set of other texts by Hemingway that present very similar diegetic material' (Robert Scholes, *Semiotics and Interpretation* [New Haven, Conn.: Yale University Press, 1982] p. 121). Scholes is here justifying his critical procedure with regard to 'A Very Short Story'.
7. William Boelhower, '"See You Around": Hemingway's Cartographic Modernism', in Sergio Perosa (ed.), *Hemingway e Venezia* (Florence: Leo S. Olschki, 1988) pp. 82, 96.
8. Sheldon Grebstein contrasts 'Soldier's Home', for instance, with the

African stories to suggest an opposition between 'the decayed "indoor" values of America' and 'freedom, courage, danger, joy, potency', those outdoor values he identifies with Africa. See 'The Structure of Hemingway's Short Stories', *Fitzgerald/Hemingway Annual* (1972) p. 183.

9. H. R. Stoneback, '"Mais Je Reste Catholique": Communion, Betrayal, and Aridity in "Wine of Wyoming"', in Susan F. Beegel (ed.), *Hemingway's Neglected Short Fiction: New Perspectives* (Ann Arbor, Mich.: UMI Research Press, 1989) p. 213.

10. Ibid., pp. 218–19.

11. Warner Berthoff, '"The Flight of the Rocket" and "The Last Good Country": Fitzgerald and Hemingway in the 1920s', in Boris Ford (ed.), *American Literature*, vol. 9 of *The New Pelican Guide to English Literature* (London: Penguin, 1988) pp. 422, 430.

12. See David Wyatt, *Prodigal Sons: A Study in Authorship and Authority* (Baltimore, Md.: Johns Hopkins University Press, 1980) p. 56.

13. The relation between nature and culture is complicated here by the presence of the wardens as nature's protectors and by Nick's first harmful action.

14. See Philip Young, 'Hemingway: The Writer in Decline', in Donald R. Noble, *Hemingway: A Revaluation* (Troy, NY: Whitston, 1983) p. 231.

15. Richard King, *A Southern Renaissance: The Cultural Awakening of the American South, 1930–1955* (New York and Oxford: Oxford University Press, 1980) p. 117.

16. Thirty of Hemingway's Civil War dispatches, written for the North American Newspaper Alliance, were republished in *The Hemingway Review*, vol. 7 (Spring 1988) no. 2.

17. See, for instance, James L. Kastely, 'Toward a Politically Responsible Ethical Criticism: Narrative in *The Political Unconscious* and *For Whom the Bell Tolls*', *Style*, vol. 22 (Winter 1988) no. 4, pp. 535–58. What is, though, noticeable is that the political aspects of the novel arise primarily from the immediate context of the protagonists' position within the war. Charles Molesworth's statement that Hemingway 'sidesteps the social and political complexities of Spanish history' prior to, and crucial to an understanding of, that war, stays true. See his 'Hemingway's Code: The Spanish Civil War and World Power', *Salmagundi*, vols 76–7 (Fall 1987–Winter 1988) p. 94.

18. I am using terms here taken from Allen Josephs, 'Toreo: The Moral Axis of *The Sun Also Rises*', where he bases his reading of the bullfight on Mircea Eliade's study of ritual and sacrifice in *The Myth of the Eternal Return*. See Harold Bloom (ed.), *Modern Critical Interpretations: Ernest Hemingway's The Sun Also Rises* (New York: Chelsea House, 1987). I quote pp. 165, 158. See also Michel Leiris, *Manhood* (London: Jonathan Cape, 1968) pp. 63–9.

19. Josephs, 'Toreo: The Moral Axis of *The Sun Also Rises*', pp. 158, 164. Leiris, *Manhood*, pp. 64–5. There is a problem with that phrase 'original time' here, which suggests a move beyond culture. Ritual can be seen as a way of mirroring nature's repetitions.

20. Stanley Diamond, *In Search of the Primitive: A Critique of Civilization* (New Brunswick and London: Transaction Books, 1987 [1974]) p. 129.
21. Ronald Weber, *Hemingway's Art of Non-fiction* (Basingstoke: Macmillan, 1990) pp. 53-4.
22. See Gerry Brenner, *Concealments in Hemingway's Works* (Columbus: Ohio State University Press, 1983) pp. 70–1. See also Brenner's psychoanalytic reading of Hemingway's fascination with Spanish values and bullfighting (pp. 98–106).
23. Hubert Zapf, 'Reflection vs. Daydream: Two Types of the Implied Reader in Hemingway's Fiction', *College Literature*, vol. 15 (1988) no. 3, pp. 296–7.
24. Hugh Thomas, *The Spanish Civil War* (New York: Harper and Row, 1961) p. 50.
25. Fredric Jameson, *Marxism and Form: Twentieth-Century Dialectical Theories of Literature* (Princeton, NJ: Princeton University Press, 1971) p. 412.
26. Both quotes taken from Scott MacDonald, 'Implications of Narrative Perspective in Hemingway's "The Undefeated"', *Journal of Narrative Technique*, vol. 2 (January 1972) pp. 1, 11.
27. Zapf, 'Reflection vs. Daydream', p. 297.
28. See Scott Donaldson, 'Hemingway's Morality of Compensation', in Bloom (ed.), *Modern Critical Interpretations: Ernest Hemingway's The Sun Also Rises*, pp. 84, 78. This whole article is on the economic motif in the novel.
29. Lawrence R. Broer, *Hemingway's Spanish Tragedy* (University of Alabama Press, 1973) pp. 14–15.
30. Berthoff, '"The Flight of the Rocket" and "The Last Good Country": Fitzgerald and Hemingway in the 1920s', p. 433.
31. My comments here are necessarily dependent on the version of the text as it presently appears in published form.
32. Fredric Jameson, *The Political Unconscious: Narrative as a Socially Symbolic Act* (London: Methuen, 1983 [1981]) p. 217.
33. Haraway, 'Teddy Bear Patriarchy', pp. 25–6, 52. In what follows, I apply to Hemingway the terms and ideas Haraway uses in her article (pp. 20–64), where appropriate.
34. David D. Anderson, 'Hemingway and Henderson on the High Savannas, or Two Midwestern Moderns and the Myth of Africa', *Saul Bellow Journal*, vol. 8 (1989) no. 2, p. 66.
35. Weber, *Hemingway's Art of Non-fiction*, p. 73; and see, too, A. Carl Bredahl, 'The Body as Matrix: Narrative Pattern in *Green Hills of Africa*', *Midwest Quarterly*, vol. 28 (1987) no. 4, pp. 455–72. The longer non-fiction works on Spain also escape conventional generic boundaries. The sustained focus on 'Hemingway' as protagonist in the African text, however, significantly differentiates it from the former.
36. Haraway, 'Teddy Bear Patriarchy', p. 50. Haraway does not discuss Hemingway. Again, I use her terms to fit my context.

37. Such an interpretation is uncomfortable in the role it grants the native African: associated with nature or culture depending on the perspective taken. This points in the direction of problems over the nature–culture binary, especially where notions of the 'primitive' are concerned.

38. Bredahl, 'The Body as Matrix', pp. 469–70

39. Quoted in Scott Donaldson, *By Force of Will: The Life and Art of Ernest Hemingway* (New York: Viking, 1977) pp. 132, 71. One should perhaps amend Hemingway's words to 'part of half of the human race'.

40. Brenner, *Concealments in Hemingway's Works*, p. 88

41. Haraway, 'Teddy Bear Patriarchy', pp. 23, 50.

42. *African Journal* is an immense and unfinished manuscript. Sections of it were published in *Sports Illustrated* in the early 1970s. See bibliography for details. 'The Christmas Gift' (*Look*, 20 May, 4 April 1954; reprinted in *Byline*, pp. 429–71) can be read in conjunction with these excerpts.

43. Which even the final mention of 'the hunt having taken a bad turn' (*AJ3*, 50) cannot destroy.

44. Ray Cave, 'Introduction to *An African Journal*', *Sports Illustrated*, 20 December 1971, pp. 40–1.

45. Hemingway reported these injuries in quasi-comic fashion in 'The Christmas Gift' (see *Byline*, pp. 454 and 465, for instance). In fact, he was very badly damaged in the crash. The link between these injuries and others (the skull fractured in London in May 1944 and so on) and the mental problems he suffered at the end of his life are a matter for speculation (see the Jeffrey Meyers biography, pp. 505, 540–6).

46. Haraway, 'Teddy Bear Patriarchy', pp. 50, 45.

47. Kenneth S. Lynn, *Hemingway* (London: Simon and Schuster, 1989) p. 434. See too pp. 431–6. Mark Spilka's 'A Source for the Macomber "Accident"' is an interesting counter-reading on the subject of Margot's motives – *Hemingway's Quarrel with Androgyny* (Lincoln: University of Nebraska Press, 1990) pp. 315–26.

48. Matthew J. Bruccoli (ed.), *Conversations with Ernest Hemingway* (Jackson: University Press of Mississippi, 1986) p. 180.

49. Jameson, *The Political Unconscious*, pp. 213, 160. See also p. 218.

50. Quoted in Glen A. Love, 'Hemingway's Indian Virtues: An Ecological Reconsideration', *Western American Literature*, vol. 22 (1987) no. 3, p. 205.

51. This is Glen Love's phrase; in 'Hemingway's Indian Virtues', p. 205.

52. Godden, *Fictions of Capital*, pp. 59, 48.

53. Mary Welsh Hemingway, *How It Was* (New York: Alfred A. Knopf, 1976) p. 356.

54. Glen A. Love, 'Hemingway's Indian Virtues', p. 205.

55. Ibid., p. 209.

Chapter 6   Coda: *A Moveable Feast*

1. Jackson J. Benson, 'Down For the Count: Posthumous and Revisionist Hemingway', *Resources for American Literary Study*, vol. 15 (1985) no. 1, p. 19.
2. Roger Asselineau, 'An Interim Report on Hemingway's Posthumous Fiction', in Sergio Perosa (ed.), *Hemingway e Venezia* (Florence: Leo S. Olschki, 1988) p. 175. Asselineau confines his remarks to *Islands in the Stream* and *The Garden of Eden* here.
3. Jacqueline Tavernier-Courbin, 'Hemingway and Company', *Canadian Review of American Studies*, vol. 18 (1987) no. 3, p. 389. See also Gerry Brenner, 'Are We Going to Hemingway's Feast?', *American Literature*, vol. 54 (1982) no. 4, pp 529–30, 534.
4. See Tavernier-Courbin, 'Hemingway and Company', p. 386, and Michael Reynolds, *Hemingway: The Paris Years* (Oxford: Basil Blackwell, 1989) pp. 5, 179, 251.
5. See Jeffrey Meyers, *Hemingway: A Biography* (London: Macmillan, 1985) p. 165.
6. Louis Renza's stimulating comments in 'The Importance of Being Ernest', *South Atlantic Quarterly*, vol. 88 (1989) no. 3, pp. 661–89, influence my reading here. I acknowledge my debt to this article, which I use as a base for my own supplementary critical work.
7. Ibid., p. 663.
8. Ibid., pp. 668, 667, 665, 682.
9. 'On Writing' is that part of 'Big-Two Hearted River' cut out of Hemingway's final version, but reprinted under this title in Philip Young's 1972 edition of *The Nick Adams Stories*.
10. Renza, 'The Importance of Being Ernest', pp. 670–2, 676, 681–2.
11. Hemingway mainly worked on the *A Moveable Feast* manuscripts between 1957 and 1960. See Meyers, *Hemingway: A Biography*, p. 533.

Select Bibliography

HEMINGWAY'S MAJOR WORKS

The Essential Hemingway [1947]. This contains the most accurate version of *In Our Time* [1925] published in the Grafton editions. It omits, however, the introductory sketch, 'On The Quai at Smyrna', which Hemingway added in 1930.

The Sun Also Rises (published as *Fiesta* in Great Britain) [1926].

Men Without Women [1927].

A Farewell to Arms [1929].

Death in the Afternoon [1932].

Winner Take Nothing [1933].

Green Hills of Africa [1935].

To Have and Have Not [1937].

For Whom the Bell Tolls [1940].

Across the River and into the Trees [1950].

The Old Man and the Sea [1952].

A Moveable Feast [1964].

The Nick Adams Stories. Preface by Philip Young (Charles Scribner's: New York, 1972).

Islands in the Stream (London: Book Club Associates, 1970).

The Dangerous Summer [1985].

The Garden of Eden [1986].

Interviews, Letters and Collections of Journalistic Writing Etc.

African Journal: excerpts in *Sports Illustrated*, 35 (20 December 1971) pp. 40–52, 57–66: abbreviated as *AJ1*; 36 (3 January 1972) pp. 26–46: *AJ2*; 37 (10 January 1972) pp. 22–30, 43–50: *AJ3*.

Hemingway: The Wild Years, Ed. Gene Z. Hanrahan (New York: Dell, 1967 [1962]).

Byline, ed. William White [1967].

Writers at Work, Interviews from *Paris Review* selected by Kay Dick (Harmondsworth, Middx.: Penguin Books, 1972) pp. 175–96.

Ernest Hemingway: Selected Letters, 1917–1961, ed. Carlos Baker (London: Granada, 1981).

SECONDARY CRITICISM

Bibliography

Hanneman, Audre, *Ernest Hemingway: A Comprehensive Bibliography* (Princeton, NJ: Princeton University Press, 1967), and Supplement (1975).

Critical and Biographical Studies

Baker, Carlos, *Hemingway: The Writer as Artist* (Princeton, NJ: Princeton University Press, 1952).
—— (ed.), *Hemingway and his Critics: An International Anthology* (New York: Hill and Wang, 1961).
—— *Ernest Hemingway: A Life Story* (London: Collins, 1969).
Beegel, Susan F. (ed.), *Hemingway's Neglected Short Fiction: New Perspectives* (Ann Arbor, Mich.: UMI Research Press, 1989).
Benson, Jackson J., *Hemingway: The Writer's Art of Self-Defence* (Minneapolis: University of Minnesota Press, 1969).
—— (ed.), *New Critical Approaches to the Short Stories of Ernest Hemingway*, with a checklist to the criticism, 1975–1990 (Durham: Duke University Press, 1990). [This book was received after my manuscript was complete but deserves bibliographical mention.]
Bloom, Harold (ed.), *Modern Critical Views: Ernest Hemingway* (New York: Chelsea Press, 1985).
—— *Modern Critical Interpretations: Ernest Hemingway's The Sun Also Rises* (New York and Philadelphia: Chelsea House, 1987).
—— *Modern Critical Interpretations: Ernest Hemingway's A Farewell to Arms* (New York and Philadelphia: Chelsea House, 1987).
Brenner, Gerry, *Concealments in Hemingway's Work* (Columbus: Ohio University Press, 1983).
Broer, Lawrence R., *Hemingway's Spanish Tragedy* (University of Alabama Press, 1973).
Cooper, Stephen, *The Politics of Ernest Hemingway* (Ann Arbor, Mich.: UMI Research Press, 1987).
Donaldson, Scott, *By Force of Will: The Life and Art of Ernest Hemingway* (New York: Viking, 1977).
—— (ed.), *New Essays on A Farewell to Arms* (Cambridge: Cambridge University Press, 1990).
Griffin, Peter, *Along With Youth: Hemingway, The Early Years* (New York and Oxford: Oxford University Press, 1985).
Johnston, Kenneth G., *The Tip of the Iceberg: Hemingway and the Short Story* (Greenwood, Fla.: Penkevill, 1987).

Kert, Bernice, *The Hemingway Women* (New York and London: W. W. Norton, 1983).

Lee, A. Robert (ed.), *Ernest Hemingway: New Critical Essays* (London and Totowa, NJ: Vision and Barnes and Noble, 1983).

Lynn, Kenneth S., *Hemingway* (London: Simon and Schuster, 1989 [1987]).

Meyers, Jeffrey (ed.), *Hemingway: The Critical Heritage* (London: Routledge, 1982)

—— *Hemingway: A Biography* (London: Macmillan, 1986 [1985]).

Nagel, James (ed.), *Ernest Hemingway: The Writer in Context* (Madison: University of Wisconsin Press, 1984).

Noble, Donald R. (ed.), *Hemingway: A Revaluation* (Troy, NY: Whitston, 1983).

Raeburn, John, *Fame Became of Him: Hemingway as Public Writer* (Bloomington: Indiana University Press, 1984).

Reynolds, Michael, *The Young Hemingway* (Oxford and New York: Basil Blackwell, 1987 [1986]).

—— *Hemingway's First War: The Making of A Farewell to Arms* (Princeton, NJ: Princeton University Press, 1976).

—— *Hemingway: The Paris Years* (Oxford and Cambridge, Mass.: Basil Blackwell, 1989).

Smith, Paul, *A Reader's Guide to the Short Stories of Ernest Hemingway* (Boston, Mass.: G. K. Hall, 1989).

Spilka, Mark, *Hemingway's Quarrel with Androgyny* (Lincoln and London: University of Nebraska Press, 1990).

Wagner, Linda W. (ed.), *Ernest Hemingway: Six Decades of Criticism* (East Lansing: Michigan State University Press, 1987).

Wagner-Martin, Linda (ed.), *New Essays on The Sun Also Rises* (Cambridge: Cambridge University Press, 1987).

Weber, Ronald, *Hemingway's Art of Non-fiction* (London: Macmillan, 1990).

Young, Philip, *Ernest Hemingway* (New York: Rinehart, 1952).

—— *Ernest Hemingway: A Reconsideration* (University Park: Pennsylvania State University Press, 1966).

Critical Articles and Chapters in Books

Bredahl, A. Carl, 'The Body as Matrix: Narrative Pattern in *Green Hills of Africa*', *Midwest Quarterly*, vol. 28 (1987) no.4, pp. 455–72.

Elbaz, Robert, 'The Mechanics of Repetition in the Discourse of Ernest Hemingway', *Zagadnienia Rodzajow Literackich*, vol. 27 (1984) no. 1, pp. 77–90.

Girgus, Sam B., *Desire and the Political Unconscious in American Literature* (Basingstoke and London: Macmillan, 1990) pp. 194–223.

Godden, Richard, *Fictions of Capital: The American Novel from James to Mailer* (Cambridge: Cambridge University Press, 1990) pp. 39–77.

Goodman, Paul, *Speaking and Language: Defence of Poetry* (New York: Random House, 1971) pp. 181–90.

Jones, Robert B., 'Mimesis and Metafiction in Hemingway's *The Garden of Eden*', *The Hemingway Review*, vol. 7 (1987) no. 1, pp. 2–13.

Kastely, James, 'Toward a Politically Responsible Ethical Criticism: Narrative in *The Political Unconscious* and *For Whom the Bell Tolls*', *Style*, vol. 22 (1988) no. 4, pp. 535–58.

Lodge, David, *The Modes of Modern Writing: Metaphor, Metonymy, and the Typology of Modern Literature* (Ithaca, NY: Cornell University Press, 1977) pp. 155–9.

Love, Glen A., 'Hemingway's Indian Virtues: An Ecological Reconsideration', *Western American Literature*, vol. 22 (1987) no. 3, pp. 201–13.

MacDonald, Scott, 'Implications of Narrative Perspective in Hemingway's "The Undefeated"', *Journal of Narrative Technique*, vol. 2 (January 1972) pp. 1–15.

Messent, Peter, *New Readings of the American Novel: Narrative Theory and its Application* (Basingstoke and London: Macmillan, 1990) pp. 86–129.

Raeburn, John, 'Skirting the Hemingway Legend', *American Literary History*, vol. 1 (1989) no. 1, pp. 206–18.

Renza, Louis A., 'The Importance of Being Ernest', *South Atlantic Quarterly*, vol. 88 (1989) no. 3, pp. 661–89.

Scholes, Robert, *Semiotics and Interpretation* (New Haven, Conn.: Yale University Press, 1982) pp. 110–26.

—— *Textual Power: Literary Theory and the Teaching of English* (New Haven, Conn. and London: Yale University Press, 1985) pp. 25–73.

Schwartz, Nina, 'Lovers' Discourse in *The Sun Also Rises*: A Cock and Bull Story', *Criticism*, vol. 26 (1984) no. 1, pp. 49–69.

Schwenger, Peter, *Phallic Critiques: Masculinity and Twentieth-Century Literature* (London: Routledge and Kegan Paul, 1984) pp. 36–50.

Strychacz, Thomas, 'Dramatizations of Manhood in Hemingway's *In Our Time* and *The Sun Also Rises*', *American Literature*, vol. 61 (1989) no. 2, pp. 245–60.

Tanner, Tony, *The Reign of Wonder* (Cambridge: Cambridge University Press, 1977) pp. 228–57.

Wyatt, David, *Prodigal Sons: A Study in Authorship and Authority* (Baltimore, Md. and London: Johns Hopkins University Press, 1980) pp. 52–71.

Zapf, Hubert, 'Reflection vs. Daydream: Two Types of Implied Reader in Hemingway's Fiction', *College Literature*, vol. 15 (1988) no. 3, pp. 289–307.

Index